Grass Roots

Grass Roots

From Prairie to Politics:

The Autobiography
of
Alice Sachs Hamburg

CREATIVE ARTS BOOK COMPANY
Berkeley • California

Grass Roots is published by Donald S. Ellis
and distributed by Creative Arts Book Company

For information contact:
Creative Arts Book Company
833 Bancroft Way
Berkeley, California 94710

ISBN 0-88739-297-0
Library of Congress Catalog Number 99-64156

Printed in the United States of America

Dedication

In loving memory of my son, Aron, whose short
time on this earth brightened the lives of many.

His death brought me to a deeper awareness
of all human suffering, to which I have always tried
to respond.

And to all my associates, past and present, whose
heroic efforts continue in the pursuit of a peaceful
and just world.

TABLE OF CONTENTS

Family Life

I. Hardship, Joys, and Tragedy: 1905-1924

II. A New Life in California 1924-1948

III. From Personal to Political: 1948-2000

Political Life

IV. The Women's Peace Movement

V. Oral Histories, Free Speech Radio, and the Future: 1984–2000

Appendices

Taking Stock: Essays on Local, National, and Global Concerns

I began my life in North Dakota as a child
of pioneer Jewish homesteaders.
I married a pioneer Jewish farmer from Palestine.
Yet throughout it all, I had aspirations outside the farm.

—ASH

"It is good to know that the people who lie beneath
the markers with the Star of David are not forgotten...
It is important that
their [stories] be recorded..."

—Frances Wold, at the cemetery
outside of Wing, North Dakota

Introduction

*"In a sense, the journey from your beginnings to the present moment
...describes what usually requires several generations to achieve..."*
—Josephine Carson, author

My grandchildren occasionally ask about how things were in "the old days," but I never considered my answers as anything more than family lore until 1984, when I took my first oral history course. Suddenly the thought occurred that I consider writing my story. Instead, the pursuit of documenting oral histories took over. I completed a number of histories of Bay Area activists, and ultimately devoted some time to a biography of my late husband, *Sam Hamburg: Agricultural Pioneer in California and Israel*, which was published in 1989 by the Western History Center of the Judah L. Magnes Museum. Yet I had read somewhere that the greatest gift a grandmother could give would be the written record of her life. My grandchildren gave me the needed push to start writing my history. While looking over the manuscript of my book on Sam, my grandson, Ted Ruehl, commented, "This doesn't mention anything about you, Grandma." My nephew Gary had lost his father at the age of nine. He had many questions about his father's life and the family's history and was one of those who encouraged me in this writing project.

In 1986 granddaughter Julie Goldsmith interviewed me for a feminist course she was taking at Yale. Ten years later, while I was still debating how to handle some of the most troublesome and tragic aspects of our family's history, Julie offered to help. Early one morning during a vacation in Berkeley, she and her brother David appeared, he with his tape recorder and she ready with questions to get me started. Julie focused on the most difficult issues of family relationships. At first I resisted. Who but family members would know, or care, about our lives? How could I relive some of my most painful recollections?

Encouraged by their enthusiasm, however, I began to search my memories. In five morning sessions, ably engineered by David, I began the first uncertain steps toward this written self-reflection, a history not only of my life, work, and family, but also a story intended to illuminate some of the great and trying moments of the last century, from my point of view.

I wanted readers to learn of the struggles immigrants like my parents faced as they established themselves in a strange foreign land, and of the conditions of poverty and deprivation which our family, like so many others, had endured.

Perhaps, I thought as I prepared to write, my grandchildren will then experience sympathy for the many homeless and helpless they see on our streets today. I hope my lifelong efforts to help bring about a more peaceful and just society might serve as incentive for their future involvement in social movements and political struggle. I hope this story will give young people a better understanding of my life experiences in the context of changing times. Perhaps they will become more aware of our American heritage, and come to realize that our forefathers and mothers underwent great hardship to create and pass on to us their dream of a democratic and peaceful society.

Why do I recollect more than a half-century of activism only now, as I begin my tenth decade? I have been unwilling to disrupt my ongoing activities for long enough to record the many changes I have witnessed, the fascinating individuals I have met, and the historic events in which I have played a role.

In this memoir, I wish to explore the influences that have shaped my life and reflect on where I am now in relation to my family, friends, neighbors, and the contemporary world. As I grow older, I am more conscious of the limits of time. Aging forces one to face mortality. The process is both exhilarating, frustrating, and at times, painful. Now is the time for taking stock.

I have attempted to emulate my mother in her concerns for others, primarily her family. Although her life was full of the struggle for survival, mine has been more complicated, in that the question for me has been how to meet my children's needs, and at the same time deal with problems affecting not only family, but also community. This conflict was never discussed in our family. When my children read this, perhaps it will help them to better understand their mother.

I have used several sources, in addition to my own files, in the writing of this autobiography. I begin with the story of my parents, who came to this country in the early 1900s to settle on a homestead in North Dakota. Fortunately, I did not need to rely entirely upon my own recollections for this story. The discovery of my father's memoir was my most immediate inspiration for beginning to write.

When my parents were living in Los Angeles in the late 1930s, my father asked me to help him write his life story. At that time my children were young; it was impossible for me to remain away from home for the length of time required to do the job. I was then living in the small San Joaquin Valley town of Los Baños near the ranch that my husband, with great effort, had acquired. I still regret that I was unable to fulfill my father's request. Fortunately, my older brother Charlie later discovered the life story of our father, Herman Sachs, on a dusty shelf in a storeroom on his own ranch near Los Baños. Our father had dictated the account to a friend in 1941. It was handwritten, in a red-bound notebook. This surprise gift was presented to me on May 7, 1989, at the reception hosted by the Judah L. Magnes Museum, marking the publication of my book on the life of my husband.

It distresses me deeply that I never told my father how much he inspired me during his lifetime. Only now do I realize the true breadth of his gifts and abilities. Although unable to provide well in the material sense for our family of six, his considerable sacrifices sustained us. His skill with languages enabled him to adjust fairly quickly to the new country. My mother had greater difficulty, yet with considerable effort, her native intelligence bridged the gap between Yiddish and English, at least enough to enable her to communicate with non-Jewish neighbors.

Charlie, who worked many jobs throughout his early years, made it possible for the rest of us to remain in school. For this I am very grateful. Perhaps by writing this family account—Charlie's, brother Ben's, sister Rae's, and my own—the debt I feel toward my parents will be lightened.

In 1987 I transcribed an oral history of Charlie. This transcript provided me with many stories of our early life on the North Dakota homestead. Charlie's memory was excellent and he continued to answer my questions and augment my recollections of those long-ago days.

Charlie died in March 1996. My activities kept me from visiting him as frequently as he wished. I never got to say good-bye. The entire family and his many friends gathered for a beautiful, summer-day memorial in the garden of my daughter, Tanya Goldsmith. We laughed and cried as we shared many wonderful family memories, carrying on Charlie's own favorite pastime, storytelling. I miss him dearly.

I would like to pay tribute to Sophie Turnoy Trupin, a Dakota contemporary, with whom I reunited nearly sixty years later in the East Bay. Her book, *Dakota Diaspora*, influenced me. Our families were neighbors from 1902 to 1914 in the pioneer Jewish settlement in Burleigh County, North Dakota, a farming experiment with little chance of success. Soon, my family moved to Minneapolis, while Sophie's remained in North Dakota for several additional years. Recently, she graciously shared some of her memories, and introduced me to the writer Frances Wold, whom my family and I visited in 1987 in her Bismarck, North Dakota, home. Although not Jewish, Frances dedicated years to researching and compiling the history of our community of Wing-Regan-Canfield. Her work has been of great value to me.

During our visit, Frances reintroduced my family and me to the town of Wing and its surroundings, which had been our early family home. To our surprise, very little had changed. The population remained approximately two hundred. However, streets were now paved and there were sidewalks. A residence stood where my father's general store had been constructed in 1911, the town's first permanent building. For years it had also housed the Post Office.

Frances referred us to Norman Kamins, who drove us out to the Jewish cemetery in nearby Regan, Canfield Township. The cemetery was established in 1903 and incorporated by a committee of settlers, including Kamins' grandfather and my Uncle Abram Sachs. The weathered gravestones and the absence of recent additions give mute testimony to the waning of the Midwestern Jewish community. Frances died in 1996. Sophie died the next year.

In my life there has been a continuous thread. The struggle to subsist off the land began in North Dakota as a child of pioneer Jewish homesteaders. My father broke stones in the barren land of North Dakota, while my husband, a later immigrant, began his farming career in the more fertile soil of California's Central Valley. He struggled no less, but the rewards were far greater. These commitments may have contributed to the perspective of our late son, Aron, who went to Brazil and Nicaragua to learn about their farming conditions in hopes of bringing knowledge of advanced agricultural techniques to their people.

Despite this legacy of life on the land, I always had aspirations outside the farm. Since my childhood I yearned to work for peace, for better living conditions for all, while my husband's focus was to change the world through agriculture. Reflecting on our family relationships, I sometimes wonder if the children may at times have felt deprived of my attention, because so much of it was channeled toward social issues. My justification was that they, and their generation, would later benefit from a more peaceful and just world.

It gives me great pleasure that my granddaughter Julie Goldsmith is both a scholar and an activist with a doctorate in sociology with the thesis, "Working the System," on welfare policy, in which she used the techniques of oral history. I appreciate her interest throughout. I wish to express appreciation to her brother, David, whose computer expertise has guided me through the technological minefield of the 'Mac.' My grandsons, Ernie Jr., Ted, and Paul Ruehl have encouraged me in this writing and indicate their eagerness to see the results. I hope this gives all of them a better understanding of my lifetime involvement in social activism.

Over the years my daughters, Tanya and Sonya, and I have come to a better understanding. As they reared their children they have developed greater awareness of the stresses and strains inherent in parent-child relationships. At this stage, we benefit from a greater tolerance and mutual respect. I consult them frequently and profit from their advice. We are friends.

In my lifetime, I have seen many changes—in my own economic circumstances, as well as in the transition from a largely agrarian economy to one of high technology, including revolutionary developments in agriculture. The invention of cotton, tomato, and almond picking machines was comparable to the onset of the computer era—it changed the fate of the workforce on the farm, taking jobs from the unskilled. This was the early stage of converting the tomato into a squarish shape and texture that could withstand the impact of the conveyer belt, as well as maintain a longer shelf life. (Was this early food engineering?) They were then trucked from the field to the cannery in Tracy. In this century, the country has evolved from horse-drawn farming to mechanized agriculture, from mail by horseback to email, from radios to satellites to the information superhighway, the Internet.

This story concerns the transition from youthful idealism to a time for reflection about the past and the ways in which it influences the future. Life for ordinary people has changed more during my lifetime than during the entirety of prior history. Having lived through these tumultuous times, I now wonder how the advances in technology and communication have been of benefit to the average person. Unfortunately, progress has come at the expense of the environment: large scale deforestation, drought and soil depletion, the rising incidence of related health problems, and the displacement of numerous indigenous peoples throughout the world. We must seek an end to this continuing environmental degradation that clouds our future.

Change is not only the background for my story, it is also the foreground. I have attempted to familiarize myself with modern thought in such areas as childrearing, health, language, transportation, and communication. I have tried to be active in such fields as politics, welfare, and world affairs. But without the support of able, like-minded, and inspiring people in a number of organizations, I would have been helpless.

Although the privilege of meeting celebrities such as Martin Luther King, Jr., and his wife Coretta, W.E.B. DuBois—who helped lay the framework for the Black freedom movement, and Paul Robeson was gratifying, I would like to pay tribute to those less-sung individuals, most of them women, with whom I have also been privileged to work. These are the people who persevered over the years, whether the day-to-day struggle was for integration, stopping nuclear testing, or ending the Vietnam War. No matter how hopeless the struggle seemed, they never faltered.

I would like to pay tribute to the following Women's International League for Peace and Freedom (WILPF) members. In San Francisco, there was Katharine Cole, an elegant woman who had earlier been involved in the anti-war, anti-racist efforts of the Unitarian Church in Los Angeles; whose husband Lester was a blacklisted Hollywood writer. Deeply concerned about the Native American struggles, she took up the case of Leonard Peltier, who was charged with murder at Pine Ridge Reservation in South Dakota and imprisoned for more than twenty-years, despite evidence pointing to his innocence.

Enola Maxwell, an African American and lay Presbyterian minister, became a leader in the San Francisco community after having moved here from the South. Fearless, blunt, and outspoken, Enola is the longtime Executive Director of the low-income Potrero Hill Neighborhood House. She alerted us early to the connections between the failing educational system, unemployment, drug use, and violence.

Frances Shaskan, a consumer advocate, was our legislative liaison to the mayor and city supervisors. Along with Sylvia Siegal, she helped found TURN, The Utility Reform Network, a citizens watchdog organization that monitors utility rates for consumers.

Frieda Salzman, wife of Milt Wolff, the last commander of the Abraham Lincoln International Brigade, raised thousands of dollars for medical relief for Cuba and Nicaragua. As president of the California Gray Panthers, she was identified with the "single payer" health plan for universal coverage.

Among those who have kept WILPF a presence in San Francisco, are Stella Paton, Ethel Von Hermann, Rhoda Norman, Karen Talbot, Miriam Rothschild, Grace Hamilton, and Aileen Hernandez, who was first president of the National Organization for Women (NOW).

In the East Bay, WILPF and Women Strike for Peace members have worked together on many projects, among them Edith Laub, Miriam Bloomberg, Leonore Veltfort, Lorene Lamb, and Lynne McDonald. Among the editors of the joint newsletter, recognized as one of the most informative in the field, have been Libby Mines, June Naboisek, Beth Wilson and Lillian Nurmela. I reflect sadly on those who are no longer with us—Frances Herring, Erna P. Harris, Leona Bayer, Frances Shaskan, Celia Yanish; and my friend Walter Gillen, who died in 1998. Both Celia and Walter made bequests to the women's peace movement.

I hope that my friends and colleagues will find some interest in the project that has kept me so occupied. Throughout this book I have attempted to acknowledge the contributions of as many of them as has proved practical. I apologize to those I have overlooked.

Perhaps some of my readers will find a resonance between my memories and their own, that this tale might evoke stories to share with their families, and, ultimately, inspire a passion for peace and justice among generations to come.

I wish to acknowledge my indebtedness to Amy Swerdlow for her excellent history, *Women Strike for Peace,* published by the University of Chicago Press in 1993. I have relied on her vivid descriptions of the beginnings of the movement, especially on the East Coast. Swerdlow's delineation of WSP's role in bringing together the various aspects of feminism during the sixties and including peace as one of its demands has been especially helpful.

In writing this account of my life, I have identified many people. In order to protect the privacy of certain individuals, I have taken the liberty of changing a few names.

About Alice

"There is only one solution if old age is not a parody of our former life, and that is to go on pursuing ends that give our existence a meaning, devotion to individuals, to groups or to causes, social, political, intellectual or creative work...One's life has value so long as one attributes value to the life of others, by means of love, friendship, indignation, compassion..."

—Simone DeBeauvoir, *Coming of Age*

"At 93, Alice Hamburg is the oldest member of Bay Area WILPF and Women for Peace," writes Barbara George, fellow activist, "but a list of her current activities would be daunting for a person half her age: researching, writing, and giving speeches about the latest wars and pending legislation; mediating at KPFA; consulting with numerous groups; keeping up with heavy correspondence; cooking, gardening, doing yoga, and tending to a tight-knit family. Her determination to live a life of meaning led her to make extraordinary contributions to her community and the larger world..."as a phenomenal force for peace and social justice."

"Alice is a richly complex character who...never sits still, either physically or intellectually," comments Alice's long-time assistant, Barbara Stack. "She continues actively to reinterpret her life and the times in which she has lived. She has standards, and that can sometimes be very tough on the rest of us. Alice makes a most astute characterization of her own political posture: activist. In her writing, this precision dictates...that the word must be exactly the right word, the just word, the kind word...Efficiency and thrift dovetail with Alice's concern for the environment, justice, and the redistribution of wealth on both a macro and micro scale. This justice is tempered by *rachmones*, the Yiddish word for compassion. Alice knows, she has not forgotten, what it means to struggle for food, for warmth, for a home."

"As an historian and author," writes Cathy Luchetti, a close friend and collaborator with Alice, "I had only witnessed history through journals, diaries, and old photographs. The pioneer days are gone, I thought. Then, in meeting Alice, I realized that a single life could not only span the changes in this country, but could also connect them. She had turned radical liberalism and the fight against war and injustice into one long quilting bee. She brought North Dakota to Berkeley, and given the chance, would do the same in reverse.

Given her outstanding background, it's almost surprising to find a woman so accessible and warm, interested in every detail of an individual's life, ready with support and encouragement at every step.

Seldom do friends, mentors, activists, and advisors come in one package, yet this is Alice's gift. She turns every environment into a small, cozy village. Suddenly everyone knows everyone else, people are connected, jobs are offered, concerns are voiced, all because of her deep humanitarian concern...She is a woman who embodies more than anyone the words, 'we are family.'"

Acknowledgments

In confronting the difficult task of writing about my life, with its many joys as well as tragedies, I have been encouraged by the following people, and I wish to recognize their contributions to this project.

I appreciate the help of anti-nuclear activist and editor Barbara George, whose early interviews and organizational skills were useful. The work was brought to completion by my longtime assistants, Barbara Stack and Cathy Luchetti. Barbara "noodged" life into some of my stories by challenging me with her humor, sparking new ideas, and creativity with her unexpected Yiddish references. Cathy Luchetti, award-winning author and cultural historian, brought her enthusiasm, patience, insights, and editorial facilities to this endeavor.

My neighbor, journalist Frances Starn, had interviewed me for a story in *The Berkeley Gazette* after my third trip to the Soviet Union in 1983. More recently, she offered helpful suggestions and pointed out the book's "vivid memories" and "socio-political" interest.

In the early days of this endeavor, Dorothy Benson and I were still using typewriters—only one of many things we had in common. My early childhood story resonated with hers; we both had experienced the hardships of growing up on marginal farms during the Depression. Her memories have helped me recall my own stories.

Political analyst William Mandel assisted with his critique of the final essays. Thanks to Matthew Lasar, author of *Pacifica Radio*, for his suggestions on the KPFA chapter.

My friend Ying Lee, following her recent return from Washington, DC, where she was a long time senior legislative assistant to our Congressman Ron Dellums, and legislative director for Congresswoman Barbara Lee, has provided invaluable editing assistance in the final stages of this book. Her fresh insight and probing questions helped me clarify a number of issues.

Grass Roots

Family Life

I. Hardship, Joys, and Tragedy: 1905-1924

"To most Jewish immigrants New York was America. Some dared venture as far as Chicago. But the Jews who settled in North Dakota at the turn of the century were different. They were a special breed. Each was a Moses in his own right, leading his people out of the land of bondage. Only this was no land of milk and honey—no land of olive trees and vineyards. This was a harsh, forbidding land, with bitter winters and stubborn, rock-strewn soil."

—description of *Dakota Diaspora* by Sophie Trupin,
    Alternative Press, 1984

Chapter 1
From a Russian Shtetl

"The Jewish Agriculturists' Aid Society of America's aim...was to help people leave the enslaving sweatshop or unpromising and degrading peddling in the city and start out as farmers."

—Hyman L. Meites, *History of the Jews of Chicago*

My father, Herman Sachs, was born in 1870 in the *shtetl* of Skopishok, Kovna Gobernia, Lithuania, which was part of Russia at the time. In his last years, he described his early home:

I first saw the light of day in a very unsanitary three-room house in which three families lived. There was one small kerosene lamp to illuminate the room. The house had no floors at all, just dirt. No sanitary fixtures or water. We had to carry our water from a well that was four blocks away. For waste water disposal, there was a ditch nearby. For a toilet we had none, just anywhere in the backyard. No privacy at all. For our baths we went to a Turkish bath house which was steam heated by throwing water onto rocks which had been previously heated by fire. It cost us three kopeks, or one and a half cents. We hung our clothes on a high stick to kill the vermin. The men took their baths first, the women later. For rinsing there was a large hole in the ground filled with cold water. The water was never changed. You can imagine the smell.

Herman, like all other young boys, attended the local *yeshiva*, where he studied the Talmud and showed a gift for languages. He describes his school as similar to the hovel he lived in, his school was "a bedlam of many boys rehearsing their lessons at the same time." Punishment was quick and certain by way of a big leather strap on the table.

When we grew older, we had to go to school at night after supper and return home when the streets were pitch dark. During the rainy season the mud was knee-deep, and in order to illuminate our way we used to make paper lanterns. Is there a wonder that when we did grow up we hated the whole system?

Illness, malnutrition and lack of sanitation cut short my father's traditional schooling. Looking toward earning a livelihood, he decided to apprentice himself to a local tinsmith. His mother was strongly opposed to his learning a trade, which was considered a family disgrace. His father had enjoyed the respected position of *shached*, a ritual butcher. His father's early death had left his mother with three young boys, and Herman felt he had to make a practical decision.

Following his apprenticeship, he worked in construction for several years, and at the age of nineteen, restless and hearing of possible work in Finland, packed his meager belongings and headed north. After an arduous, lengthy trip he met his future employer, an unpleasant and bitter alcoholic. Adding to my father's apprehension was his discovery that Jews were *persona non grata* in Finland. It was dangerous for them to be seen in public. As a dark-haired, poorly-dressed foreigner, Herman could safely venture out only at night.

He faced other dangers. Herman almost lost his life one winter night when he and another young man were sent to frozen Lake Ladoga to fetch a tub of water. His partner slipped and fell into the icy water, pulling Herman in with him. They called for help but no one heard. Desperate to find a handhold in the darkness, Herman felt a piece of horse manure frozen into the ice, grasped it and pulled himself and his coworker out. When they returned with their clothes frozen to their bodies, their employer rebuked them for failing to bring back the water.

In addition to work as a journeyman tinsmith, Herman also became a longshoreman, which enabled him to earn enough to reach Sweden, where Jews enjoyed greater acceptance. By this time he was fairly fluent in Finnish, and welcomed the challenge of further travel and language study. However, his stay in Sweden was cut short when his older brother, Louis, summoned him home. Their mother was ill. With his twenty-first birthday approaching, and fearful of being drafted into the Russian army, Herman nevertheless heeded the call and returned home. He was immediately drafted into the army for a five-year stint, although he was granted a leave to attend to his dying mother.

My father served in the cavalry, an exhausting and dangerous job. His training as a tinsmith stood him in good stead, however, as it facilitated transfer to the foundry, where he cast metal food containers carried by the cavalry while on maneuvers. In his diary he tells of the cruel discipline and brutal treatment accorded Jews in the army. Enlisted men were portioned four slices of bread a day, but they often received only one or two, because officers were stealing and selling supplies. Forced to eat grass to survive, at times he contemplated suicide.

After completing his service in 1900, Herman returned home. It was time for him to marry, and the enterprising *shotchun* (matchmaker) took up his case. Marriages were generally arranged in those days, love and future happiness not necessarily the most important concerns. When the *shotchun* settled the bargain and the parents on both sides were satisfied, plans began for the wedding. Shortly thereafter, Herman married Hannah Shmuelson, from the nearby village of Pokroi. Local people were a bit wary of his worldliness—it was said that "he wore his cap at a rakish angle"—yet Hannah was in her mid-twenties, an old maid by local standards! Many years later, my father's cousin, Sarah Lipkin of Oakland, told me what a beautiful bride my mother was, with her wavy light brown hair and flawless fair complexion.

My mother's family owned a dairy and was slightly more prosperous than my father's, but her childhood had not been easy. Girls received very little formal education, the lack of which hampered my mother throughout her life. Her own mother died when she was very young, and she was raised by a stepmother. She became devoted to her younger brother, BenZion, who later emigrated to South Africa. Recently, my cousin Hannah wrote me from South Africa that BenZion talked often of his sister and especially treasured her sweet singing of Yiddish songs.

It must have been a particular comfort to my mother to have BenZion with her when her first child, Choskel (Charlie), was born in 1901, because my father was about to leave for the United States. He planned to send for her and the baby as soon as he was able. BenZion had progressive ideas about child rearing and advised her not to swaddle the infant as was the custom of the times. It would be two years before Hannah and Charlie would join Herman in the new country.

Chapter 2

A Perilous Time for Jews

"Tears came to his eyes as he recalled the days of the Czar, the days of the knout, pogroms, ignorance and superstition. But the tears were tears not only of sorrow, but of happiness, for Abe had seen the hopes of a lifetime fulfilled in the country of his birth. He had lived to see the most oppressed colonial people throw off the chains of bondage. He is happy that in his humble way, he did what he could to see that day when the dream of his youth became a reality..."

> —A friend honoring my uncle, Abram Sachs, at his 70th
> birthday celebration in Minneapolis

In August of 1902 my father left Russia, soon to be followed by his younger brother Abram, who was escaping service in the army. The war with Japan loomed on the horizon. It was a period of great unrest in Russia and a perilous time for Jews, a persecuted minority. Herman saw no future for himself or his family in Lithuania; many were leaving for the promise of a better life in America, the land of opportunity. It was inevitable that he would join them.

Herman was in his early thirties when he crossed the Atlantic on a freighter. As the ship neared New York harbor, all the bedding was thrown overboard. The company was not licensed to carry passengers and all such evidence was discarded. After arriving in America, Herman went first to Denver, where he had a contact, then to Chicago, looking for work. He only found jobs requiring little skill, for a pay ranging from $1.25 to $2 per day. While working for the Armour Packing plant in Chicago he injured his left eye, the effects of which he felt for the rest of his life. He received no treatment since workers were not compensated for any work-related injury and he had little money.

In Chicago he learned that the Jewish Agricultural Society, which administered funds donated by an Austrian philanthropist, Baron de Hirsch, was encouraging poor Eastern European Jewish immigrants to settle on new homesteads in the United States and Canada. The fund offered low-interest loans for minimal housing and tools—perhaps a cow or two and some horses—to people who had nothing when they came to the United States. Under the Homestead Act of 1862, each applicant was allowed to register for ownership of a 160-acre parcel, and was required to "prove up" the claim by developing the land and remaining on it for five years.

Herman received travel funds from the Jewish Agricultural Society, which landed him near Wilton, North Dakota. He arrived there in 1903, soon to be followed by his unmarried brother Abram. They applied for adjoining plots of land in an agricultural settlement of some fifty Jewish families.

Difficult though pioneer life proved to be, Herman preferred it to working in the city. The extreme deprivation of his childhood and youth left him well prepared for the hard times confronting him on the barren, rocky soil of North Dakota. It was very difficult to scratch out a living. For four years, all through the frozen months of winter and spring, Herman and Abram took leave of the homestead to work at the Washburn Lignite Coal Company Mine near Wilton. They lived in a shack provided by their employers. Work in the mine was backbreaking: dust everywhere, winter temperatures dropped to forty degrees below zero. The mine was a dangerous place. In the years Herman worked there, three men were killed in accidents.

When not on call at the mine, Herman tried his hand at other jobs: he was a bridge carpenter on the Soo Railroad Line at $2.10 per day. During the summers, he and Abram collected their wages and headed for the farm.

The land was marginal at best—more productive acreage had long since been claimed by earlier settlers. The treeless landscape was daunting, a panorama of small hills and gullies surrounded by heaps of rocks and boulders. On particularly frigid mornings, Herman and Abram would build a fire around a boulder, causing it to crack. Inserting a heavy chain into the crack, they broke the rock apart and hauled the chunks away to the edge of the property. In winter, the entire landscape was marked by rock piles protruding from endless fields of snow. Two years passed before Herman was able to send for Hannah and Charlie.

After six weeks in steerage, enduring overcrowding, filth, sickness, and hunger, my mother came through Ellis Island with baby Charlie and whatever worldly possessions she could carry—featherbeds, linens, and baby clothes. Also included in this assemblage was an accordion, which she had played in happier times, although I don't recall ever hearing her play it.

When she followed my father to this country, Hannah left her family behind in Lithuania—never to see them again! She only communicated by mail with her brother and sister, who had settled in South Africa about the same time. Mother traveled by train across the United States with Charlie, to be met by Father in Wilton. Since there was no house on the land, she and Charlie boarded with another settlement family, the Handlemans. There she was thoroughly miserable as conditions were crowded and primitive, and food scarce and strictly rationed. As a toddler, Charlie, to Mother's deep embarrassment, tattled on her for having taken two eggs for their lunch. He recalled walking with Mother to visit Father, in his dilapidated shack on the grounds of the coal mine.

Chapter 3

Coyotes and Coal Mines

"Two inches of snow drifted onto our bed. The wind could blow 50 miles an hour in the winter. Summer winds were no less troublesome because of the danger of prairie fires."

—Herman Sachs

I was born on November 25, 1905, in Wilton, North Dakota, in the coal mining company hospital. By then, our growing family definitely needed a home. With money earned from their work at the mine, Herman and Abram were able to buy lumber and supplies to rebuild and reinforce an abandoned, weather-beaten shell of a house that stood on their land, enlarging it to include a granary in the rear. They put down a well, and a year after my birth our family moved in. The wind, rain and snow blew in, but it was a shelter. The eerie howl of the coyote disturbed our nights. My mother, new to the prairie, was terrified.

Our greatest dread on the farm was prairie fires. They would come suddenly, approaching by leaps and bounds. On the treeless prairie, a blaze could be seen for miles. When neighbors saw one coming, they would rush to start a backfire, but often it was too late. Many families watched everything they owned go up in a blaze. My father, who was very careful about planning for possible dangers, plowed firebreaks around the house. One hot summer day, he spotted a fire in the distance. He led us to safety in a freshly plowed field and ordered us to lie face down in the dirt. Fortunately, the flames veered off in another direction. To this day, strong winds, lightning, and thunder conjure up the nightmare of fire destroying everything in its path. As a child, my response to lightning was to crawl under the bed and pull the covers over my head.

13

I have no idea how my mother managed on the homestead. When my sister Rachel was born in 1907, Mother was assisted by "Dr." Kongursky, a Russian-Jewish immigrant and neighbor trained as an orderly. He earned his livelihood by traveling from farm to farm performing the services of a midwife in return for several weeks' lodging. Rachel's birth was the first to be registered in the town of Wing.

Ma was always busy, keeping the family clothed and fed. At her treadle Singer she sewed baby clothes and made diapers out of flour sacks. To do laundry, she heated water on a coal-burning kitchen stove and then scrubbed, using a washboard and a tin laundry tub which doubled as the family bathtub. I helped her spread the laundry on the grass to dry. There were neither clothes lines nor trees on which to attach them.

In addition to the daily household chores—caring for us, preparing meals—she fed the animals, milked the cows, gardened, and generally kept things going. Mother loved animals and seemed able to communicate with them: a calf on the farm followed her around like a dog. She also raised chickens, ducks, and turkeys. One of my early terrors was of being pursued by raucous and belligerent turkey gobblers. When they came near me, I scurried away as fast as I could. Charlie's chore was to search their nests and bring in eggs. When the baby chicks were hatched, however, I could not resist picking them up and cuddling them. After I smothered one or two, the henhouse became strictly off limits for me.

Our farm diet was the product of our own efforts, and consisted mainly of homemade bread, potatoes, corn meal, eggs, and poultry. Mother was really the one who should have been the farmer. She could always make things grow. No matter where she lived, Mother raised potatoes. Years later in Los Angeles, she added avocados to her list of produce. She was also a lover of flowers, and even raised geraniums on the farm.

We bought staples such as flour, cornmeal, oatmeal, and sugar, but we had no canned goods. We always kept some potato "eyes" to plant for the next year's crop. Eggs were carefully preserved for the winter in salt-filled crates. I remember helping chop cabbage for sauerkraut and pickling watermelons for a special treat during the winter months. Pickled produce was stored in the root cellar in large crocks weighted down with rocks. The cellar was filled with heavy burlap sacks bursting with potatoes and onions.

When the long-awaited summers came, we children quickly discovered the treasures of Haystack Butte. There, we found beautiful pink prairie roses, the North Dakota state flower, and chokecherries, which we gathered and took home for jelly-making. The jelly, relished on special occasions with tea, brought a shine to the eyes of us children.

When the lakes and ponds froze solid in winter, the men and boys would carve out blocks of ice and cart them home in wagons. Ice was kept in a storehouse connected to the main quarters, and packed with mounds of sawdust to prevent melting. This ice preserved a certain amount of meat for special occasions. We never had any surplus of food. Beef or chicken were luxury items. To this day, when served a meal, I always eat the vegetables first and savor the meat, although today, I favor vegetables!

When I was very young, I had the bad habit of sticking foreign objects in my mouth. One day while helping my mother do laundry, Charlie hit me. When I started to cry, I swallowed a very small corsage pin, much to the alarm of Mother and a neighbor. They were terrified! What was to be done? My father hitched up our horse Molly for the buggy ride into town. On the way, he tried to make a deal with me, hoping to avoid the expense of a visit to the doctor. He asked, in Yiddish of course, "Are you sure you swallowed the pin? If not, we'll buy you a doll." Since I insisted I had, we continued on to Dr. Tillen's office. He advised feeding me an abundance of potatoes and bread to aid the natural course of things. The outhouse never yielded the missing object, but, miraculously, I survived.

About the same time, Charlie, still a young boy, was having problems with his vision. A neighbor suggested a "sure-fire" test. Pointing at horses about a half-mile down the road, he asked, "Charlie, do you see horses out there in the field? What direction are they headed?" Having failed the exam, my brother was taken sixteen miles into Wilton and an additional thirty-five miles by train to Bismarck for an examination. He felt badly about Pa having to spend $10—a small fortune—for his new glasses.

With little cash to pay hired help, mutual assistance among prairie settlers was essential for survival, especially during harvest season. Late summer was a crucial time. Farmers kept a wary eye out for storm clouds on the horizon. As the wheat ripened, swaying in the wind, farmers took turns with the horse-drawn threshing machine, helping each other load wagons with grain-filled sacks, which were then hauled away to the granary for later transfer to flour mills in Minneapolis. Money from the crops would buy the following year's supplies and the cycle would begin again.

When Father worked long hours on the neighbors' threshing crews, his clothes got so grimy that he hesitated to enter their kitchen for meals. He chose to sleep in the barn at night. At this time, women came from nearby farms, accompanied by their children, and prepared to help feed the hungry men. Threshing went on from sunup to sundown—an abundance of food was consumed! I still recall the huge platters heaped with pancakes, eggs, potatoes, and homemade bread, pots of oatmeal, gallons of coffee, and pitchers of cream. These gatherings marked the end to the year's labors and sparked a feeling of mutual goodwill. Despite the merriment, my mother, not able to understand English and new to the country, felt uncomfortable in the presence of so many rough men.

The summer harvest also included wild grasses, which were used as fodder for the stock. As Charlie recollected:

They would mow and rake, then pile it in the barn, and you had a thing you could put the hay on. There'd be a thousand pounds of hay in one stack. With a team of horses and a rope you'd pull the hay... A stack would line up to 10 feet high, maybe 12 feet wide, and could be even 20 feet long. You would top it off with burlap so that the rain and snow could run off. The outer edges might be ruined, but 90 percent would be O.K.

Dakota winters were unremittingly harsh. If lost in a snowstorm, settlers were warned to find a haystack and burrow in for the duration. The rule was, always carry matches—either to start a fire, signal for help, or to burn a haystack to keep from freezing. In winter's endless months, it seemed as if the snow would never stop. Blizzards raged, and the drifts were very deep. No matter how severe the storm, farmers had to feed their livestock. Some would tie a rope from the house to the barn to avoid getting lost. Tragedies occurred. One night, a neighbor disappeared in the midst of a blizzard and his body was discovered the next morning only a few feet from his door. Fourteen-year old Charlie was once lost in a snowstorm, but he had the good fortune to make it back home. During winters when our cows were not producing enough milk, it was my chore, at age four, to go to a neighbor's house for a bucket of milk. In spite of fleece-lined boots and hand-knit woolen mittens, many a time I almost froze.

A large kitchen stove heated water for cooking, while a smaller, pot-belly stove in the front room provided heat. Both burned coal, without which none of us could have survived. To obtain this precious commodity, our men were forced to navigate twenty-five miles of severely rutted roads to the mine outside of Wilton. Weather often forced them to stay overnight. At the mouth of the mine, wagons would line up, each waiting its turn before soft coal, usually of inferior quality, was shoveled into each wagon bed.

Homesteading was a hard life, with very few conveniences. Without running water or sanitary facilities, we relied on the outhouse. I remember walking out there at night in winter, a lantern in one hand and my two-year old sister's hand in the other. The Sears Roebuck catalogue served the dual purpose of entertainment and toilet paper. Indians would come by, and Mother would offer them milk or whatever food we might have. I knew little about them. To me, they seemed just like other poor itinerants.

Horses were essential to our survival and they were our most valuable asset. Father was a skilled horseman. Falling back on his experience in the Russian cavalry, he knew how to handle them, and was able to help others break and train their animals. Altogether, we had five workhorses. Pa bought Nellie and a rundown buggy with wired-up wheels for the grand sum of $5. Humorously, he described the swayback mare as "old enough to vote." On the other hand, Pa thought Molly was a great horse, although, given half a chance, she would run away. Fortunately, she behaved herself when Ma, pregnant and alone, would drive into Wilton to pick up Pa at the mine. The entire family went into mourning when Molly died from pneumonia one winter.

Life on the farm was, in some ways, a reflection of the outside world. There were horse thieves among the settlers. Horseback riding accidents occurred and medical help was not readily available. My father broke his leg twice driving the wagon to the coal mine. Once, Pa saved Ma and me from disaster when he managed to stop a runaway horse and wagon. Mother had me in her lap and Father quickly reined in, stopping the frantic horse by slamming it into a fence. "Otherwise", said Pa, "The little one would have been thrown out and probably killed." While riding his horse to the barn, our neighbor, Art Little, let go of the reins too soon. The horse spooked, and the poor man was catapulted against the barn door and literally beheaded.

Somewhat experienced in ways of the new country, my father served as a village elder. Once, when a woman was charged with shooting her stepson, my father proved conclusively to the district attorney that she didn't know one end of a gun from the other, and that someone else must have been responsible for the death.

On another occasion, a Jewish couple tried to murder their non-cooperative son-in-law. They beat him and locked him out of the house on a winter night, hoping he would freeze to death. The ruse failed and he was able to crawl to a neighbor's door, the Blumenfelds. The story got around. When the sheriff came, my father was called in as interpreter. Since most settlers did not speak English, my father, more skilled in the language, often served in this capacity. I believe the family got away without punishment.

Chapter 4

Drought and Debt

"From the beginning, the settlement had trouble..."

—William C. Sherman, ed., *Plains Folk:*
North Dakota's Ethnic History

After Father and Abram completed their five homestead years, each received title to a quarter section. By that time they were tired of the back-breaking farm work, and after an extended drought, decided to mortgage their land and try their luck in business. Herman received his naturalization paper on November 24, 1908. In 1909 they put up the first structure in what was to be Wing, North Dakota. Our building, Sachs Brothers General Store, also housed the Post Office. The family's living quarters were upstairs and Abram lived downstairs. After meeting county requirements, my father became a cream tester, and for four years the business boomed. Farmers would bring their milk to be tested by him for cream content. Milk would then be transported to the dairy in the next big town.

Abram—young, single, and restless—soon left to learn the plumbing trade as classes were being offered at a nearby Indian reservation. He then moved on to Minneapolis to set up shop. We all missed his cheerful presence.

Although I have only vague recollections of the homestead, my early memories about our life in Wing are clearer. I was only four when we moved, and remember the town growing up around our Sachs Brothers General Store, where customers included Finnish and Norwegian neighbors, as well as the approximately thirty Jewish families that traveled into town to trade or buy.

During winter we sometimes went sledding, but it was so cold that we seldom were able to play outside. The neighboring Rashie girls used to play with Rachel and me. We would mix flour and water for paste and make collages with pictures cut from the Sears Roebuck catalogue. In spring and summer we played in the barns, rigging up trapezes with ropes and swinging like monkeys. My best trick was hanging by my knees from a dizzying height. I was not afraid of anything.

Charlie, attracted by the five-cent bounty on gopher tails, offered by the county, often stopped on his way to school to fashion a noose out of twine. Jumping down from his pony, he placed it over the gopher hole, waited for the curious rodent to emerge, and then snatched the varmint. He was quite successful. On a few occasions, I pulled the string over the hole. Occasionally I served as lookout. Charlie also had a gun, and went hunting for ducks and rabbits. A sociable fellow, he had friends among the Finns and Norwegians as well as our own people, and would stay over with his pals on hunting excursions.

In those pioneer days, everyone was busy and there was little time for stirring up trouble. A sense of community prevailed. Kinship in this pioneer village transcended culture or religion. People from different parts of the world were brought together in this tiny place, united by common hardships.

Since Pa had traveled in Finland, he was able to communicate well with the Finns, who were predominant in the area. Ma was unable to speak their language, but she established friendships with a number of the neighbors. Shared difficulties helped overcome language barriers. In Wing, my mother acquired shopkeeping skills and learned to interact with customers with an ease that graced her social dealings throughout her life.

A letter to the editor of the May 15, 1985, *South Wing News* reads:

> *"I wish I could have been more attentive to what mother spoke of the first store in Wing and the Sachs. I know she liked them really well and Mrs. Sachs would ask her and Helmi to have coffee with her. Mother didn't speak English, but the friendship showed. Also Mr. Sachs could speak Finn. Mother spoke so often about the store, as it must have been a treat to go shopping.*
>
> > *Signed,*
> > *Lydia Linska"*

Other Jewish families moved from the farm to Wing, and I recall religious services held in the homes of some of our neighbors. Our house was not large enough to serve as a meeting place for the seventy-odd members of this Jewish colony, but I have memories of some social gatherings. Men played old Yiddish tunes on their fiddles and accordions, and people danced the *kazatsky*—vigorous footwork and heavy stomping on rough-hewn, wooden floors. For these occasions, women vied with each other to bring forth their best traditional dishes, including steaming platters of German strudel, Romanian polenta, Lithuanian chopped herring, Russian cabbage, and spicy brisket borscht. Although Father was not religious, Mother attempted to keep a kosher kitchen.

At these gatherings there had to be a place for small children. Charlie loved to tell about sleeping with girls at a very early age! The four Blumenfeld girls and several of us Sachs children were put down to sleep crosswise on a big bed while the adults socialized, often until morning.

One of the customs popular among all the settlers was the shivaree, a noisy pioneer celebration imposed upon newlyweds. Couples who were caught at home on their wedding night were serenaded with a cacophony of rattles and horns. The event usually ended with the hapless groom being thrown on a blanket and tossed high in the air.

Jewish women in the community would try to entice the young rabbi, Julius Hess, for a social visit. He was a handsome, red-haired man, who traveled around to different farm settlements, staying with local families. When he visited us, he would bring a supply of *schmaltz* herring, and would roast them on the coals in our parlor heating stove, not ordinarily used for cooking. The rabbi didn't trust our kitchens or our dishes to be kosher. After the rabbi left, there was always a lingering smell of fish, bearing out the popular lore that Lithuanian Jews are "herring eaters." Later, Wing had a *shached* who did the slaughtering for the Jewish community. Poultry could be handled by the settlers themselves. The first year after we moved to Wing, I recall the entire community gathered at a local hall to celebrate Christmas Eve. How the children's eyes lighted up at the sight of the tree and the colorful wrapped presents beneath! To my bitter disappointment, there was nothing there for me. My parents had neglected to describe Christmas to me and explain that Jews did not celebrate this holiday.

I remember the excitement in December 1911, when the Northern Pacific Railroad finally reached Wing and we were connected with the rest of the country! Mother's curiosity about different foods prevailed over her shyness. A fine cook and baker, she had memorized many wonderful recipes, and brought them with her to America in her head. Yet from the railroad cooks who were feeding the crews laying the tracks, she learned the art of pie-making. This clearly American addition to her baking repertoire soon became the family's favorite dessert. Almost a magician, she also knew how to improvise with the simple ingredients then available on the North Dakota frontier. The railroad brought Wing's first telephone, which was installed at the station. People waiting for the train would often ask Charlie to crank up the phone and call the preceding station, asking: "Is the train coming today?" That was the schedule! For years, we were filled with anticipation as we watched workmen lay the rails and build the station.

Shortly after the railroad was extended to Wing, Mother, pregnant with her fourth child, took my sister Rae (as Rachel was known) and me by train to Chicago to await the birth. For Rae and me, this was our first train ride, and I still recall the excitement of it all: the whistle, the mysterious destination, and the dapper, uniformed conductor. We stayed at the home of our good friends Eva and Dave Blumenfeld, one of the first Jewish immigrant families to move from the farm to the big city.

Life was very difficult for all in the Dakotas, on land that had never been highly productive, and rain was unpredictable. Some years the crops were good, but at other times a sudden hailstorm could dash to the ground a fine stand of wheat, oats, barley, or flax—a year's labor gone in a matter of minutes. 1907 witnessed a severe drought. Many of the Jewish farmers left afterwards, the average stay in the community was about five years. Margaret was born in the Blumenfeld's Chicago house.

My experiences in Chicago still seem vivid. I recall waking up and hearing the sound, "clop, clop, clop," of horses trotting down the cobblestone streets to deliver milk. When visiting Woolworths, my eyes devoured the great displays of chocolates, which I had never seen before. A huge cornucopia of luscious candies and colorfully displayed packages astounded me; until then such items had only existed on the pages of Sears catalogues. While I was not able to sample any of these goodies, I did enjoy my first banana in the city.

Shortly after we returned home, true tragedy struck. The infant Margaret died of pneumonia. She was about two months old. The next child born into our family was Paul, who died of whooping cough while still an infant. The babies' deaths left my mother distraught, grieving. She was uncommunicative and different, somehow. One day I came upon her in the storeroom, packing away baby clothes, tears streaming down her cheeks. She hardly noticed I was there.

For the most part, Mother accepted the harsh existence on the homestead without complaint. Since contraceptive information was not available, women would often resort to life-threatening methods, including jumping from high places, in order to abort. Perhaps this gave rise to the old Midwestern term for menstruation, "falling off the roof."

In 1914, the year World War I broke out, my mother gave birth to her last child, Benjamin. We children were sent outside during the labor, which was assisted by Dr. Kongursky. Mother always had difficulty in childbirth, and Ben's arrival was no exception.

Yet he was a healthy baby, and as he blossomed and grew, Ma's depression lifted.

Wing had no bank, only Mr. Kiefer, an individual money lender who would visit the homes of loan applicants. If he spotted canned goods on the shelf, he would reprimand, "You folks spend too much money. You should raise your own food!" As it became apparent that the community was not prospering, my enterprising father had the idea of sponsoring Sunday afternoon baseball games to attract business. He also generously extended credit to his neighbors for supplies—he could never refuse anyone. A trusting soul, he believed everyone and suspected no one until it became clear that an employee was blatantly stealing from the till. Once, I got in trouble by telling Anna, the clerk, that according to my parents, she was a *gonif* (thief.) When funds were discovered missing in the general store, everyone was alarmed. But real excitement prevailed when money from the post office account was stolen. This thief was never apprehended, but suspicion pointed to the postmaster.

During a severe two-year drought, farmers could not pay their debts, causing my father to lose his credit with the wholesale houses. To make ends meet, he tried his hand at hay-baling, threshing grain, and road-building. Trusting one partner after another, he consistently came out on the short end. Inevitably, creditors moved in and the store failed. Discouraged about future prospects in Wing, Father decided to follow his brother Abram to Minneapolis and join him in the plumbing business.

Chapter 5

The Katzenjammer Kids

Before leaving home, Pa would feed the cat, saying, "I want to make sure you get a good meal before I leave." He didn't quite trust us children!

The move from Wing, with a population of scarcely more than two hundred, to Minneapolis, a city of many thousands, was quite a shock. We rented a furnished flat in a ten-unit building, paid $10 per month, and spent $60 on all the furniture, fixtures, and appliances. Among the many firsts that Minneapolis offered were running water and an indoor toilet. I remember ours as a very dreary house, with a ruined "dumb waiter" shaft in the center of the wall. For the first time, our playmates lived nearby and life was different from the isolation of the farm or small town.

In Wing, both my parents had been engaged constantly in running the general store and post office, but in Minneapolis, since Father was working in Uncle Abram's plumbing shop, he was usually home on Sundays. This was the only occasion during which I remember him reading to us. We gathered around him to hear the latest adventures of the *Katzenjammer Kids* in the comics—the original funnies. They were the goofiest boys, ugly as sin, who got into all kinds of scrapes—one of my few memories of Father relaxing with the family.

We traveled by trolley to the spectacular Minnehaha Falls and attended free Sunday afternoon concerts on the shores of a nearby lake. One Fourth of July, when we were allowed to be out late, I first heard the popping of firecrackers and marveled at the colorful fireworks spreading across the night sky.

We were in touch with others from North Dakota who had also moved to Minneapolis, including the Flacks family. In the summer, my mother would take me along to visit them. Still attracted to agriculture, the Flacks later purchased a farm on a lake. When I was on a visit there, Harry, the younger son, teased me, claiming I wanted to watch him swim in the nude. This annoyed me. I was being falsely accused! I knew about sex. I had heard conversations by older women and I wasn't naive. I had no interest in him—what was he thinking?

Harry Flacks later became a boxer. Unfortunately, he was badly injured in a fight and died shortly thereafter. The lack of rules in the "wide-open" boxing arena made that sport highly dangerous. Family and friends mourned the senseless loss of this healthy young man.

I started school quite late, attending the first grade in Minneapolis when I was almost eight. My mother had hesitated to send me to the one-room schoolhouse in Wing, when Charlie was bringing home reports of the teacher throwing her overshoes at noisy pupils and freely using the horsewhip on slow learners. Also, some six and seven-year-olds were being denied entrance, as the school was too crowded.

I entered Harrison Grammar School that winter, wearing a new home-sewn coat. On the farm and later in the town, Mother made clothes for my sister Rachel and me on her Singer, using catalog-purchased fabric. Patterns were a luxury and unfortunately, she was not a great seamstress. The coat was wool, to keep out the cold, and long, in anticipation of my future growth. But its length proved a hazard. To my consternation, the boys at school teased me, stepping on the hem as I walked up the steps—most embarrassing!

Mother taught me to knit, and she and I finished many pairs of socks for the Red Cross to send to soldiers fighting the Great War in Europe. Although removed from the fighting, we realized that it was impossible to be unaffected by the specter of war.

At age twelve, brother Charlie was already contributing to the family budget by working odd jobs, from hauling coal and ice to pin-setting in a bowling alley. I looked forward to contributing to the family income as well. As a girl, I realized that my contribution would result from my education. I longed to study and approached schoolwork with great enthusiasm.

Even though I was somewhat deficient in English, and in spite of my unfashionable clothes, I always made friends at school. Sister Rachel, though bright and attractive, found fault with others and tended to carry a chip on her shoulder. Charlie and Ben were often subjected to harassment, as anti-Semitism was directed more toward boys than girls. Although I do not recall any words of praise from my father, I knew that he was pleased with my progress in school. He was also interested in my sports activities and he took time to watch my fledgling ice-skating efforts.

Pa could not tolerate discord, which generally erupted when his children quarreled. The bedlam of four kids at mealtime was too much for him. He attempted to keep the family peace by his own calm example. Once, when I was sassy, he tried to slap me—but missed. Much to his consternation, his hand went through the glass door of the kitchen cupboard, a free-standing, pinewood-and-glass hutch. This restrained and stoic man never uttered a word!

When food was scarce and we were reduced to rice pudding or beans, my father would say, "Oh, I'll just open a can of sardines, don't worry about me at all." In the city, chicken was a luxury. So precious was this item, and so close to the edge were our lives, that my mother once accused me of having "taken" a drumstick. She had miscalculated, and upon finding the missing part, apologized. Mother did not sit with us at the beginning of the meal, following the European custom of waiting on the family first. She joined us only after everyone else had been served. Needless to say, both our parents made many sacrifices for us.

In Minneapolis, Ma's teeth, which had long been neglected, were extracted. We had no money for reconstructive dental work. As the dentist fitted her with dentures, she used her limited English to say, "Too big, too big," believing that small teeth were more attractive. Not long after, while still in her mid-forties, Ma ended her years of dangerous childbearing with a hysterectomy. But the procedure did not solve all her health problems. I heard one of her friends say, "You will never feel good after this operation."

Chapter 6

Horse & Buggy Days

"How the Jew lives and works as an agriculturist in America must be of the deepest interest to every well meaning...Jew. For the poor Jewish immigrant from Russia and Romania to rise from a peddler...it is the farm that holds the true key to a difficult situation."

—Abraham R. Levy, "Central North Dakota's Jewish Farmers
in 1903," *Western States Jewish historical Quarterly*

When we moved to Minneapolis, Uncle Abram had just begun his plumbing business. Pa found this work increasingly unsatisfactory, and it soon became obvious that he could not make a good living for the family. To Herman, the grass was always greener elsewhere. Forever restless, he yearned for greater independence and the healthier environment of country life. After less than two years, we again took to the road.

We began a series of frequent moves from one small town to another, first to Annandale, Minnesota, a town of less than a thousand people, not far from Minneapolis. But in spite of our parents' best efforts, this was not where we wanted to settle. Pa did some peddling with horse and buggy, and it was up to Ma to supplement his meager earnings. She opened a storefront where she did dry cleaning and alterations.

We were in rather dire straits in Annandale. To augment our simple diet, we went out to the country to pick potatoes and apples. I ate almost as many apples as I picked. Afterward, Ma used some for apple pie, our favorite dessert, and we stored the rest of our harvest. In the Midwest we could store apples all winter long without them spoiling.

When I enrolled in the Annandale Grammar School, it was at the fourth grade level, whereas my proper placement should have been third grade. To my distress, I learned that the class was working on long division while I had not even learned short division. Not to be outdone, I determined to catch up, and before too long, I had done so.

In 1916 we moved to Hecla, South Dakota, having found Annandale somewhat inhospitable. Charlie remembered the anti-Semitic atmosphere being "so thick you could cut it with a knife," yet, he was pleasantly surprised that when we were leaving, his schoolmates came down to the station to see him off.

While preparing for the move, Pa heard of special rates for farmers moving West and arranged to ship our team of horses, plus wagon and equipment, by rail. Charlie recounted his excitement at riding in the caboose and caring for the horses, making friends with the trainmen and helping to stoke the engine.

Hecla was a town of several hundred, with a mix of nationalities. As most of the farmers were Finnish or Swedish, Pa got along well with them because of his familiarity with their languages. He was still pursuing his dream of settling among the hard-working Finnish families of the American West.

We were the first Jewish family in a town that had never before met Jews, and they were curious about us. Charlie and Ben were teased and made to feel uncomfortable. A large building was being erected next to our house. As a small boy, Ben enjoyed playing around the site. The men who worked there were rough types, and both boys were subjected to anti-Semitic teasing. Derogatory jibes were common, although sometimes masked by other arguments. Though already a believer in non-violence, I found myself in a scuffle with Myron, a fellow sixth-grader. We fought over a swing, but the true issue was his teasing me about my being Jewish. Myron lost the encounter, walking away with a scratched face. I was not fazed by his father's lament that I had "scarred his son for life." His family were also immigrants.

Such behavior was not uncommon. Pa, already an inveterate follower of the news, was shocked at Henry Ford's widely circulated, anti-Semitic (and anti-black) diatribes in the *Dearborn Independent*. Ford was noted for the introduction of the eight-hour day, the five-dollar wage, and the common man's dream, the inexpensive Model-T. Unfortunately the writings of this genius and great innovator appealed to the hidden prejudices of the general population.

As usual, Pa traveled the area peddling his wares to farm wives. He expanded from notions and dry goods to a more practical business: buying cattle hides for the Ribnick Western Fur and Hide Company in Aberdeen. He and Charlie also dismantled old steam engines for scrap iron, a product highly prized in the war effort.

In Hecla we occupied a simple house directly across from the school. Once again we were without indoor plumbing. Pa built a barn on the outskirts of Hecla to shelter our horses, while Ma operated a small dry goods store and continued doing alterations. At Thanksgiving time we all worked at plucking turkeys for the local market. It was a daily struggle for survival.

Children who grow up in poverty are often unaware of their deprivation until later. I had never owned a doll, and only after finding an old photo of my sister holding one did I realize that, somehow, a dollar had been found to indulge in this luxury. But the outdoors offered countless delightful diversions. As my friend Valeda and I walked along the railroad track between Hecla and the next town, Houghton, we picked fragrant prairie roses for bead making. Our arms filled with flowers, we immediately placed them in a pan on the stove, cooking up a wonderfully scented, viscous mass to roll into balls and pierce for stringing.

Valeda was four days older than I, and was a virtual "peeping Tom," spying on her parents in their bedroom and reporting to me. Perhaps we were both eager to learn about adult life, and what it might have in store for us! In those days, anything having to do with sex was not spoken of. To this day, I do not know the Yiddish word for menstruation. In the days before the advent of Kotex sanitary napkins, my mother would bring out the Sears catalogue, from which we ordered most essentials, and point out a sanitary belt to be worn with the strips of cloth which would equip me for my period, or "monthly," as it was called in those days. For years when my birthday rolled around, I would often wonder about Valeda's whereabouts.

Among the citizens of Hecla, education was not a leading priority. A single, nondescript wooden structure housed both the elementary and high schools. There were, however, outstanding instructors. Mrs. Singer, my fifth-grade teacher, took an interest in me, occasionally inviting me to her home and loaning me books. In the absence of a public library, I was thrilled to begin reading American and English classics and became an avid reader. For lack of other materials, I was also attracted to cheap adventure magazines. When not reading about werewolves, I daydreamed. One dream in particular comforted me, seeming to compensate for my trials and tribulations: some day I would come back to Hecla as a glamorous movie star. That would finally show up the kids who had taunted me.

I was quickly snapped out of my daydreams one day when Mrs. Singer announced, "Class, we have some unwelcome visitors with us. Some pupils are coming to school with head lice. Please ask your mothers to examine your hair." Did she mean me? I was profoundly embarrassed, but grateful for her discretion. My poor mother immediately set to work, exterminating the vermin with kerosene and a fine-tooth comb.

As the older daughter, I was assigned the task of assisting Ma in the "war against bed-bugs." This was truly a battle, as these repulsive, wingless insects hid in the cracks of old houses. In warm weather they would creep out to find their victims. Although not as prevalent as mosquitoes, their tiny bites could transmit disease. Each month we would dip rags in kerosene and carefully clean every inch of the mattress, killing the nits.

Since our parents were always working to keep body and soul together, and Ma was preoccupied with her chores, we children were rarely supervised. I loved the adventure of meeting new people, and was pleased to accept invitations to accompany the local veterinarian, Dr. Hayes, as he made his rounds to treat livestock on surrounding farms. What an experience! I had never ridden in a car before, and his shiny automobile, a new Metz, dazzled me. In retrospect, it seems that my parents were surprisingly trusting and naive, giving no thought to the possible dangers inherent in such a situation. After all, Dr. Hayes was an older man.

The same trust was extended to the young boys from a neighboring farm who were called in to "tend" us. They were not much older than I, and took improper advantage of me to learn the anatomical differences between girls and boys. I did not know enough to complain. We were ignorant of the possible dangers of child molestation. The fear, so rampant today, did not exist then.

Around the age of twelve, I went to work folding papers for Frank Young, the local newspaper publisher. At the same time, I became acquainted with Lola Young, the publisher's wife, and spent a school year as a live-in helper to this childless family. Ma thought I would become more familiar with American customs, living with a professional family such as the Youngs. This was my first introduction to a truly middle class, non-Jewish, American family. My companion at the Young's was Buster, a Boston bulldog whom I cared for in the family's absence. Although alone, I was not worried. There were no robberies and doors were never locked. In payment, I received room and board and several pretty dresses fashioned by Mrs. Young.

I also cleaned house and babysat for the Methodist minister. In the spirit of investigation, I surreptitiously browsed through graphic books on human sexuality in his library, learning what my parents never told me. I also babysat for another family, the Greens, whose house seemed to me a virtual palace, with an upstairs and an indoor bathroom. Oddly, I was never paid. Naively, I was surprised when Mrs. Green presented me with a jar of cold cream, purchased at Woolworth's as compensation. I had no idea what to do with it.

One of my classmates in grammar school, Elva Featherhuff, was part Indian. We competed at the footraces, a festive part of community picnics, though she always won. I wondered if it was because she was a "fleet-footed Indian," a common stereotype. Her family, regular churchgoers, often invited me to attend services at the local Methodist church. Although Ma was uncomfortable about my exposure to a different faith, she did not forbid my going. The congregation's hymns failed to stir me—I did not belong. I experienced similar emotions at school and other community events, when an inner voice reminded me that my parents would not approve of my singing songs about Christ. Nevertheless, I had read the Bible and was inspired by the ideals of early Christianity—the principles of a just society that cares for those in need. The Golden Rule was non-sectarian. Was this the beginning of my humanitarian aspirations?

In the seventh grade I had an excellent teacher, Charlotte Noteboom, who was also the principal of our grammar school. An innovative administrator, she was dignified, soft-spoken, and faultlessly attired, every hair in place in a perfect chignon. Once, in a current events class, she left a lasting impression. I had remarked that something was "funny," and she immediately corrected me, suggesting that I substitute "strange" or "unusual." That embarrassing episode remained with me, and precision of speech became a goal toward which I still aspire.

Aware of my zeal for study, Miss Noteboom arranged for me to take the eighth grade county qualifying exams to enter high school a year early. When I passed with high grades, my mentor was gratified. But my joy was tempered by the fact that Miss Noteboom would not be rehired for the coming year. The reason? Resentment on the part of other mothers, who felt I had been given special consideration. Fortunately, Miss Noteboom later joined the faculty at the University of South Dakota at Vermillion, where she was appointed Dean of Women. Our warm friendship continued through correspondence until long after I was married.

Our high school was not exactly a model of decorum. The algebra teacher, Mr. Fried, would at times leave me in charge of the class while he corrected papers. One day a strapping male student, in response to a reprimand, grabbed the teacher by the collar and shook him while other students looked on. The incident was ignored by the administration. Mr. Fried left town and our class was without an instructor.

In the winter of 1918, the great flu epidemic struck. No family in our town escaped. More than twenty million people died worldwide, six hundred thousand in the United States. The only ones spared in my family were Pa and Rae, although we all survived. In those days, doctors still made house calls. The overworked Dr. Holmes, when invited by Pa to sit down, replied, "If I sit down, I'll never be able to get up."

Popular wisdom at the time called for a "fresh-air" cure for the epidemic. Instead of being kept warm and comfortable, people were warehoused in large rooms, exposed to open windows through which the icy wind blew. There was no other treatment—whiskey was considered the only medicine.

If we had any illnesses when we were growing up, we simply had to get over them. I don't recall even hearing about aspirin. However, my mother, suffered chronic headaches and relied on Bromo Seltzer most of her life. I had developed rheumatism in Hecla from the dampness of the swampy terrain where impractical Pa had built the house and store.. My illness kept me bedridden for weeks. When Rae developed scarlet fever and had to be quarantined, she and Ma went to the "pest house" for the duration of her illness. Dark and forbidding, this weathered building on the outskirts of town frightened all who saw it, but this was the only way to keep the infection from spreading. Isolation, rather than treatment, was emphasized.

Generally, we were fairly healthy children. Crisp weather and fresh air might have contributed, and we were also nourished by the fresh bread made from local wheat, seasonal produce from the garden, and by our own chickens and turkeys. Everything was organic. Those were the days before earth, air, and water became polluted—unless, of course, you count coal smoke.

In 1919, having survived the flu epidemic, my parents decided it was time for us to leave Hecla in search of better schools and a synagogue. Organized religion was lacking in our family's early history, and even later, we failed to become fully integrated into the life of the congregation. My friendships with other Jewish girls occurred mainly outside the synagogue, and some of my high school friends were non-Jewish.

We moved seventy miles away to Aberdeen, South Dakota, a town of about thirty-thousand.

Chapter 7
Poetry and Poverty

*"I wandered lonely as a cloud
That floats on high o'er vales and hills..."*

—"The Daffodils," William Wordsworth

In Aberdeen, we found a good high school, the Northern State Teachers College, about fifty Jewish families, a synagogue, and our old friend, the erstwhile traveling Rabbi Julius Hess, whom we knew from the days in Wing. Even then, Rabbi Hess had urged us to move closer to a synagogue. My non-religious father, however, felt that his early Torah education had not proved helpful. He was too busy eking out a living to attend services. Our participation at synagogue in Aberdeen was typically limited to the High Holy Days. Although Charlie studied Hebrew, I did not, as it was not the custom for girls. Bat Mitzvah for girls was unheard of in our part of the country. Pa did not try to teach me to read and write Yiddish or Hebrew, which I now regret. At the time, it was a matter of some embarrassment that my parents spoke English poorly, with a Yiddish accent. Although I speak Yiddish, I am not fluent. Still, I find myself searching for Yiddish words and phrases, and take a great deal of pleasure in this form of expression.

Life in Aberdeen was difficult. We had a two-story house on 6th Avenue, and Mother opened a small grocery store on the first floor. It was my job, in the summertime especially, to rise early and open up the shop. When I heard pounding on the door, that meant I had to get up. The sound of birds chirping in the trees was the only compensation for my loss of sleep.

Aberdeen was a hub for more than twenty railway lines, and our store was on a direct route from the train station to downtown. Many itinerants riding the freights would come looking for handouts. I invariably gave them food, which earned me much scolding. This habit has continued throughout my life. I'm a soft touch. I even gave away one of Ma's colorful quilts to a shivering transient, for which I was soundly reprimanded. Although my charity was sincere, I regret not having a single one of her patchwork creations to pass on to my grandchildren.

I enjoyed the new technology in Aberdeen, such as the store's telephone, which I used to place grocery orders. One of my earliest crushes was on the salesman who took orders and delivered stock. I also liked going to the occasional five cent Saturday movie, although my father discouraged it, fearing the corrupting influence of motion pictures. One day, I was comfortably seated in the movie house, watching a "Perils of Pauline" serial adventure film. Just as Pauline lay bound and gagged on the train tracks, my name flashed on the screen, a signal that meant I must leave immediately because my irate father had come to take me home. He had forbidden my attending the movie that day. To my surprise, he had followed through on his threat. Reluctantly, I walked out without learning Pauline's fate. I never attended the films again without his permission.

Father continued to travel, driving his team to various farms and also buying hides, whose distinctive odors he brought home. Fortunately, we had a bathtub! In the summer, Charlie accompanied him. During the school year, he was able to remain in class, unlike so many of his friends who were compelled to work. Education was a high priority in my family.

My high school experience was not very pleasant. I yearned to be more like my "American" friends with Anglo names and I envied people who were better off. I was also embarrassed about our parents' faulty English as well as some of their habits. For example, one winter, when I was badly in need of a warm coat, my mother took me to Pred's Clothing Store, owned by a Jewish family, the Predetskys. I blushed when I was waited on by the owner's handsome son, Dave, who, under different circumstances, had given me my first kiss. Mother and I selected a new suede-like "Chappie" coat, trimmed with a fur collar—very warm and expensive. Then, to my horror, Ma proceeded to bargain with him for a better price! Every time I wore the coat I felt uncomfortable. Yet I was determined to advance my own education as rapidly as possible, thus helping my family attain a better life.

As young girls often do, I daydreamed constantly. Although I did have my secret loves, I was never carried away by them. Once, Charlie was quite concerned about a certain boyfriend of mine named Harold. He let me know, in brotherly fashion, that he was aware of the potential dangers inherent in boy-girl associations. In high school, my only decent dress was of a black-and-white check pattern, which I wore almost daily and which attracted "Dutch" Arnesy, a football hero, who referred to me as his "checkerboard girl." This caused Charlie to redouble his protective efforts.

During my sophomore year at Aberdeen Central High School, we lived next door to another poor family from Russia, the Antons. Their eldest child, Rose, was bright and quite attractive, with black hair and sparkling dark eyes. While a sophomore, Rose quit school to work in the local candy factory. She considered herself quite grown up, although at fifteen she was not much older than I. She challenged me to follow her. "What a fool you are. Why do you want to waste your time in school? You could earn five dollars and have a lot of fun." I ignored the siren's call. I did, however, work briefly at the local Woolworth's store selling dime novels and a variety of items. I lost my job when the floorwalker caught me chatting with some young men and fired me on the spot.

I greatly admired my third-year English teacher, Betty Kraft, a small, neatly dressed woman in her thirties with a prominent nose and an abundance of hair piled artfully atop her head. She introduced us to the poetry anthology, *Palgrave's Golden Treasury*, which I loved. I set out to memorize all the poems in the book, and came close to doing so.

I began to write in English class, despite my lack of training in formal grammar. Again, my pervasive feeling of inadequacy prevailed—part of my "foreignness," poverty, and perhaps, my adolescence. Shy and insecure, I was driven to excel in my studies. "There is no other way!" I admitted to myself. I wanted to use my academic achievements to overcome a sense of inferiority. I appreciated being considered intelligent and was able to form strong friendships. My greatest ambition was to develop myself by doing good work in the community. This shaped my life.

I thought of myself as unattractive. Having gained some weight, during my late teens, I was utterly humiliated one day when a neighborhood boy called out, "Hey fatty!" Stunned, I decided to go on a diet, subsisting mostly on rye bread and skim milk. I grew thinner, and as a result, my periods stopped. Mother insisted on consulting a physician, Dr. King, whose attentions proved a bit too personal and frightened me back to a normal diet. Imagine, living so many years on limited rations and then going on a starvation diet!

Unlike me, sister Rae had difficulties in school. She would frequently complain of the teachers' unfairness in not giving her credit and singling her out. It was not until late adolescence that she began to show signs of mental disturbance.

Rae and I, though friendly, were not close, although we seldom argued. When you have very little, there is more of a tendency to share. We both simply accepted our situation, even taking turns with our single pair of dress-up shoes without quarreling.

During high school I began to gain more knowledge of society and its power structures, and this led to an interest in law. I dreamed of being able to represent working people. However, I thought law school out of my reach, and aimed to get my education at a local college while living at home.

I was thinking seriously of what I could do to earn money, so in addition to the regular college "prep" courses, I also enrolled in commercial studies. I learned Gregg shorthand, a universal language for secretaries which I still use today. I took courses in bookkeeping and typing. It was a big thrill when we were able to buy a portable Corona typewriter, my pride and joy. Charlie always changed the ribbons for me, and to this day, I shy away from anything mechanical.

Rae and Ben were progressing in school, but Charlie was struggling. He had started at the local Normal School and complained that the English teacher, Miss Meade, was prejudiced against him. Although I experienced no overt anti-Semitism in Aberdeen, my brothers were not so lucky.

Pa, with Charlie's help, started another small store across town, near the Northern States Teachers College, formerly known as the Normal School. Because of our proximity to the college, we named our business the "Normal Grocery." Pa, always willing to take a chance, put in an order for Eskimo pies, an absolutely new concept, which proved to be a "hot" item among students. Candy bars sold for a nickel and the pies cost a dime.

After school, I tended this store while my mother ran our home-based operation. Work gave me an opportunity to meet people from the college. Occasionally a professor would come in, ask me about the sandwich menu as well as what my plans were for attending college.

Late one fall afternoon, arriving home bedraggled after a long day at the Normal Grocery, I opened the door to the enthusiastic greetings of "Happy Birthday, Alice!" It was a total surprise! My mother had arranged this festive event, complete with her fancy frosted cake, for my sixteenth birthday. All my friends were there. The party remains one of the happiest memories of my youth.

When I was working at the grocery after school, and later when I was going to the teachers college, I had to walk nineteen blocks twice daily, since the streetcars had been quite mysteriously removed and there was no other public transportation. In winter it was rough going, in spite of the warmth of my Chappie coat. Years later, I was disgusted to learn why the electric streetcars had disappeared. The oil companies and the auto and tire manufacturers had banded together in the 1920s to force cities all over the US to tear up the tracks, eventually replacing them with high-polluting diesel buses.

In 1923, I graduated from Aberdeen Central High School, having completed both the commercial and academic programs. Following graduation, I took charge of the Normal Grocery all summer, and in September, enrolled at the college full time.

Chapter 8

Learning the Ways of the City

"[Alice Sachs] debated at Sioux Falls for the Normal School of Aberdeen. Her team won both debates held by the girls' intercollegiate teams. The debate on the home floor was a lively one."

—Sioux Falls, South Dakota newspaper, 1924

My introduction to higher education began with a course in economic history. The professor used the text, *The Significance of the Frontier in American History*, by Frederick Jackson Turner. His concept of the frontier combined history, geography, sociology, statistics, and economics, opening up new intellectual vistas to me. Turner viewed the frontier as a process, constantly changing, just like the adventures of my own family.

Growing up, I had heard many stories about Russia from my father and uncle Abram, an avowed socialist like many other young Jewish men who were opposed to the repressive Czarist regime. A number of his friends were in jail, and Uncle Abe left Lithuania just ahead of the *gendarmes* and the Russo-Japanese War. I have a letter of his from the 1930s, in which he wrote glowingly about the success of the Communists in the Soviet Union. In Minneapolis, he married Gertrude Lippman, raised a family, and became an established member of the local progressive community, although he never made a great deal of money. I wish I had asked him more about early life in Russia.

Father was always interested in politics, though he had little time for philosophical or political discussions. He was a supporter of Eugene Debs, a presidential candidate and socialist rabble-rouser who spent years in jail because of his opposition to World War I. Pa thought things out for himself, but didn't say much.

In all the places we lived nobody ever attempted to proselytize or indoctrinate me with socialist rhetoric, but I could see the effects of poverty and poor education, particularly on the lives of women. It seemed natural that people would accept the principles of socialism: that everyone should be treated equally, that resources should be available for all, and that it is wrong for a few to accumulate wealth without sharing with those less fortunate.

I was fascinated by the world-shaking events still unfolding in Russia, and when the subject for the inter-collegiate debating team was posted as, "Resolved, that the United States Should Recognize the Present Russian Government," I was determined to try out. I was able to overcome my extreme nervousness, and was thrilled to make the team. Disregarding the anti-socialist propaganda prevalent in the United States following the 1917 Bolshevik takeover, we debated in several college towns, defending the unpopular position of *"for* recognition." We consistently won.

My English teacher, Paul Osgood, introduced us to George Bernard Shaw and other well-known modern writers. He arranged to have Shaw's *Androcles and the Lion* produced at the college by a visiting company. I was on the committee in charge of this event. During the class review of this production, I was embarrassed to confess that I had missed the performance even though I had read the play. It was never my custom to return to the campus for evening events. The long, wintry walk, coupled with my heavy study load, made it impossible. Professor Osgood was disappointed, but not half as much as I was. From then on, I decided I would make every effort to break my usual routine and be part of the theater audience at the several campuses I attended.

Even with two stores, our family was barely making expenses. We rented out a room to John Murray, a fellow freshman. Although taking in boarders was a common practice, it was unusual for us to have a non-Jewish person living in our home. I have a photo of the two of us in costumes for the Halloween Homecoming Celebration. This shot of me in a long, flowing skirt and a gypsy bandanna is one of my earliest photos.

Charlie, always outgoing and enterprising, had established a popular summer refreshment stand in Melgaard Park, on the outskirts of Aberdeen. Many road-weary drivers, en route to California from various points in the increasingly impoverished middlewest, would stop at the stand, tired of the slow, 25-mile per hour pace. Here, exhausted travelers would sample my brother's refreshments, including drinks and ice cream. One of the Mayo brothers, of the famed Mayo Clinic, stopped to *shmooz* while enjoying a corned beef sandwich on his way West. Soon my brother, too, was responding to the "call of the West."

Uncle Abram had invited Pa to join him in an exploratory trip to Los Angeles to visit their successful cousins, the Tyre family. Charlie enthusiastically went along, and they all set off by train. After a short visit, Uncle Abe returned home to Minneapolis, but Pa and Charlie decided to remain in California and try their luck.

Pa and the Tyres were first cousins. Their entire family had emigrated from Lithuania with eight or nine children, including two sets of twins. Passing through Ellis Island, their name was changed from an unpronounceable one to Tyre, which in Yiddish means "dear" or "expensive."

In fact, this name change presaged a dramatic difference in family fortunes. Herman and Abram were impressed by the four brothers, Ben, Jack, Morris, and Sam, whose success in the glass business during World War I had earned them their first million. The Los Angeles-based Tyre Brothers Glass Company had branches in Fresno and Seattle. As an expression of the solidarity among immigrant families, they offered Pa and Charlie jobs in the big plant, installing plate glass, producing windows and mirrors, and repairing auto windshields. Later, the firm also employed my brother Ben.

Other Tyre family members volunteered help as well. Sisters Ida Suplin and Esther Romm, whose husbands were part of the family enterprise, generously offered to put up my father and Charlie. A third sister, Sarah Lipkin, whose husband managed a glass store in Oakland, would welcome me when I later attended UC Berkeley.

The following spring, as I was completing my first year in college, Pa wrote suggesting that we prepare for a trip West. Charlie returned to collect us. We were unable to sell the Normal Grocery because of the depressed local economy. Instead, we just closed it up. We managed to sell our house, but the family that bought it sent us very few payments. Money was scarce in the Midwest.

In the fall of 1924, Charlie purchased our first automobile, a Ford, for under $500. An open touring car wasn't exactly open: it had plastic-like isinglass windows, which could be snapped into place. Outfitted with camping and cooking equipment, bundles tied to the running boards, two spare tires clinging to the back, and the Ford crammed full of our belongings, we ventured toward California. Ma had baked beans and packed other food. We struggled to find space for my little Corona and a modest supply of clothing. Somehow, we all managed to pile into the car—Ma, Rae, Charlie, Ben and I, along with our fox terrier, Fanny, and her five squirming newborn pups, which were suspended in a basket from the roof. With high hopes we began our slow, tedious journey West, Charlie behind the wheel.

The trip was a true test of my brother's skills, determination, and fortitude. There were no interstate highways, very few road signs, and steep, torturous routes from one rutted trail to another. The trip was so grueling we wore out four sets of tires. There were few motels along the way, but no matter. Our budget did not allow for such luxuries! At night, the boys would simply curl up in the car, while Ma, Rae, and I huddled on blankets inside our tent. Our license plates were stolen, sometime during the eighth night out. Even though Charlie heard a noise, he was fearful of bears, or worse, and did not get up. The next day we drove without a license, which made us nervous and insecure. Along the way a local sheriff issued a temporary certificate.

We stayed overnight in Yellowstone National Park, one of the country's most spectacular sights, and nearly froze to death in a sudden autumn snow storm. Frost covered everything, our breath hovered in the icy air, but we were undaunted. The idea of going West and the adventure of travel was all we could think about. The next morning, fascinated by Old Faithful Geyser, I took photos with my new Brownie camera—a typical tourist.

We also stopped in Salt Lake City for a bit of sightseeing, which included the Mormon Tabernacle, a cold, cavernous, impressively solid building unlike anything we had seen before. Farther west, the desert heat proved too much for one of the puppies, which we buried in the sand by the side of the steaming road. We saw many abandoned cars, their engines blown by the white-hot desert temperatures. From then on, like the rest of the heat-fatigued travelers, we rested in the daytime and drove mostly at night.

Despite the many hardships, my only disappointment was crossing the California border, where, instead of the rolling, endless vista of beautiful flowers that filled my imagination, we found only desert. However, the highways were brightened by oleanders. Rae and I took a train from Barstow to cover the last several hundred miles, as we aimed to reach Fresno by the opening of school. Preparing for the family's arrival, Pa took over the Fresno branch of Tyre Brothers Glass Company.

Pa had just learned to drive and collected us at the Fresno station in his dusty little Ford pickup. Not long after, Charlie pulled up to our new home on Fourthcamp Avenue, his car full of panting puppies and their worn-out mother. Ben and Ma weren't in such great shape either. We were finally reunited in the golden land of California.

II.
A New Life in California
1924-1948

"We decided that when Alice will be through with her school and...ready to come home the whole family will come to Berkeley with our machine and we will all return home, the whole mishpocka, and that will be my vacation and Ben's and Ma's, too..."

—My father, 1927, planning the vacation he never took

Chapter 9

Meeting Sam

A striking personality, Sam stood out with his booming voice, piercing dark blue eyes, and restless manner.

In September 1924, Fresno, the heart of the Central Valley, became our home. Its abundant fig orchards yielded the largest harvest in the country, and its lush grapes supplied the wine industry. This natural desert, developed by man, is bounded by snow-topped mountains looming to the east and distant foothills to the west.

Here, life took a new turn. Here, my children would be born and reared. At the time, however, my greatest concern was getting to college. Upon arriving in Fresno, Rachel entered high school, Ben started grade school, and I enrolled as a sophomore at Fresno State—the second of the four colleges I would attend before graduating. My grades had been all A's, but I worried whether the California system would recognize them. Such fears soon vanished; my credits were accepted everywhere I went.

College in Fresno was a new and exhilarating experience, offering many freedoms and much diversity, different from the small-town schools I had experienced previously. I was meeting and making new friends, including two Asian girls, the first I had ever met. One day we were waiting for a streetcar and I asked them if they were sisters. Hilarious laugher followed, as they explained that one was Chinese and the other Japanese!

This was not my only cultural hurdle. As a newcomer, I stumbled over the spelling of names such as "Joaquin," which was hardly phonetic! Other Spanish words were equally puzzling and I resolved to study the language.

I met several interesting professors at Fresno State, including my political science instructor, Dr. Hubert Phillips, an eloquent lecturer and highly idealistic person. Fresh from a teaching post in Chicago, he was ruddy-faced, enthusiastic, and dynamic. We were both new to campus, and quickly became friends. He had a much broader view of life, and I was so impressed that I would often linger after class to talk to him. He was the sponsor of the Bohemian Club, which promoted discussion of world and local events.

Another fascinating personality on campus was my geology instructor, anthropologist T.T. Waterman. Recently arrived from UC Berkeley, he had collaborated with Alfred Kroeber, a prominent UC scholar and patron of the famed Ishi, the last survivor of his Native American tribe. Waterman, a student of Native American languages, was called in to decipher Ishi's speech—no one else was up to the task. During Kroeber's frequent absences, Waterman assumed responsibility for Ishi. He became his protector and remained with him during the Native American's last days, when Kroeber was out of the country. Waterman's wit and humor enlivened the study of even the dullest rocks and minerals on our geology field trips. Later, when I applied for my first teaching job, he wrote a glowing recommendation.

Other teachers were less inspiring. The bacteriology instructor, Dr. Thompson, seemed insecure. She had been brought in as an interim instructor, due to the lack of trained professors at the college level. Although women were well-represented in grammar and high school, their numbers in college were limited. Even though she was in her late fifties, this was her first teaching job. Occasionally, she would leave me in charge of the laboratory in her absence—and this was my first science class!

Expecting greater cultural and religious understanding in this impressive state college—in a more diverse state—I was taken aback when my Spanish instructor, Mr. Coburn, proved to be rather narrow-minded. When I notified him that I would be absent on the Jewish holiday *Yom Kippur*, he replied in a mocking tone, "Why don't we *all* take a holiday!"

Father had taken over management of the Tyre Brothers Glass Store on Broadway, next door to the Public Library. Using skills he acquired in the big plant, he was also the store's glazier. When Professor Phillips, visiting the Library, learned that my father was next door, he called on him to talk about my academic future. To say that my usually undemonstrative father was thrilled is an understatement!

Our parents felt we should join a congregation. They were concerned, as we got older, that we needed to meet more Jewish people. We joined Temple Beth El, where Rachel and I were both quickly enlisted as Sunday School teachers. With virtually no religious background, we worked diligently to keep ahead of our classes. This was one of the rare collaborations between Rae and me.

At the time, I had been seeing Max Flacks. A son of the North Dakota Flacks family, Max was a traveling music instructor who generously offered to give me violin lessons. I willingly accepted, and signed up for the elementary orchestra class at college. I was not an adept music student, as was illustrated by an unkind comment by my instructor, Mr. Chambers. "Alice," he said, "it's all right to tap to the music, but you are off the beat!" I dropped orchestra at the end of the semester, bringing to a close both a romantic episode and my short-lived musical career.

One Friday night following services, Rabbi Segal introduced me to his close friend, Sam Hamburg. I often wonder what fortuitous turn of fate caused us to meet, since neither of us attended regularly. He was a recently-arrived immigrant student from Palestine who was worldly and knowledgeable, with a strong artistic bent, different from anyone I had ever met. We began seeing a great deal of each other while I was completing the first half of my junior year. Instead of regular dates, he would pick me up and then we would join his friends at Hart's Cafeteria, a smoke-filled hangout of the local intelligentsia.

Born in Poland, Sam had been sent to Palestine (pre-state Israel), for his secondary school education, but was unable to return home after the outbreak of World War I. In the forefront of the *kibbutz* "back to the land" movement, at age eighteen he helped start a commune. He remained intolerant of shopkeepers and business people who were interested only in making money, and wanted to prove that Jews could be successful farmers, so he came to California to study modern agricultural methods at UC Davis, later transferring to UC Berkeley. He intended to return to Palestine eventually to resume activity with the kibbutz movement.

Disappointed that his academic courses had not proved practical, Sam was looking for "real" farming experience. He landed summer ranching jobs near Fresno and was able to visit his mentors, Dr. Meyer and Rae Wahrhaftig, more frequently. Settling in Fresno during the New Deal era, the warm and friendly Rae would arrange frequent local soirees to which we would be invited.

Sam and his politics reinforced my own socialist leanings. His background in literature, art, and music helped him overcome linguistic difficulties with English, which was for him a third or fourth language. He would hold forth dramatically on subjects ranging from Rodin's sculpture and Vivaldi's compositions to his favorite, the writings of Tolstoy.

Sam and our local rabbi had met as members of a small group that would gather to discuss the progressive *The Nation* magazine (to which I still subscribe). Sam, who was steeped in European-Jewish culture, would often help the young rabbi with his sermons.

In turn, his friend introduced Sam to individuals who would later be valuable contacts for his farming ventures.

Not everyone was as impressed with Sam, however. About this time, several Jewish women, members of the Beth El Congregation, warned my mother. "You have a nice daughter and we understand she's seeing Sam Hamburg. Be careful, he's a Communist."

That didn't bother my parents. They were impressed with Sam. He and my father had developed an intellectual friendship and shared a mutual interest in politics. Pa thought Sam ambitious, and Sam praised Pa's ability to converse in Hebrew, despite Pa's lack of practice since his *Yeshiva* days. To my knowledge, Sam never spoke Yiddish with Herman or anyone else.

That summer of 1925 we were all trying to earn money. Charlie was employed as a packer by Sunmaid Raisins at fifty cents an hour while Rachel set up a lemonade stand at the downtown Farmers' Market. She added her own freshly squeezed juices to the tables groaning with luscious peaches, figs, grapes, raisins, and other local produce.

After finishing my first year at Fresno State, I went through several jobs, first, as a waitress at the popular Wilson's Restaurant in downtown Fresno. This proved to be one of my toughest experiences. I've never understood why I was harassed by the male waiters. Was it because I was young and small, or simply fresh from the country? I didn't stay there long.

Next, after a short stint clerking at a dry goods store, I heard of an opening for a typist with the Krasner Fruit Company in a huge, gray building recently equipped with the latest technology: air conditioning. Since summers in Fresno were oppressively hot, I would be thoroughly chilled when coming in from the blazing outdoors to an ice-cold atmosphere. (I still suffer negative effects from extreme changes in temperature and am subject to respiratory problems.)

My Aberdeen dentist had advised me to have my wisdom teeth extracted, but was unwilling to perform the surgery, claiming the "lack of proper instruments." Later, seated in a dental chair in Fresno, I discovered why he had declined. The procedure which I endured that summer seemed interminable, my mouth propped open with braces past the point of misery. As the dentist pounded away, we suddenly heard a thump. It was my poor mother, who, terrified by the sound of the mallet, had fainted. I was left unattended while my tormentors rushed out to the waiting room to care for her!

After living in Fresno for a year and a half, the family grew restless. Ma was not in good health, and found the valley heat unbearable. Since the lease on the Tyre Brothers' store was about to expire, Pa was free to leave. That winter, 1926, we departed for Los Angeles, in what would be the final move for the family.

Rachel, with only a half year left to finish high school, was invited to remain in Fresno with Ben Tyre's family. Their lifestyle was far more lavish than ours, and the contrast was marked. When Rae was suddenly plunged into this different environment, she was overwhelmed. At seventeen, she was impressionable and sensitive, and found it difficult to adjust to the Tyre's affluence. She must have felt left out, in contrast to her three confident, well-groomed girl cousins. I often wonder whether this experience might have contributed to her later emotional problems. That fall, after she joined us in Los Angeles, Rachel started junior college but soon dropped out. She had a good mind, yet lacked patience and was unwilling or unable to exert the effort necessary to succeed. Perhaps Rae thought that Pa tended to favor me because of my scholastic drive. Her contrasting frame of mind was best exemplified by her attitude toward our parents.

When we were growing up, I would do what needed to be done without brooding about the unfairness of life. Weren't our parents doing the best they could for us? Although dependent on them for most of her life, Rae freely flouted their standards and beliefs. She would often prepare bacon in the kitchen, despite Ma's attempts to maintain a kosher home. Not only was bacon *verboten* by our religion, but the smell itself was an insult to them. Her lack of consideration for our parents seemed to grow as time went on.

Chapter 10

The $25 Ring

We wanted to save the family the expense of a regular wedding...

In Los Angeles, Father continued to work as a glazier for Tyre Brothers. When handling glass, he would frequently cut himself. His cuts healed slowly, but, grateful for a job, he never complained. He also suffered from blood poisoning on at least one occasion, a potentially fatal condition in the days before antibiotics.

Around 1930, the family bought a home in southwest Los Angeles for $3000, a large sum at that time. Mother went back and forth by streetcar to City Hall for permits to bring the house up to code. She was also busy with the kitchen vegetable garden, which was bordered with flowers, and with the chickens she kept—even in the city. I admired her greatly. She had stoicism and dedication, and unlike many people today, refused to allow poor health to interfere with her total dedication to our welfare.

Since coming to California our standard of living had improved somewhat, but Pa could not accept that new reality and continued to wear hand-me-down clothes. It never occurred to him to buy from a store when perfectly good (and better) suits and shoes were given him by his cousins. Often, these items were several sizes too large. Style was not an issue for him. In light of his history, he felt fortunate to be adequately clothed.

Now a young man, Ben still suffered embarrassment at our family's lack of status and our parents' foreign accents, and felt that Pa paid too little attention to modern standards of grooming. For example, Pa did not follow a regular schedule for bathing. Ben was fastidious and sensitive in many ways. Although friction brewed between him and Pa, he always got along beautifully with Ma, who tended to favor him. After dropping out of junior college, Ben pursued a musical career while continuing to work various jobs. After several years of private singing lessons and some out-of-town operetta performances, he was forced by the Depression to find steady employment.

Charlie was unhappy working for relatives, and wanted to go it alone. He decided to start a glass business in San Bernardino, which proved unsuccessful for lack of capital as well as a poor choice of a business partner. Was he repeating his father's mistakes? While in the San Bernadino desert, he established friendships with local ranchers who welcomed his help on weekends. He loved horses—in keeping with our family's devotion to animals—enjoyed working with them, and began practicing fancy rope tricks.

As usual, I was studying diligently, now at the Southern Branch of the University of California (UC), later called UCLA. I expected my professors to be geniuses, but found them less inspiring than several of my Fresno instructors. I was also greatly disillusioned when the contract of my economics professor, Dr. Hilmer, was not renewed because of suspected left-wing leanings. This was a harbinger of the coming battles over faculty loyalty oaths during the decades of the "red scare" and the later McCarthy years.

Now in the second semester of my junior year, I majored in economics and also began taking education courses. Instead of law, I was now preparing for a teaching career. Determined to earn top grades, I studied virtually non-stop. To escape noise and family conversation, I moved my books to a screened porch at the back of the house where there was scarcely room to sit. I hadn't counted on the colony of ants that stung me for invading their territory, but, like a true bookworm, I stuck it out.

Seeing me hunched over my books, Pa would repeatedly remind me, "Sit up straight!" Later, when I was at Berkeley, he would write, "You shouldn't work so hard. It takes a strong body to carry a big load of education." I realize now how similar I am to my father—the same drive, the same interest in current affairs—I even move fast, as he did. After his semi-retirement, he was always off somewhere on a streetcar. At home, he would listen constantly to news on radio.

At UCLA, one of my classmates was Agnes DeMille, the future world-famed choreographer and niece of the great director, Cecil B. DeMille. Her father was a follower of Henry George, the renowned social reformer. Shyly, I watched her from a distance.

Ever since the summer in Fresno and my first encounter with air-conditioning, I have had trouble with my sinuses. One day after school I took the streetcar out to a free medical clinic and had a minor operation on my nose, not because of its shape, but to improve my breathing. Wanting to avoid the expense of a private physician, I failed to tell Mother. I was not about to have her spend money, nor did I want her fainting in the waiting room! When I came home, holding the bandage to my bleeding nose, she was beside herself, chiding me for my folly, angry that I hadn't let her in on my plan. Happily, the free clinic did a good job.

Sam and I kept up a correspondence after I moved to Los Angeles. He was struggling to get started as a tenant farmer in Merced County near Dos Palos. In 1925, his first farming venture—growing lettuce in Chowchilla—had failed. The next year he made a fresh start on the San Juan Ranch, owned by the Miller & Lux Corporation. Henry Miller and Charles Lux were successful German immigrants, wholesale butchers who had amassed well over a million acres. They were the largest landowners in the San Joaquin Valley, with holdings so vast that, reportedly, a cattle drive beginning in Canada and ending in Mexico could camp every night on their property. Legend had it that some of their land was acquired by a certain stretching of the Swamp Act, which granted homesteaders ownership of all the land that could be reached by rowboat. Miller and Lux bypassed this detail by attaching a boat behind a team of horses, thus acquiring a great deal of land, swampy or not.

The San Juan Ranch was heavily wooded, with many marshes. A popular nesting place for wild ducks, it also echoed with the harsh cries of blue herons and cranes. Other flocks of wild birds foraged in grain fields and roosted in shallows, safe from predators. Sam was attracted to the land because of the supply of canal water for irrigation, and the availability of credit, since banks and other businesses in the adjoining towns were also then owned by Miller & Lux, his landlords.

At the end of the spring semester, Sam persuaded me to visit, and then talked me into going to San Francisco to get married. He argued this would relieve my parents of the expense of a more elaborate home wedding. In retrospect, I realize I might also have been sparing myself a public ceremony—I was still extremely shy. Sam bought a white gold wedding ring with diamond chips for $25.

I was twenty and Sam was several years older. In a ceremony conducted by Judge L. S. Jacks, on June 15, 1926, we were married in the lovely San Francisco home of Sam's friend, businessman Maury Segal. I recall the beautiful setting, overlooking the sparkling bay.

Returning to the ranch, Sam wrote my parents the news. His letter was most undiplomatic. While he tried to reassure them, telling them that we were the "only ones concerned," in retrospect, the message seemed heartless, as if they no longer mattered. His progressive political ideas had not mattered to them, but our failure to include them in this important event caused great pain. My parents had never interfered with our plans, never questioned Sam's background, never asked how much money he was making, which, at the time, was hardly any. They trusted me to make my own decisions. They were unhappy because they had not been included in our wedding. What we thought was consideration for their financial condition was interpreted as rejection. I had not yet realized how important it was to voice my ideas in the face of Sam's sure-fire opinions. Because of my insecurity, there was no dialogue—he made all the decisions. In this case, the result was my parents' unhappiness. This was a lesson for me for the future.

My parents' main concern was that I complete my education. Sam wholeheartedly agreed with these plans, since he felt confident that his farming operations would be successful eventually. Today, a "free" education such as I enjoyed would be impossible—tuition rates throughout the University of California system are skyrocketing and admission is highly competitive.

Chapter 11

At Last! The University at Berkeley

Berkeley is the most exciting campus—intellectually and culturally—I've ever seen. It's hard for me to imagine being anywhere else but Berkeley.

Sam and I spent our first summer together living in a tent on the Dos Palos ranch and taking our meals in the workers' cookhouse. Once again I found myself making the familiar trek to the outhouse! By summer's end we were able to move into the weather-beaten cookhouse, and I struggled to turn it into a home. In these surroundings we entertained friends from the Bay Area and Fresno, including the Wahrhaftigs, Robin Lampson, a popular writer of the time, and several local artists.

Sam and I had not discussed starting a family. The problem of birth control was made no easier by the attitudes of the times. I had read Margaret Sanger's practical book, and when I asked my husband to buy the recommended items at the Dos Palos drugstore, he was embarrassed and refused. But he drove me into town. When I asked the druggist's wife for the items I needed, she looked shocked, but proceeded to fill my order.

Intent on pursuing my education, I transferred to UC Berkeley in the fall, as it was closer to the ranch than UCLA. Also, my heart was set on earning a prestigious Berkeley degree. I had two alumni scholarships, one of which had been established by the prominent San Francisco Heller family. I continued to use my maiden name, which made me a "Lucy Stoner," in the tradition of the first woman to retain her name after marriage. There was no objection from Sam. I received my diploma as Alice Sachs.

After driving the 140 miles to Berkeley by way of the Pacheco Pass, we rented an apartment on Durant, near the campus. We were inexperienced in apartment living and Sam, after finding that we had run out of toilet paper, ran down the hall to ask the manager for the item. Puzzled, she looked at him, "You have to furnish your own, but here's a roll anyway." I knew even less than Sam about city apartment life.

Zev Hassid had arrived in Berkeley from Palestine not long after Sam, and they became fast friends. Where Sam was flamboyant, Zev was reserved. They liked to recall their days washing dishes in exchange for meals at one of the university fraternities. As soon as he was able, Zev enrolled at Cal in Biochemistry—he would achieve national prominence in this field. Since he roomed nearby, he was expected to keep an eye on me after Sam returned to the ranch.

I lived on the busy corner of Durant and Telegraph until my graduation in 1927. On holidays I would travel back and forth to the ranch, often boarding the Southern Pacific at Oakland's 16th Street Station, but Berkeley continued to be my home. Sister Rae came from Los Angeles for a lengthy visit. Having learned to write Yiddish, she was able to correspond with Ma, who sent us packages of goodies and messages of cheer.

One weekend when Sam was visiting, we took the ferry over to San Francisco to buy me a coat at the Emporium, a well-known store. After several tries, Sam picked a $35 coat with a fake fur collar, which did not seem becoming, but he was impatient. "That's fine, that's fine, let's go." I had not yet gained sufficient confidence to stand up to him. Even though Sam had excellent taste in art and literature, it did not extend to my wardrobe! This was my first experience shopping in a big city. In the past, we had purchased mainly through the Sears Roebuck catalogue. I was overwhelmed by the choices, the glitter, the great variety. It was my entrée into a new life.

In the late twenties and thirties, San Francisco's Fillmore Street was the heart of the Jewish neighborhood, filled with several wonderful Jewish restaurants. There Sam introduced me to the Menuhins, whom he had known earlier in Palestine. Moshe, the father of the musical prodigy Yehudi, was the head of the Central Hebrew School. Yehudi played his violin for us, and I marveled at the beauty of his playing. At nine, his musical ability had already created a sensation when he performed with the San Francisco Symphony. Years later, we visited his parents in their Los Gatos home. Not only was Yehudi a musical genius, he also became known world-wide as an advocate for universal peace.

Sam had many wonderful *avant-garde* associates from his student days in Berkeley: Joan London, the daughter of Jack London, the world-famed Oakland writer, was a close friend. She was married to Charles Malamuth at that time, although they later divorced. Charles was the first western journalist to interview Russian dictator Joseph Stalin for *Time* magazine. Joan tried her hand at writing and lecturing, but to my mind, she was more impressive for her ability to create fine meals with little money.

One of Sam's earliest contacts was poet and UC lecturer Eda Lou Walton, who had helped him assimilate into the new culture and with whom he had earlier been involved romantically. In pursuit of her career, Eda Lou left Berkeley for a professorship at New York University. She and I became friends and she often visited us during the summer. Through her, we would later meet Henry Roth, her *protégé* and author of *Call It Sleep*.

Others I met through Sam included UCB Professor Robert Brady, a radical economist, and St. Mary's College professor Gregory Silvermaster and his Russian-born wife, Helen Witte. I would later serve as witness in her citizenship proceedings. Helen's brother, a leading agronomist from the USSR, visited the ranch to observe Sam's farming methods.

I was dazzled by all this brilliance—Alice in Wonderland. Though I was also making contacts, I was full of insecurities about my wardrobe, my cooking, my own intellectual credentials. That being said, I found myself influenced by a number of strong women. Among the outstanding professors during my senior year at UCB was the dashing Barbara Nachtrieb Armstrong, the first woman to serve on the Boalt Law School faculty, under whom I studied social economics and law. In her spare time she was an amateur actress whose photo hangs on the wall at the UCB Women's Faculty Building. At this time, the birth control controversy swirling around Margaret Sanger was at its height, and Professor Armstrong, the mother of an only child, anticipated the struggle that would take place for freedom of choice. It was also in her class discussions that I came to realize the injustice of capital punishment, which has prompted my lifelong opposition to the practice. Recognized for her scholarship, she was called to Washington by the Roosevelt Administration in the mid-thirties to help write the landmark Social Security legislation. There she worked closely with Labor Secretary Frances Perkins, the first woman cabinet member.

At mid-year I was elected to Phi Beta Kappa. This unusual recognition of a recently transferred student was undoubtedly due to the recommendation of my mentor, Economics Professor Jessica Peixotto, the first woman to attain full professorship at Berkeley. She was also one of the founders of Oakland's Children's Hospital, an institution established in the early part of the century by women, mostly nurses and community leaders. Its origin has been obscured by subsequent male administrative boards. In the spring of 1927 I graduated with Highest Honors in Economics. I am grateful to the memory of both women who served as role models.

Mother had looked forward to my graduation with great anticipation. Arriving by train from Los Angeles, she was informed at the Oakland Station that the streetcar to Berkeley had just completed its final run for the day! The conductor, sensing her distress, decided to take her anyway, as his sole passenger. I hope he was not reprimanded for this act of kindness. As she and Sam sat outdoors among the crowds at the Greek Theater, watching me receive highest honors, she must have felt great pride.

The first summer after graduation I worked for the American Trust Company in San Francisco. Since this was before the Bay Bridge was built, I commuted by ferry, beginning each day with time to read the morning paper. Later I worked for their Los Baños branch before returning to Berkeley for my Master's Degree.

When Dean Charles Lipman interviewed me for graduate school, he asked whether I "knew a Herman Sachs." Lipman had been a consultant for the Baron de Hirsch Fund and remembered reports written by a "Sachs" about the progress of the community of Jewish farmers from the Wilton, North Dakota area. He routinely read these reports, remembered my father's writing, and was pleased to admit this pioneer's daughter to graduate school. This story delighted my father enormously!

Although my application to the UC School of Social Welfare had been accepted, I changed my mind. After having experienced the difficulty of commuting back to the ranch on weekends, I decided on a teaching credential for work closer to home—I needed to devote all my time to my studies, as I wanted to earn an M.A. in Economics as well as a Special Adult Education Credential. Had we lived in the city, I would have gone on to study for a Ph.D., but that would have meant several years away from the ranch, which was my home. A teaching job, on the other hand, would permit me to remain in the valley. For practice teaching I ended up choosing English for adults instead of high school history. Although the former was a breeze, I failed to obtain the experience that I would later need in teaching high school students.

Joan London and Charles Malamuth's house on Panoramic Way became my "home away from home" on frequent visits to the Berkeley campus. This enabled me to attend the theater in San Francisco. On one occasion, I was thrilled to be in the audience and hear the beautiful voice of Paul Robeson in *Othello*. Joan and Charles and Zev Hassid and his wife Billie Fenigsten would sometimes spend weekends on the San Juan Ranch. We were delighted with Joan's luscious fresh fruit pies. My own repertoire was sadly limited.

I had briefly been a reader for Professor Paul Taylor, who was later employed by The Farm Security Administration to document the miserable conditions of farm labor in California, with particular emphasis on the San Joaquin Valley. He was to become the great proponent of the 160-acre limitation on farms receiving subsidized canal water from the Central Valley Project (CVP). This five hundred mile-long water distribution system, completed in 1951, favored farming interests at the expense of cities and the environment. This battle for water, filled with twists and turns, continues to this day.

Under Professor Peixoto, I wrote my M.A. thesis on Economic Policies of the Soviet Government between 1917 and 1926. A member of my committee, Professor Kerner of the History Department, had emigrated from Czechoslovakia and was no admirer of the Soviet leaders. He criticized what, in his opinion, was my positive account of the Bolshevik Government's policies. The Soviets had not initiated land reform, he insisted. Such improvements had begun under the Czars before the 1917 Revolution. He referred me to reports that were published by the International Agricultural Academy in Rome. Through the UC library I was able to access these papers, cite them, and thus satisfy the demands of this member of my committee. It took all summer, but I was finally granted an M.A. in Economics to the satisfaction of Professor Peixoto and the third member of my committee, a literature professor, the Russian-born George Z. Patrick. Upon deep reflection, perhaps I was too much influenced by my desire to see the world transformed under socialism.

Chapter 12

Teaching at the San Juan Ranch Cookhouse School

*"I remember you as my teacher on the San Juan ranch, and so did my sister
Virgilia. When you and Sam moved to the new ranch, our family went along."*

—Gilbert Padilla, retired United Farm Workers treasurer

I began teaching in 1929, in a small school on the San Juan ranch. My students
were children of migratory farm laborers, mostly Mexican. I had children of all
ages, and found them eager to learn. Absorbed and excited by my new work, I
could not imagine the far-reaching effects of the stock market crash, which occurred
at this time and which I read about in the *Fresno Bee*. Since we lived in a small town,
we were somewhat removed from its initial effects. Many local people had truck gardens and were self-employed. They managed somehow.

Through my students, I became aware of the serious lack of medical care for farm workers and their families. In 1930 I made contact with a field nurse, Eva Barnes, of the Council
of Women for Home Missions, a national organization with an office in Oakland. We
arranged for transportation to the Merced County hospital for the most needy cases.

When I obtained a teaching position in the Joint Union High School in nearby Dos
Palos, Sam and I moved into town. At first we lived in the ramshackle old Cordova, the
town's only hotel. As I became friendly with the owners, the Richards, they asked me to
take over during their vacation. The week before my teaching job started was spent making up beds and filling in, but I was happy to help my friends.

For the next two years, 1930 to 1932, I taught history, earning the magnificent salary of

$1900 the first year and $2000 the second. Since Sam was supporting me, we were able to send most of the money I earned to his family in Poland. I was proud to have this job, although I felt ill-prepared to handle high school students. They were used to a strictly disciplined, question-and-answer style, while I encouraged discussion, using topics not always covered by the text. They were at a rebellious age and often difficult to handle. California children enjoyed more freedom than those of the midwest, it seemed. Also, Dos Palos was a "frontier" kind of town, drawing rowdy children from the farm as well as from the city.

The early 1930s proved a test for Sam. As a tenant farmer, he had been experimenting with growing cotton on Miller & Lux land, working long hours. It was a struggle just to survive. Like most farmers, he needed to obtain advances on the current crop in order to plant for the following year. At one point, we lived on $75 a month, and even that was borrowed! Sam lacked funds, but he had the imagination, enthusiasm, and self-confidence to obtain backing from several sources, including the Bank of America, founded in San Francisco by an Italian immigrant, A.P. Giannini.

Dissatisfied with tenant farming, Sam was able to finance the purchase of eight hundred acres on the west side of Merced County, about fifteen miles from Dos Palos, and 140 miles south of San Francisco. The ranch was eventually enlarged to almost six thousand acres, and remained the site of Sam's farming operations until his death in 1976. "Sam Hamburg Farms" can still be found on today's Thomas & Sons California Maps.

The new farmland stretched for miles along the foothills of the Santa Cruz Mountains: in spring it was covered by a mantle of green that turned to purple under the last rays of sun. Golden poppies carpeted the hills, dancing in the morning sunlight. Before Sam bought it, the acreage had belonged to the White family of San Francisco. Sam was friendly with their son-in-law, who was head of San Francisco's Painless Parker chain of dentists. Up to this time, Basque farmers from Spain had been running sheep on this land. It had also supported light grain plantings. Sam envisioned a land that could, with irrigation, produce many other products including cotton, which by 1970 was the leading cash crop of California.

With bulldog determination, Sam managed to cajole creditors into advancing the necessary funds for the installation of extremely deep wells for irrigation. Dissatisfied with the high electric rates charged by PG&E [Pacific Gas & Electric] for pumping the water, he once drove to Sacramento to protest before the State Railroad Commission, the precursor of the California State Utility Commission.

In the late 40s, Sam was one of the first farmers to benefit from the lower water rates of the Central Valley Project (CVP), which currently supplies and distributes one-fourth of California's water. This favoritism toward agriculture has been the source of much controversy, since the irrigation water is supplied to farmers at rates below cost while city users pay more per unit. Sam was experimenting with raising cotton, which required more irrigation water than other crops. He wanted to learn all about farming in order to take his knowledge back to the land that is now Israel.

I lost my teaching job in 1932 because the trustees believed that married women should be supported by their husbands. The Depression had finally hit home. Also, I may have been a bit too outspoken in some of the discussion groups held outside of class, in which taboo topics such as birth control were brought up. After my job ended we moved to Los Baños, which was closer to Sam's new ranch, and rented a small two bedroom house on 6th Street. I did some substitute teaching and developed a friendship with our next door neighbor, Carmelita Luke, a divorced woman of Spanish and Irish descent, the mother of two sons, and a talented cook.

I was at loose ends. I did not care for Los Baños social life, which centered around women's bridge parties. Having no interest in bridge, I was not a part of Los Baños society. In Dos Palos, I had several good friends, including Blanche Lucas, the down-to-earth, humane principal of the grammar school, and other people who had interests somewhat similar to mine. That town reminded me of the midwest because of its absence of minorities. In Los Baños, however, there was a division between "white" Americans and "foreigners"— Portuguese and Italians. Although the predominantly southern Europeans were dairy farmers and land owners, not field workers, I still sensed real prejudice against them. I joined a number of concerned people working to overcome widespread opposition to a swimming pool that was to be "open to all." The pool was finally constructed in the newly-established city park and came to be enjoyed by *all* the city's children.

Los Baños, like nearby Dos Palos, had been a Miller & Lux company town. By the twenties, it had diversified and a number of independent enterprises were owned by Italians, Portuguese, and Chinese. However, Los Baños preferred to maintain its public image as a western-style cowboy outpost. The annual Mayday Parade featured the area's finest citizens mounted on horses as cowboys and cowgirls, bringing back memories of its colorful past. Everyone dressed in western gear, and the kids, with their ponies and wagons, had a ball.

As an avid reader in socio-economic affairs, I was so impressed by the 1931 autobiography of the famous muckraker, Lincoln Steffens, that I wrote him. I eagerly accepted his invitation to visit in his Carmel home, where he lived with his young British wife, author

Ella Winters. I was interested in his account of how our democratic institutions had been taken over by selfish entrepreneurs. This was particularly evident in the cities, many of which were dominated by corrupt politicians. What had happened to the ideals of equal opportunity for all? I came away with a better idea of the gulf between political and economic theory and the reality of American politics. At this time, my father, living in Los Angeles, was caught up in the campaigns of another muckraker, Upton Sinclair. His book, *The Jungle*, exposed conditions in the meat-packing industry and led to the nation's first pure food law. Sinclair made several unsuccessful attempts to win the governorship of California.

I also enjoyed music and theater, and attended programs in Fresno whenever possible. We reveled in the rich music of Feodor Chaliapin, a Russian opera singer, famous for interpreting *Ivan the Terrible* and *Mephistopheles*. Sam loved hearing Russian, his first language.

Back in Los Baños, I sought out several interesting women who were leaders of the California Federated Women's Clubs. It was the only other game in town! That was before I had children or had become active in school affairs. I was appointed Head of the Youth Conservation Section, which concerned itself with saving children from delinquency. I wrote newsletter articles about the lack of educational opportunities for poor children, which led to delinquency, unemployment, and sometimes, the break-up of the family. This remained my area of concern for several years. Ellen Jensen, then president of the local chapter, and I would travel around the Valley speaking to other clubs and conferences. This large Swedish woman with an attractive face and blond hair was a marvelous cook, and of such proportions that her new Chevrolet had to be rebuilt with a special seat.

My interest in health care was not far removed from Youth Conservation, and I pursued both during my years in the Valley. After the mission nurse Eva Barnes left, I became friendly with her replacement, Miss Huffnagel. These hard-working professionals spent their days driving from one farm camp to another, dispensing medical advice and first-aid to workers and their families.

I was learning more about ranching, and often accompanied Sam on his frequent, short trips in the area, checking the progress of his fellow farmers. Since this involved a great deal of waiting around, I developed the habit of never leaving home without reading material in hand. In the early days, ranchers exchanged machinery, tractors and tools, and Sam, who was just getting started, was a frequent borrower. He often stopped to look over his neighbors' crops to see what had been planted, pointing out good, straight rows of cotton or alfalfa. If they were not straight, he would comment, "He's not a very good farmer!" I saw so much acreage, I could have drawn maps in my sleep. Barley and other grains depended on seasonal rains, which came only during winter and spring—"sky farming." Other crops required irrigation. In California, water is the life blood of the country and the cause of continuing battles between urban and rural users. Farming was a most risky and grueling way to make a living and it began to take a toll on Sam. In the early years he drove the tractor himself, often working all night, only taking time to sleep by the side of a ditch.

Sam had become friendly with Russell Giffen, whose extensive acreage was the model of what was to become "corporation" farming. Russell's father, Wiley, had been a pioneer raisin grower in the Valley and the founder of the Sun Maid Growers Association, the earliest cooperative in this part of the country. Russell was a large-scale farmer whose neat attire resembled that of a city banker. He was once featured in *Fortune* magazine as the largest grower of diversified crops in the country. He was one of the first to plant large acreages in Mexico, a practice still popular as farmers from the US take over some of the most productive land south of the border. Who could have foreseen that this practice would be a first step toward the globalization of industry and trade?

At this time, I sensed a change in Sam's thinking. He had been very progressive when we first met, but as he identified with his fellow ranchers, he became less open to new ideas. Giffen wielded the greatest influence over Sam and may have been responsible for my husband beginning to question some of his original convictions. Sam's earliest training had been in the Kibbutz movement in Palestine. But those socialist concepts were now in conflict with the practical reality of farming. He began to see these earlier ideas challenged in his dealings with landowners, PG&E, and bankers.

During the Depression, farmers were deep in debt and constantly under threat of losing their land. President Roosevelt's Agricultural Adjustment Authority (AAA) was part of the New Deal's effort to restore stability to the farm as well as the city. The policy was to restrict the acreage planted to major crops, in order to boost prices. Later, subsidies for certain crops, including cotton and sugar, were also introduced, enabling growers such as Giffen and Sam to begin realizing substantial returns on their operations. While Giffen complained about the red tape involved in government programs, he nevertheless welcomed the payments. However, he never had a kind word for Roosevelt or the New Deal. Sam's farming was also beginning to pay off. With our newly-acquired acreage we could begin to clear our credit and plan for the future.

Chapter 13

"Go Back, You're Not Wanted!"

I'm just a lousy vagabond,
See, that's the way they made me be,
And there's no cotton crop for you
Unless it's picked by bums like me.

—popular song of the day, quoted by B. Traven,
The Cotton Pickers, 1969

One day in the early thirties, when Sam opened the door, he found himself face to face with the county sheriff who proceeded to "warn" him about the pending visit of two "dangerous subversives." Friends of Eda Lou Walton were known to be coming to visit us from New York. One was the novelist Henry Roth. "Communists!" the sheriff warned. Communists, especially from New York, were no doubt a threat to the town's safety! Even though Sam had met some of Eda Lou's friends earlier, he was apprehensive, and his wavering seemed to be a harbinger of future conflicts between us. Should they be turned away? I put my foot down, "Absolutely not! They're friends of Eda Lou's and we are not sending them back!" They stayed with us for about two weeks. The town survived.

This year also marked the beginning of serious labor unrest in the Valley. In the early years of the Depression, farmers across the country, including California, were going broke, except for those with substantial holdings. Large farmers were favored by banks and consolidated food processing companies, who also offered crop financing.

Times were now propitious for investors from the cities seeking favorable tax shelters in agriculture. In 1939, writer Carey McWilliams described these large-scale corporate

69

holdings as "Factories in the Fields." Migrant labor traveled from farm to farm, planting, cultivating, and harvesting whatever crops were in season. For a long time, ranch productivity had depended mostly on Mexican hands and a sprinkling of Sikh laborers from India. The main irrigators on the ranch, they worked the land and could be identified by their carefully-wound white turbans.

But as the Depression deepened, many farm laborers were unable to survive, even though every family member worked, including children. Some were forced to return to Mexico. Dust Bowl refugees were straggling in from abandoned farms, primarily in Oklahoma and Arkansas. Their battered vehicles scarcely made it to California, where they hoped to obtain jobs. Over time, workers of many nationalities arrived, including Chinese, Filipinos, and East Indians. Marginal laborers, barely managing to get by, were threatened by the new arrivals. These displaced farmers were greeted by freeway billboards warning "Go Back! You're Not Wanted!" Even those lucky enough to have jobs earned only about fifty cents an hour.

Who would predict that some among these poor "Oakies and Arkies" would later become landowners, a few also occupying political positions? Among them was my former student from the ungraded school on the San Juan ranch, Gilbert Padilla, whose primary school education enabled him to serve as treasurer of Cesar Chavez' United Farm Workers Union (UFW), and whose eight children would become skilled or semi-skilled professionals. This is a tribute to the quality of education in the days before the 1979 passage of California Proposition 13,which placed limits on property taxes and precipitated the steep decline in funding for California schools.

Early attempts to organize labor occurred in other parts of the Valley, including Fresno and as far south as Bakersfield. Although unsuccessful, this was the area where charismatic labor leader Cesar Chavez would, thirty years later and assisted by Dolores Huerta, begin the long struggle to organize the oppressed migrant workers. Some farmers became vigilantes. Much greater bloodshed would have occurred if Chavez had not followed the Gandhian principles of non-violence from the beginning.

The Communist Party had fought many battles alongside labor and the poor, and was active in the Valley. One of its most involved members, Meyer Baylin, had been a fellow student during my senior year at Berkeley. We had been active in the Cosmopolitan Club, where social issues of the day provoked many lively debates. In 1928 I remained in Berkeley to begin graduate studies, while Meyer, devoted to the Communist cause and primarily interested in labor organizing, left the university. Although a US resident since early childhood, Meyer was denied citizenship and a passport until the 1970s because of his political activities. As an alien, he often found himself under threat of arrest while trying to organize workers.

Confronted with the deteriorating situation of the unemployed farmworkers in the Valley, Meyer returned to his home in Los Angeles and from that base threw himself into efforts to improve agricultural labor conditions. He planned and launched two hunger marches: one, in 1929, ended in San Francisco; the other reached Sacramento the following year. He selected Pat Chambers, "straight off the bread line," and a dynamic, attractive young woman named Carolyn Becker to spearhead this work. Carolyn was "obviously of another world," according to Meyer—she seemed more a sophisticate than an activist. Diminutive and blonde, her appealing Southern air endeared her to the workers, who hung on her every word and trusted her implicitly.

So successful was Carolyn's organizing work that she was arrested and spent time in Tehachapi Women's Prison in the California desert. Later, she married one of her attorneys. I visited her following her marriage and was interested to learn that she had become a devoted housewife and mother. Her husband had been connected with the famous Harry Bridges case: Bridges, an Australian dock worker, was one of the nation's most successful labor leaders and the founder of the International Longshore and Warehousemen's Union (ILWU). In 1934 they were able to immobilize all of San Francisco by calling a one-day strike.

In the nineties, Ernie Bessig, retired Northern California ACLU Director, interviewed Meyer for the UC Regional Oral History Library. In this session, Meyer recalled that during the Depression, Sam, half in jest, had urged him to persuade his "friend," Stalin, to invite him to Russia to introduce new farming methods there. Despite Sam's departure from his earlier Socialist roots, Meyer and Sam had remained friends over the years. In 1930, when the hunger marchers were passing through the San Joaquin Valley on their way to Sacramento, Sam obtained milk and cheese from a nearby dairy for the strikers.

The 1933 labor strike in the southern San Joaquin Valley was the largest and most successful action among migrant workers. At that time, Meyer and Sam were in touch. Sixty-three years later Meyer recalled the dilemma which had faced my husband who was aware that fellow growers, members of the reactionary "Associated Farmers," were organized to oppose pro-labor activity in the Valley and would use force if necessary. Although never a member, Sam realized they would "raise hell" with him if he expressed support for the strikers. Although he proudly referred to himself as a "Jewish man of the soil," in reality, he was an anomaly. Aware of his tenuous situation and dependent on the Bank of America which was now financing his farming operations, he knew it would have been risky to express openly any sympathy with the labor movement.

During this troublesome time, violence had erupted on a ranch near Fresno where the cotton strike had started. Two workers were killed by the police. Later, their fellow pickers refused to pick cotton on that particular acreage. Ranchers thought of themselves as the "last frontiersmen," willing to take the law into their own hands. A large-scale farmer kept a machine gun in the garage, threatening to use it in the event of trouble. One winter morning, a neighbor coming upon a *bracero* stealing gas, brought out his shotgun and blew the man's head off. He was never charged!

The strike was successful in raising wages: pickers who had been earning thirty-five cents per hundred pounds were asking seventy-five, and settled for sixty. As Meyer told me in a recent conversation, "Sam felt it was only fair to pay a decent rate." Union organizing efforts fell apart soon afterward, leaders were jailed, and the Communist Party's focus unfortunately shifted away from agricultural workers and back to the cities.

Years later, Cesar Chavez would issue his call: "Once people understand the strength of nonviolence, the force it generates, the love it creates, the response it brings from the total community, they will not easily abandon it."

Chapter 14

Settling Down, Having Children

"We mothers
rock into the heart of the world
the melody of peace."

—Nelly Sachs, in *Mother to Daughter,*
Daughter to Mother, Tillie Olson,
The Feminist Press, 1984

In 1932, Charlie had set off for Tucson, where once again he opened a glass business. As before, he spent his weekends riding horseback on the surrounding ranches—a striking figure in his chaps and cowboy boots—performing fancy rope tricks for the amusement of ranch hands. He loved to tell the story of the town's encounter with John Dillinger and his gang. One morning, while eating his customary fried eggs at a downtown cafe, he saw a building in flames. Several rough-looking characters were tugging a huge trunk down the fire escape of the nearby hotel. They were Dillinger's gang, escaping! The spectacle aroused immediate alarm and the police were called. An inspection of the trunk revealed the arsenal of John Dillinger. These outlaws were rounded up and jailed while others in nearby hotels also came under the sheriff's net. Subsequently, they all escaped.

The Depression hit Tucson hard. Banks failed and Charlie was forced to give up his business. His heart had always been in farming, and he had discussed with Sam the possibility of acquiring some land near our ranch. Without resources or western farming experience, it seemed logical for him to begin to work at the Sam Hamburg Farms.

The Mexican laborers were feeling insecure in their jobs due to the influx of migrant Dust Bowl workers. Sam invited Charlie to try his hand at the job of farm manager, since he needed a responsible person who could handle worker conflicts, which invariably arose. Charlie, with his quiet manner, was often able to step in, reconcile differences, and restore peace. But not all conflicts on the ranch were so easily settled.

Among the Dust Bowl itinerants was a contentious "Oakie" family, the Lesters, consisting of a father and several sons. Sam eyed Walt, a strapping fellow with farming experience, as a potential foreman. Problems later arose about the delegation of responsibility between Charlie and Walt. Sam would play one off against the other; as time went on, there was much jockeying for position.

Signs of Sam's instability were noticeable. His deferential attitude toward Russell Giffen contrasted with his treatment of other farmers. The differences Sam and I were experiencing were reflected in his attitude toward Charlie. Sam would make unreasonable demands on my brother without fully explaining what he expected. Having been raised on a North Dakota farm, Charlie was scarcely prepared for some of the situations he encountered on this highly-mechanized California enterprise.

In farming, calamities arise: early frosts, grasshopper invasions, and drought create perpetual crises. There were also human tragedies to be handled. Late one Saturday afternoon, following payday, a Mexican worker was killed in a brawl. What was to be done? No one else volunteered, and it was left to luckless Charlie to transport the body to Los Baños in his pickup. Unfortunately, it was late and Dr. Collier, the town physician, was not to be found. After driving around for some time, Charlie managed to persuade the mortuary to accept the body, pending an autopsy.

During its long growing season, cotton requires numerous applications of pesticides. Sam had built a landing strip to accommodate crop-dusting planes. On one of these flights, the low-flying plane hit an electric wire and crashed, killing the pilot. The entire ranch mourned the death of this young man.

Tensions continued to develop. Sam and I had been so preoccupied with our separate goals and worrying about the future of his family in Poland, that we had never discussed the question of starting a family. Concerned about our compatibility and our future together, I privately doubted the wisdom of bringing children into the world. He also had some doubts. This issue was finally raised by Dr. Meyer Wahrhaftig, friend and family physician. "Isn't it about time you start thinking about having a baby? "

Sam and I finally decided to begin our family and soon I was pregnant. In March of

1935 Sam drove me to Los Angeles to await the birth of our first child at my parents' home. Instead of relaxing, I continued my activities. As a frequent visitor to Los Angeles, I had often attended meetings of the progressive John Reed Club in Hollywood with friends, with whom I had become acquainted at UC. I enjoyed these gatherings of left-wing intelligentsia.

I had gained considerable weight, in contrast to my cousin Beatrice, who also happened to be pregnant at that time. Quite tall, she appeared svelte by comparison. On several occasions, noting the difference between us, Sam had asked, "Why are you so large?" Halfway through my pregnancy, I had reason to believe that I might be carrying twins, but my Los Angeles physician Dr. Fearon insisted, "No, you're just going to have a large baby."

On the morning before delivering, I visited the doctor who had again pronounced me not ready. That evening I attended a concert with my friend, Alma Hokinson, a former WW I nurse who was concerned about my climbing all those steps to the "Peanut Gallery" at the Philharmonic Auditorium. But I did not want to miss the cultural offerings of the city. Later that night, I felt the first contractions. Ben drove me to Queen of the Angels Hospital while Pa called Sam. The next day, April 6, after a protracted labor, we became the parents of twin daughters, Sonya and Tanya, named for Sam's cousins in Warsaw. When the twins were announced, I was thrilled but still groggy from having delivered two girls who tipped the scale at a joint weight of 12-$\frac{1}{2}$ pounds. "We'll be lucky if we raise one!" I murmured. The doctor, embarrassed and apologetic for his miscalculation of the delivery date and the fact I had been carrying twins, remarked, "I'm not going to charge you for the second baby." I think the entire doctor's bill came to $125. I enjoyed the luxury of a twelve-day hospital stay, during which time there was no emphasis whatsoever on breast feeding, to my later regret.

I remained in Los Angeles for a number of weeks after the babies' arrival. Inexperienced and overwhelmed by the demands of twins, I suddenly needed two of everything, having prepared only a scant single layette. I found myself unusually dependent and in need of help. Unfortunately for me, my mother was now occupied with campaign work. Jewish immigrants tended to be political, and my mother had caught the spirit. In spite of her imperfect English, she had been recruited to walk precincts for the local Democrats who were gearing up for FDR's 1936 reelection. I'm certain the dual obligations created a conflict in her mind; thrilled with her first grandchildren, but still dedicated to her political work. Somehow, I managed.

I stayed on with my parents for a while, until Sam, who was impatient about having to fend for himself, called and startled me with his brusque demand: "Well, the parade is over. Come home!" He had just suffered the loss of an entire barley crop in a severe hailstorm at the end of March.

The twins were about a month old when Ben drove us back to the Valley, a hot trip of approximately three hundred miles. Mother, proud of her first-ever washing machine, insisted on sending it home with me, saying, "You need it more than I do." She then went back to scrubbing her sheets by hand. The washing machine was called the "Easy" and had a spin dryer attachment. This was a luxury for me. During wet Valley winters, it would have been impossible to dry the dozens of soggy diapers.

Throughout the 30s, economy was called for. I had learned to dry clean with cleaning solvent sold by the gallon at service stations. I used a tub in the backyard and wore rubber gloves to handle the solvent, now a recognized pollutant and no longer available for home use. I always "dry-cleaned" out of doors. Occasionally, in the effort to economize, I would also do Sam's suits.

My next door neighbor, Carmelita Luke, fell in love with my two little girls and became an indispensable part of the family. She was so dedicated and she did not set an actual wage for her baby-sitting services. Quite independent, she preferred to come and go as she pleased. Sonya and Tanya knew her as their beloved "Kuku." We kept in close touch with her even after we moved away, until her death from cancer many years later.

Housekeeping was difficult for me. As a girl, my only concern had been my studies. I'm embarrased to confess that Mother had done all the family cooking. Now, although Carmelita prepared special dishes, it was up to me to cook. Attempting to imitate my mother's wonderful style, I improvised, making stock-pot soups in which simmered every vegetable in the market.

I had done some canning with my mother and found the abundance of lush, summertime fruit and produce in the Valley irresistible. I preserved fruit of all kinds: peaches, grapes, pears, figs as well as vegetables. Our cellar shelves were lined with jams, jellies, and preserves. During the winter, we also ate pickled herring by the pound. The Rosenburgs, a Jewish family that had recently joined the local merchants in Los Baños, would make frequent trips to The City, bringing back herring in 25-pound kegs, along with kosher salami, one of Sam's favorites. I would clean, cut up, and pickle the fish. Sam also loved dill pickles, which I put up in crocks.

I organized a mother's group in town, sharing literature about child-rearing, and solicited members to subscribe to *Parent's Magazine.* The articles prompted lively discussions among us new parents. I also volunteered at the state-supported Well Baby Clinic, where San Francisco Pediatrician Dr. Anita Faberman examined infants and young children. Until then, child development was taken for granted. At these clinics, mothers were introduced to the practice of regular health checkups and inoculation against common childhood diseases. Although I had been single-minded about my own education, now the children became my primary interest. To my deep disappointment, Sam could find no time to read any of the literature about parenting. Farming was his all-consuming interest: He rarely came home when the children were awake. He had left his parents' home at thirteen and lacked experience with family life. Simply, Sam was waiting for the children to grow up.

Some time after returning to Los Baños, I realized it was time for the twins to have a checkup. I decided to visit Dr. Van Wagenen, a well-known pediatrician, in Fresno. Sam seemed perplexed. "What do you need to go to Fresno for? Are the babies sick?" It was a trip of seventy miles, and fortunately a friend was able to drive us.

That summer Sam's New York Uncle Saul Lehman, his wife Esther, and their two college-age sons Jesse and Elliot, planned to drive out to California in a brand new car. A tall, imposing man and a great storyteller with a deep, melodious voice, Saul owned the Georgian Press on Varick Street in Greenwich Village. Several days before their expected arrival, I received a telephone call from Saul, who informed me that the motor had literally dropped out of their new Buick. Could Sam pick them up in Nevada? Sam, at that time, was driving East to Merced on business, though fortunately not in his pickup truck. Frantic, I phoned the Highway Patrol, who agreed to flag him down. I waited expectantly, hearing nothing until the weary travelers arrived at our doorstep hours later. After being notified of the Lehman's predicament, Sam had decided to "rescue" the family, taking the shortest route—the mountainous road through Yosemite and over Tioga Pass—in spite of his fear of heights. The pass was so steep that he attached a blanket to his side window to block the terrifying view! Imagine the emotional scene in which the stranded and anxious family was saved by their heroic cousin Sam. When these grateful New Yorkers arrived at our little house in Los Baños, they could not have been happier had they been received at the Ritz.

We insisted that Saul and Esther make themselves comfortable in our bedroom, and their boys took the smaller one. We moved the crib into the living room, alongside the couch where Sam and I slept. The twins, however, had developed a routine in which Sonya cried by day and Tanya by night. None of us could sleep. Sam, the good host, announced to his guests, "Come on, we're going to the hotel." Upon which, Aunt Esther appeared in her robe, arms akimbo, and countered, "Sam, we are staying right *here*!!" We finally managed to get some sleep. Sam took the Lehmans on several trips to Southern California and the desert, but in the end, these inveterate New Yorkers were eager to return to the comforts of their beloved city.

By now, Charlie felt his presence was no longer needed on the ranch and he was able to fulfill his lifelong dream of acquiring a small acreage not far from ours. This upset Sam. He felt challenged, even though my brother made no attempt to compete with him. Around this time, Charlie was also working part-time for the Merced County Farm Security Administration, part of FDR's New Deal in support of the country's farmers. He proved to be an innovator as one of the first in the area to plant rice. He also raised the crop near Woodland, in the Sacramento Valley.

Charlie, the perennial bachelor, had been introduced to a young friend, Gertie Stein, by our old North Dakota neighbors the Blumenfelds, who had moved to Los Angeles not long before us. The Steins were a large family, also. The father, Philip, was head of an insurance firm and a prominent member of the Los Angeles Jewish community. The courtship developed.

In 1937 the twins and I attended the wedding of Charlie and Gertie, who married in a traditional Jewish ceremony in a Los Angeles synagogue. They then settled into the old, weather-beaten bachelor house on his ranch. Although a city girl with a Physical Education degree from UCLA, Gertie willingly accepted the rugged life of a struggling farmer's wife.

The couple had no telephone. When the call came from Los Angeles reporting Gertie's father's death, I had the sad duty of delivering the news. Within a couple of years, they were forced to abandon the old farm house and move into a small cottage in Los Baños where Charlie was willing to make a daily, fourteen-mile drive to his farm. Their son, Philip, was born in 1939, and daughter, Dorothy, in 1942. Charlie had happily returned to farming—his first love—and was raising a family.

Chapter 15

The Effects of the Holocaust

"We know you're hiding Jews! Bring them out or we'll shoot you!"
Thus tragically ended the lives of Sam's mother and sister.

—Letter from Uncle Josef Limone

Tanya often asked why we had not attempted to rescue her father's family in Poland. What could we answer? We were no wiser than the rest of the world. In 1938, a year before the Germans invaded Poland, Sam was finally able to visit his family there, having been informed of his father's pending surgery. Uncle Saul had made frequent trips to Poland before the war—it was now time for Sam to go. Charlie assured him that he would look after the ranch. Although I was expecting for the second time, I was getting along well.

Although for years we had been sending his parents what help we could afford, Sam was shocked at the depth of the deprivations he observed. Tragically, this was to be his only visit home. His father, Aron, died later that year. Our son, born the following January, was named after him. Upon his return from Poland, Sam brought with him beautiful needlework, including exquisite outfits for the twins made by his sister Rosa, an art teacher. He also returned with an 8 mm movie film of his relatives. Sadly, the film contained the last images ever taken of Sam's family, including the Goldmans of Warsaw.

In Germany, Hitler's rise to power was fueled by turbulent domestic conditions. Unmanageable WWI reparations levied on the government contributed to high unemployment and runaway inflation. Hitler, in an effort to find a scapegoat, blamed big business, especially those sectors dominated by foreigners and Jews. Conditions were so chaotic in the 30s that the German people willingly followed his leadership.

Leaders of the western democracies, including industrialists and prominent British and US bankers, were lulled into a sense of false security by Hitler's assurances and their own vested interests. He promised to restore order in Germany, which would include settling some "border disputes." In fact, many big-business relationships between the Germans and Allied countries continued throughout the war and afterwards. The Allies refrained from bombing the railroad tracks even after they became fully aware of the crimes against humanity being committed in Nazi death camps. In retrospect, it is difficult to understand how the genocide resulting in the slaughter of six million Jews, as well as other minorities, could have continued as long as it did.

When Hitler's army quickly overran Poland in 1939, it was not long before Jews from all over Warsaw were forced into cramped ghettoes established by the invaders, and cut off from the rest of the city. Suffering from disease and starvation, inmates were terrorized by German guards. Jan Karski, a Christian Pole, risked his life to enter the ghetto illegally, eluding German security guards in order to observe its true conditions. He noted with horror the daily "pile-up" of corpses. After two visits, overcome by what he had seen, he resolved to inform the world of these atrocities.

In April 1943, about sixty-thousand Jews remaining in the ghetto revolted. The Germans retaliated, setting the miserable quarters on fire. Thousands perished. The few who survived escaped through the sewer lines, and then attempted to join the Polish underground. Most were rejected—mainly because of religious prejudice.

As Karski told his story in England, he was confronted with disbelief. Even though rumors of the concentration camps continued to filter out of Nazi-occupied territory, a news blackout about the terrible slaughter of civilians kept this information from us. Karski traveled to the US, in hopes of speaking to Roosevelt. Unable to see FDR directly, he met with Henry Morgenthau, the Treasury Secretary, who happened to be Jewish. To his bitter disappointment, the Pole failed to convince him and no action was taken. It was only after the surrender of the Germans that the remaining death camp survivors were freed and the shocking truth of the Holocaust came to full public attention. It is estimated that six million Jews were slaughtered in the camps. When Hitler first came to power, few could have foretold the lengths to which his followers would go to destroy entire populations. Even if Holocaust prisoners were to escape, where could they go? Although England controlled Palestine by mandate, no Jewish immigration was allowed at that time. The future of this territory was uncertain because of rival Jewish and Arab claims. Yet, against all odds, some Jews managed to make their way there clandestinely.

What had happened to Sam's family in Pinsk? During the turmoil of the war, all lines of communication were cut off. For years we had no knowledge of their fate. Saul Lehman's brother Josef, newly settled in Palestine, had closer contacts in Poland and was the first to learn of the decimation of the family. The Goldmans, Sam's cousins, were among the thousands who perished in the Warsaw ghetto. The entire family was lost, including their four grown children—a pianist, a writer, and two teachers—whose lives and talents were abruptly ended. Sam's mother Shana and sister Rosa had been protected by a Polish farm family throughout the war years. In the desperate final days, the retreating Germans had heartlessly ordered the Poles to surrender any Jews they might be holding. Thus his mother and sister were gunned down.

Among the survivors of the Holocaust in Sam's family were a few young cousins. Stenya, who had been sent to study in France, joined the underground during the occupation and settled in Montpellier. Another, Mania Mayerson from Kielce, had escaped with a group of Young Zionists. Michael Garin, Mania's future husband, fled Poland on foot, ending up in France and eventually finding work on a British cattle ship that transported beef to Palestine. Forbidden to land, he entered the territory surreptitiously. These young people were never again to see their families. Mania and Michael are Israeli citizens.

Sam's cousin, Helena Rubinstein, also from Kielce, saved her two small daughters and herself by posing as Christians. Of the two thousand Jewish children living in the area, these two girls were the only survivors. "In broad daylight, with the Gestapo surrounding the ghetto, my Mother took us by the hand, one on each side of her, and marched out of the gate. Her attitude was, 'If we die, then the three of us will die together. If we live, then we all live.'" In order not to attract suspicion, Helena took the girls to mass regularly. Changing their names, they would later become Anita and Janet. Both came to accept their new identities.

Anita, whom I interviewed for an oral history project years later, was young, impressionable, and unfortunately had absorbed the constant barrage of anti-Semitic remarks filling the air in occupied Poland. Even today, she has been unable to overcome her own anti-Jewish feelings, a residue of those terrible formative years among the mostly Catholic Poles. In her own words, "I became strongly anti-Semitic. To this day, this background leaves me with a great deal of confusion regarding my religion."

Her sister Janet, who was somewhat older, has no trace of this identity conflict, although they all lived in constant terror of discovery. Not until mother and daughters were traveling safely by train on their way to a French refugee center could the mother tell the girls that their father had been killed while fighting in the Polish underground, in the very forest through which they were passing. Anita remembers watching the countryside as she listened to the story of her father's betrayal. He was forced to dig his own grave and was shot in the back of the head. "In this forest your father was killed,"She recalls her mother saying, gazing out the window. For Anita, everything had turned gray.

After some difficulty, Uncle Saul and Sam, were able to bring the three out of Europe. Because they lacked proper visas, the Immigration and Naturalization Service (INS) in New York requested a $5000 bond to guarantee their appearance at a future hearing. When Saul's wife, Esther, arrived with the funds in hand, she was dismayed to be told, "Well, if you have that much money available, you could easily forfeit it to keep your relatives here forever." The INS refused the bond. Sadly, the refugees' trials were not yet over. With assistance from the family, they were able to enter and remain in Cuba, where the girls enrolled in school until they obtained proper documentation for entry into the US.

When they settled in New York, the girls continued their education and Helena found employment in a mattress factory. Later, she married and settled in Canada while her daughters remained in this country. Janet married an American rabbi and raised a family. Anita pursued a business career with Revlon before entering a doctoral program in history at New York University. It was my privilege to give some assistance to Anita while she completed her degree. She is now an administrator with the New York City Board of Education. Although she is a contemporary of my daughters, her life, and that of her sister, has been so different, because of a tragic turn of fate.

Chapter 16

Look Out For Enemy Planes!

Once up in the tower, Ellen and I could discuss club affairs, and enjoy our "rationed" sandwiches, while surveying the Valley and watching for planes that were on their way to bomb us. Fortunately, they never came.

I was concerned about who would care for the twins while I was in the hospital awaiting the delivery of the new baby, and asked Carmelita for help. Always independent, she nevertheless offered to step in during my absence. The day before New Years' 1939, Sam drove me to the Burnett Hospital in Fresno where Aron was born. It was a long and difficult labor—a breech birth. He was over nine pounds and just missed a New Year's birth date. The twins, who were about three and a half, welcomed their little brother with great excitement. A lovely baby with curly blond hair, his sisters doted on him. Sam now had a son who could carry out his dream by taking over the ranch.

I needed help with a new baby in the house, so I engaged Jenny Allen, a tiny young woman freshly arrived from Oklahoma. Expecting a child, she had been abandoned by her husband while traveling West. As I observed the poverty of the Dust Bowl victims and the inequities of our system, my sense of social injustice grew. My early years had not been too different from theirs. The townspeople's prejudice against the newcomers was marked—I overheard Jenny 's family referred to by their landlord as "a passel of squirrels" because of their small stature.

I was sometimes able to help our ranch workers who needed medical attention. Occasionally I would drive ill or injured people to the Merced County Hospital, some fifty miles away. At that time, the roads approaching the ranch were not yet paved, and there was no telephone. Our home in Los Baños often served as a communications center. At times I would deliver urgent messages from the hospital concerning critically ill workers or family members. On one occasion, following arrangements made to repair a child's cleft palate, I arrived early, ready to transport the youngster to the hospital. The mother, Mrs. Segura, met me at the door. Obviously nervous, she held her little girl safely behind her. As an illiterate laborer's wife, knowing little about her adopted country, she was afraid of modern hospitals and feared Isabelle would never return alive!

During the 1930s, I learned a great deal about the farmworkers' struggles from Professor Paul Taylor, who, with his wife, famed photographer Dorothea "Dorie" Lange, was preparing reports for the Farm Security Administration on the deplorable living conditions of migratory laborers in the Valley and throughout California. She had formerly been married to Maynard Dixon, the renowned western landscape painter, and had given up her San Francisco portrait studio in order to photograph the bread lines, common during the Depression. A childhood polio victim, Dorie walked with a noticeable limp and appeared in voluminous, Mexican-style skirts or pants and her ever-present Mexican silver jewelry as she trudged through the fields, taking photographs of the workers. No women professionals were hired for the project, so Dorie began as Paul's typist, but her real purpose, was to create a visual record of the dust bowl families. Her photographs have been acclaimed worldwide. She is considered one of the great women of the century.

The Taylors frequently came to our ranch on weekends. We still cherish Dorie's portrait of Sam, taken in the field, which I used as the cover photograph for my biography of him. Clark Kerr, who served later as Chancellor of UCB from 1958 to 1967, occasionally accompanied the Taylors on their visits. Dorie introduced me to the well-known Imogen Cunningham, who photographed my children in her San Francisco studio.

Concerned over the tents, shacks, and vehicles in which many migrants had been making their home, Paul Taylor persuaded the government to establish a model rural housing camp for these workers—the first in California—in the nearby town of Firebaugh. He heartily approved of Sam's plans to build forty modern, air-conditioned houses for the year-round ranch workers. There was even a swimming pool as well as indoor plumbing, electricity, and refrigeration in each unit.

Others were opposed to Sam's expenditures, predicting, "Those people will never take care of the houses." They were proven wrong. Sam was proud to contribute to a higher standard of living, and maintained a paternalistic attitude toward his employees. He would simply walk into their homes and peer into the refrigerator, curious if the women were preparing nourishing food for their families. Also, when presented with a hard luck story, he never turned down a request for an advance or a "loan." His impulses were generous. He felt that his expenditures had been worthwhile because he had reliable workers, good people. When Sam constructed his model group of homes, he also built a dormitory for single men, a grocery, and a recreation hall, where the local Catholic priest would often conduct Sunday mass.

Ma and Pa looked forward to my bringing the children to Los Angeles for visits. Weighed down with sand pails and Hannah's corned beef and turkey sandwiches on homemade bread, we would head for Santa Monica Beach. We spent wonderful days watching the children play in the sand while Ma swam. As a young girl she had accompanied her family to the lovely beach near Riga, Latvia, and was an avid swimmer. Having taken few vacations in his life, Pa never wearied of building sand castles with the children or answering their endless questions.

While in Los Angeles, we also visited my old friends from UC, the Feider family, who owned a pharmacy in the Boyle Heights section, then a Jewish-Russian neighborhood. Triplets Mary, Sophie, and Flora were by this time professionals; two of them pharmacists, the third a teacher. Multiple births were such a rarity that these girls had been treated as near-invalids by their mother, Bella. I had always been fascinated by twins, especially now that I had my own, and loved to compare notes with Bella. My daughters were using a secret "twins" language with one another. Had her triplets done the same?

In the late 30s, my father was among the first to receive the long-awaited Social Security retirement benefit, $24 a month! Still active, restless, and eager to maintain his financial responsibilities, he then hired on as watchman at the Tyre Brothers San Pedro plant, and also worked odd jobs.

When the twins were still toddlers and Aron an infant, we moved the short distance from 6th to 338 "K" Street in Los Baños—to a grand old house with a large yard. I decided to organize a play group as a kind of experiment, both social and educational, in which I might test the many theories from my psychology courses at Cal. I wanted to get to know other young mothers. Lacking experience, and with few models, I turned to *Parents* magazine and books on child rearing. Spock was yet to publish his seminal baby book, and Sam was yet to recognize his own role!

Enthusiastically, I bought several types of playground equipment: slides, swings, and a jungle gym. I was able to draw children and mothers from all around town, including another set of twin girls, and eagerly observed the interactions between children from different backgrounds. At that time, few women worked outside the home. One, Pearl Johnson, was married to a local highway patrol officer, and we would later be co-leaders of a Brownie troop. Another was Mary, the town's first female mail carrier, a woman of Armenian descent. The play group lasted for several years—long enough for swings and slides to be replaced by wagons and bicycles. In those days, children could play safely throughout the neighborhood without close supervision. Sam filmed the youngsters with our new movie camera, and later they were delighted to see themselves on screen.

The girls entered the first grade at the Los Baños public school, where I made a point of having them placed in separate classrooms to avoid possible competition. I tried to organize a PTA in the school but the idea was resisted by the principal, who feared that his authority might be threatened. I had also been a write-in candidate for the local school board. However, I did not campaign and did not win. As the children grew, I became more involved in the broader community and joined the County Recreation Commission, attending monthly meetings in Merced.

Raising the children occupied almost all of my time, particularly since Sonya suffered from every possible childhood illness, as well as many complications. How could we have known that Sam's smoking might have affected her health? Tanya, who was more robust, might have felt her sister to be the favored one because of my almost constant concern for her welfare.

One winter, Sonya developed a severe ear infection that did not respond to sulfa drugs (penicillin was not yet available). Lacking confidence in local health care, we decided to take the precarious drive to Los Angeles over the Ridge Route in the Tehachapis, which was often snowed in. After our arrival, a renowned specialist, Dr. Goldstein, performed an emergency mastoidectomy.

Even more frightening was Sonya's month-long hospitalization, at the age of six, with an undiagnosed illness. Dissatisfied with the local doctor, and with her condition worsening, we called a surgeon in Fresno. Although initially unwilling to make the night drive to Los Baños, he was finally persuaded when Sam appeared at his door. At the hospital, he immediately operated to remove her ruptured appendix. Even during the long hospitalization the local physician had failed to diagnose her unusual case! Sonya's difficulties did not end there. Later, she came down with scarlet fever, which placed the entire household under quarantine.

Nor were things going well between Sam and me. Farming had become his all-absorbing interest, and his impatience with the children cast further doubt on the future of our marriage. Communication between us was almost impossible. As the children grew, Sam loved to show them off to his friends, occasionally taking the girls on short trips. Once they were capable of the give and take of conversation, Sam showed more interest, but he soon favored Aron. One cold January night he ran out of gas—a relatively common experience for him. He and our two-year old son were stranded. When they finally arrived home, the poor child was wet and cold, almost frozen. I grew ever-more concerned about the children's welfare, given Sam's absent-mindedness and apparent carelessness in exposing them to danger.

The stresses continued. On one occasion I had planned to attend Tanya's second grade special Mothers' Day program, a very important event. But at the last moment Sam insisted on my driving the seventy miles to Fresno to pick up chemicals needed to halt a grasshopper invasion that was threatening the cotton crop. Although I broke the speed limit along the way, I was late and found Tanya in tears, a miserable moment for us both.

By then, Sam was frequenting the bar in nearby Firebaugh with his farmer friends, endlessly discussing the weather, struggles in the field, the fluctuating commodities market, and labor difficulties. In the evening, I would sometimes hold dinner for hours, never knowing whether he would come home alone or accompanied by unexpected dinner guests.

Drinking was hardly a Jewish custom at that time, and Sam did not indulge at all when I first knew him. But feeling the need to fit in with other ranchers, and to relieve the substantial tensions of farm life, he continued his socializing at the bar, which was the center of this universe, and though he did not participate in his friends' jocular "Roosevelt bashing," he enjoyed himself. Given his exuberant personality, he scarcely required this additional stimulant, nor did he handle alcohol well.

Meanwhile, I was involved in local activities, including the election attempt of my friend and former professor, Dr. Hubert Phillips, who ran for Congress in our district in 1944. I volunteered to organize our area for his campaign. In spite of my efforts, he lost. Political work was important to me.

During the war years, we occasionally traveled back and forth from Los Banos to Berkeley, often picking up hitchhikers, young men in uniform. Speaking with them we would increasingly hear, "The next war's going to be with Russia." Such talk against our former ally was shocking to us, in view of the tremendous suffering the Russian people had experienced and the important role they played in stopping the German army. But anti-Red sentiments were on the rise.

I also assisted the Rationing Board. Shortages in consumer goods had brought about domestic rationing of gasoline, meat, butter, and sugar, although farmers were exempt from the most stringent restrictions on fuel supplies. Meat rationing in the city was a true hardship. Fortunately, we could store beef and lamb in our rented locker in the town's commercial freezer, which was maintained primarily for the convenience of deer and duck hunters. Occasionally Sam would bring meat to share with our Berkeley friends.

As the children grew, my educational interests turned to after-school activities. I led the Brownies, Cub Scouts, and Campfire Girls. Despite my rural background, I still had to memorize the names of local trees, and I learned to tie sixty-seven kinds of knots. I couldn't sing—but I still led the groups anyway.

During World War II, I was a volunteer plane spotter with Ellen Jensen as my partner. It was amazing to watch this huge woman work her way up the rickety, wooden steps to the steep lookout tower. Sonya, a curious little girl, was amazed by her girth, and would walk around Ellen, wide-eyed. She had never seen anyone quite that large.

Eagle Field, the military base in Ora Loma, was near the ranch. Sam struck up a friendship with flight instructor Hal Foote and his wife Dorothy Jordan, an artist. For my birthday one year, Dorothy did a painting of the church at Volta—a town had disappeared with the coming of Interstate 5. Her second gift was a painting of the Southern Pacific Railway Station in Los Baños, later the site of the Sam Hamburg Farms packing shed. We were friendly with several Air Corps student pilots, and were saddened to hear of the death of one of them on a training flight in Colorado. This was the first war-related death in our circle.

Chapter 17

Berkeley, the Bomb, and the UN

"On July 16, 1945, a moral dimension descended, like fallout, on to science itself. Science was no longer neutral. Science, and scientists, now had the power to blow up the world."

—Cynthia Bass, novelist

Although my paramount concern has been my immediate family, I cannot remember a time when I was not avidly pursuing my interest in the outside world. As the years on the farm wore on, I grew restless and dissatisfied and began thinking about moving back to Berkeley. From the beginning, I had been drawn to the university. That appeal still held, even after completing graduate work. Because of the Valley heat, the children and I had spent several summers in Berkeley, and I had close friends there. Sam grudgingly went along with the move to the city because of the promise of better schools. The idea of divorce had not yet been raised.

In June 1944, we bought a modern style house on the upper part of Spruce Street in North Berkeley. We moved in on June 6, the day of the Normandy Beach landing. Aron started kindergarten and the girls enrolled in the 4th grade at Cragmont School. I immediately became active in the Berkeley-Albany PTA and was delighted that my children would be part of a progressive school system. Even so, I could not shield Aron from occasional incidents of anti-Semitism.

Judaism entered my children's lives, I sent them to Sunday School at Oakland's Reform Temple Sinai. Sam, a secularist, had little interest or time for religion. My own religious training left much to be desired. The children wanted to drop out of Sunday School after the first year or two and I, too busy to insist because of my growing preoccupation with civic affairs, gave in to their wishes.

During the war, the Bay Area had attracted many African Americans from the South. The labor market was booming, with a tremendous drive to produce ships, planes, and other war-related materiel. For the first time industrial jobs opened up to minorities as well as women.

Unfortunately, the influx of workers from the South triggered prejudice, even among local African Americans. The numbers of Bay Area residents who had "made it" into the middle class were reluctant to accept the many poorly-schooled newcomers. Since all children shared classes, it was necessary for parents to get together, as well. The PTA took up the integration issue. In 1943, following a campaign by African American parents, we made history by hiring Ruth Acty, our first black teacher. As an active PTA member, I initiated correspondence with a number of experts in the field, including Dr. Stewart Cole, Director of the New York Bureau for Intercultural Education. With his recommendations, I was able to propose speakers to address groups of parents and teachers. Berkeley became the first racially-mixed American city to completely integrate its schools. Voluntary busing was instituted between the years 1945 and 1968, when the board of education finally voted for total school integration.

In the family, we were fortunate to employ Fannie Thorne, a large, devout, cheerful, and outgoing Louisiana native who had settled in Richmond, when she worked at the Mare Island shipyard during the war. Lacking health safeguards, she had suffered severe hearing loss from the terrific noise of the workplace. Grateful for employment, her faith led her to accept this work-related handicap without complaint. Deeply religious, she was disconsolate when two of her children became involved with the law. One was incarcerated and the other fell victim to the crack epidemic. An excellent worker, she played an important role in my children's development. Our friendship continued until her death in 1992.

During the 1944 election campaign, I was active in the Democratic Club movement, speaking to various adult and student groups and distributing election materials in a number of North Berkeley precincts. Aron, who was about five, happily ran ahead of me handing out voting guidelines. I also joined the local League of Women Voters, an excellent nonpartisan national organization devoted to educating the public on vital issues. Their in-depth study groups on domestic and international topics interested me greatly. At election time I was asked to represent the League as a speaker, with arguments, pro and con, on state and local ballot issues. In later years, rather than confining myself solely to the League's information, I analyze a wide variety of sources and make my own recommendations, which continue to be widely distributed.

Just as I was starting to feel settled in Berkeley, I received news of my father's death. He had labored at arduous and environmentally hazardous occupations for most of his life, and suffered from heart disease. In his opinion, he had lived long enough. Seventy, in those days, was considered a ripe old age. He would often say, while preparing his morning breakfast, "Well, what is there to look forward to? Just so many more dishes of oatmeal…" He had not seen much joy in his life, although he took great pleasure in his grandchildren.

When I was younger, I had not fully appreciated my father, but as time went on I began to sort matters out. Mother was really the moving force in our family, but I realize that Father, in his own quiet, hardworking way, had done all he could and had encouraged us children. It was sad that he, always an avid follower of public affairs, died in April 1945, a few weeks before the demise of his hero, FDR, just before the end of the war. Neither lived to witness the peace.

Many of us were unaware of the implications of some events surrounding the war. August 6, 1945, the day the atomic bomb was dropped on Hiroshima, I had driven the children to Fresno and stopped to visit Rae Wahrhaftig. Upon seeing the bomb headlines in the press, Rae exclaimed, "Oh, this is a terrible, terrible thing." At that time, I failed to recognize the import of this planned catastrophe. In retrospect, this says a great deal about the naiveté of the American public, who were unaware of this tragic attack's awful significance to the Japanese city of Hiroshima. The government convinced us that the bomb would end the war and save our men, an argument still used today to justify high defense budgets. Rae, however, understood its implications. Extremely well-informed, she quickly grasped the true horror of what had happened.

That same year I went with my friend Grace MacDonald to witness the founding of the United Nations at the Civic Center in San Francisco. Although Grace was from New York and extremely sophisticated, she considered this the biggest event in her life. Next to her I felt immature, just "in from the farm." Tall and elegant, she was absolutely aglow with the prospect of a United Nations.

October 1945 was a time of great elation. The UN Charter promised to "save succeeding generations from the scourge of war"—an enormously persuasive sentiment. But a number of liberals who had played important roles throughout the period of cooperation with the USSR during the war were now under surveillance. Alger Hiss, State Department functionary and a major architect of the UN, was later accused of Communist affiliations, spent time in prison, and died without having his name cleared.

Grace was a woman of political experience and means. She and her husband "Mac" had come to California from New York City in the 30s and purchased an apple orchard in Aptos, Santa Cruz County. Their activities were scarcely confined to the orchard, however. Mac had gone to the Soviet Union shortly after the 1917 revolution to help establish their railway system. Cuthbert Olson, one of California's few progressive governors, appointed Grace MacDonald, this brilliant and effective woman, to the California Agricultural Commission.

On her visits to Los Baños, she tried to involve Sam in her efforts to improve the conditions of small farmers, with no luck. She published the _Farm Reporter,_ a monthly bulletin concerning small farm operations. We became good friends, and I drove frequently to her imposing, colonial style home in Santa Clara to obtain her wise counsel. She, in turn, relied on her friends to spread the gospel of cooperation between farmers and labor, an idea before its time.

Another visitor to the ranch in those days was Dave Jenkins, a well known San Francisco progressive, ILWU activist, and associate of founder Harry Bridges. At this time he was fundraising for the San Francisco Labor School, headed by former Stanford professor Holland Roberts. During its heyday in the late 40s and early 50s, the school signed up veterans who were pursuing their education under the G.I. Bill. On one of my visits to The City, I met Peggy Sarasohn, the school secretary, and we immediately hit it off.

In 1946, shortly after the Labor School opened a branch in Oakland, I was asked to host a benefit in Berkeley. Since the guest of honor was the aristocratic, British-born Jessica (Decca) Mitford, recently arrived in the Bay Area, Sam was pleased to co-host the affair. Unfortunately, this was the last time he and I would be involved in any type of joint political activity.

After the party, Gordon Williams, the Oakland branch director, and I were summoned to appear before the state Alcohol Control Board. We had been reported for selling drinks at the party. We devised a method of collecting for the drinks in advance, and sent out a cautionary word to the Movement: "No money at the bar!" Was this an early sign of future surveillance and harassment of left-wing groups?

In 1946, while attending a movie in Los Angeles with Ben's wife Genya, Mother suffered a cerebral hemorrhage and was taken by ambulance to the hospital emergency where she died later that day. Losing her was a terrible blow to our family, falling especially hard on Rae, who was still living at home.

Although Ma was not in good health, there had been no warning signs before her death. It was a very difficult time for me. In order not to upset the children, I attempted to hide my overwhelming grief. In retrospect, I realized it was a mistake common to my family; we tend to withhold rather than express our emotions. At Mother's memorial service, Ben was overcome by the scent of the many flowers and could never again abide lilies and gardenias, as they reminded him of that mournful event. We were all distraught and deeply felt the irreparable loss.

When confronted with some difficult situation I often reflect on my mother's life, the horrendous problems which she overcame in the early and final separation from her own family, living in a strange land, and rearing her children with limited means. Extremely resourceful, she was willing to try her hand at almost anything, and throughout it all, kept nurturing us and growing beautiful flowers. I feel indebted to her and my father for whatever I have been able to accomplish—in pursuing my education, rearing my children, and whatever small contributions I may have made to society at large.

Chapter 18

Experiments in the Israeli Desert

"Show me your worst piece of land and I'll show you what it can produce."

—Sam Hamburg to Ben-Gurion, 1951

By 1946 the ranch was not doing well. Irrigation water was bringing up deposits of salts in the soil, forming a crust and rendering crop growth impossible. The land lay fallow for two years, and we were on the verge of bankruptcy. That year we sold the Berkeley house and moved back to Los Baños. But it soon became apparent that this "reunion" between Sam and me was to be short lived. Temperamental differences led to increasing friction between us.

After considerable research, trial, and error, Sam was able to return the soil to its former condition by applying quantities of gypsum to break down the salt crust. Ruin was averted, and in 1948 I was able to move the children back to Berkeley. Although Sam was opposed to a departure that was bringing us closer to a final break, he did not stand in the way. After selling the Los Baños house, he moved to a newly built dwelling on the ranch.

This marked a turning point in our family. We bought a large home on San Luis Road with a beautiful view of the Bay. Trees brought from various parts of the world had been planted by the former owner, an army officer. A fishpond in front and a small pool in back completed our little park.

The move back to Berkeley marked a decisive change for our family. Although Sam continued to visit on weekends, we had, in essence, separated. Like typical adolescents, the girls took refuge in their room when Sam and I were arguing. Sonya was absorbed in her school work, whereas Tanya missed her friends in the Valley and was often moody. I decided to take her for a consultation with my friend Dr. Leona Bayer, who was, among other things, an expert on adolescent psychology. I hoped for some insights into the problems we were experiencing and wished to improve my relationship with my daughter. After the session, Leona reassured me in her comforting yet professional manner, "You don't have to worry about Tanya. Her hostility toward you is perfectly overt...Be patient."

As always, I tried to involve myself in the children's school activities. I joined Garfield Junior High PTA—now known as M.L. King, Jr. Middle School—where Aron was enrolled, and I was soon elected recording secretary.

Earlier, we had an opportunity to take a young man into our Los Baños home—Bernie, a Jewish refugee from Poland. He and his brother were the sole survivors of their family. We hoped he might fit in with us, but he was nervous, smoked nonstop, and bore the emotional and physical ravages of war and persecution. With three children in the house, and Sam restless and impatient, the relationship was extremely unsettling. I was torn between what I felt I should do for Bernie and what was possible under the circumstances, since, when we moved to Berkeley, he was unable to adapt to high school. Had Bernie appeared at a different time, there might have been a chance for success. Sam sent Bernie and his brother to Israel, where he felt they would adapt more readily. They were still unhappy and soon returned to the US.

Sonya and Tanya were not thrilled with the move to Berkeley. At thirteen, in junior high, they resented leaving their Los Banos friends. Tanya was rebellious and problems between us continued for several years. Aron, who was younger, had not yet established deep relationships and weathered the changes well. He was interested in science and was thrilled when a family friend, a graduate student working at the cyclotron at UC, took him to see the particle-accelerator used in the development of the bomb. If I had only known that this atom-smashing machine, used to breed fissionable materials, would end in the awful destructiveness of the atomic bomb, I would not have been pleased.

Whenever there were differences in the family, or when Sam came to Berkeley in a dark mood, the girls would retreat to their lovely room with a sweeping, panoramic bay view. I still remember them, heads together, whispering. Were they still communicating in their secret "twin" language? Was the turbulence around them responsible for their remarkable closeness, which characterizes their relationship to this day?

Sam was still supporting us. There was no way I could have managed financially by myself. It was not easy to explain the reasons for my wanting a separate life. I did my best to make the frequent trips back and forth to the ranch happy ones for the family, attempting to provide the best of both worlds for them. I had confidence in the children's ability to transcend their parents' difficulties and still feel secure.

Sam's comfortable new house on the ranch had a swimming pool surrounded by an orchard, where the children spent their summers and other vacations. He felt that they should learn to work with, and get to know, the people on the ranch. I applauded Sam's ideas in this; the results were good. Since the twins lived part-time in a small farming town, they each qualified for a rural drivers' license at fourteen. At sixteen Sam bought them a red Ford convertible with a black top, and they and Aron were able to travel to and from the Valley on their own.

Sam continued to expand his operations. In the 1950s he finally had a reliable source of water from the Central Valley Project (CVP), the largest and most expensive civil engineering project in the nation, and an important landmark in California history. The Friant Canal, which stretched from Mendota to Bakersfield, came through our ranch. Under California law, as owners of the land prior to the dam, we had special "riparian rights" to the water.

In addition to grain and cotton, Sam began to experiment with cantaloupes and vegetables, alfalfa seed for export, sugar beets, and, later, canning tomatoes. I remember a steady flow of trucks and trailers loaded down with fresh tomatoes, on their way to the cannery in Tracy. Sam was indefatigable. In 1951, at great expense, he built a cotton gin. Equipped with its drying component, the gin made it possible to pick the bolls while they were still damp, thus extending the growing season. He also constructed an alfalfa seed-cleaning mill, a grain elevator, and a cantaloupe-packing shed in Los Baños, right next to the railroad tracks.

Our first-class melons were shipped in refrigerated cars across the country to eastern cities. Generally the melons sold at local markets are of lesser quality. During the summer Aron was occupied on the ranch while his sisters labored in the packing shed, grading and labeling cantaloupes as they came down the assembly line. They also worked in the office.

The twins formed friendships with some of the so-called "fruit tramps," the elite of itinerant laborers, whose worldly wisdom made quite an impression on them. Getting to know these people of different backgrounds was an important part of their education. Tanya claims that these friendships made her the person she is today. These workers earned high wages because of their expertise in handling melons and other perishable produce. Although not well educated, most of these savvy, native-born workers could afford to live in motels during their seasonal stints rather than in labor camps or in trucks, as was the practice of other seasonal laborers.

Throughout this period Sam yearned to return to the land of his youth. The state of Israel had been established in 1948, and in 1951 he was able to take his first trip there. This would be the culmination of his dream: to introduce modern farming technology to this ancient land where he had received his early education. His Israeli cousins had been active in the formation of the new state and they introduced him to Prime Minister David Ben-Gurion, and Minister of Agriculture, Chaim Gvati. Sam was able to convince them that, contrary to the general consensus, the land could adapt to cotton culture. Over the next twenty years he demonstrated his methods for growing cotton and other crops on a section of land in the Beit Sean Valley in Galilee, later called Hawwat Shemu'el, or "Sam's Ranch."

Sam became known as the "Father of Israeli Cotton." His cotton provided fiber for a successful Israeli textile and fashion industry. Later, he would write to his children, "For the first time in my life I felt that I had not lived in vain. I realized there was a meaning and purpose in all the long years of struggle." He never took any compensation for his work, sparing no expense in his efforts. He even brought over his own engineers and mechanics to build the first Israeli cotton gin. Determined to eliminate endemic pests, Sam packed various pesticides in his luggage, an act that would be strictly forbidden today.

Sam made more than fifty self-financed trips to Israel during the next two decades, twice traveling after having been stricken with a paralyzing illness. He was often accompanied by Aron, for whom each trip to Israel proved exciting. War hero General Moshe Dayan invited Aron to fly over the country, to better understand Israel's precarious situation, surrounded on all sides by unfriendly Arab nations. Aron's youth and personality attracted many, and each trip offered a new opportunity for romance. Once, when the girls traveled with Sam, Ben-Gurion turned to Sonya and queried, "Since your father has been so much a part of our country, why don't you children make your home here?"

Chapter 19

More Deaths in the Family

"And now I mourn her. I mourn that cornerstone. I mourn her caring. I mourn the one who always hoped for me...My life now is only mine..."

—Toby Talbot , in *Mother to Daughter, Daughter to Mother* ,
Tillie Olsen, The Feminist Press, 1984

Rae was forced to live on her own after our mother's death. Brother Ben would take her out to dinner regularly, and was ever available to listen to her lengthy list of complaints about landlords, fellow tenants, and neighbors. Rae had made an unfortunate marriage in 1927 and ended up in the L.A. County Hospital after suffering a miscarriage. She was divorced shortly afterward. From then on, she lived at home, working occasionally, still dependent on the family.

After meeting Nathaniel Klein, an eccentric older man in the building and real estate business, Rae applied for her real estate license, passing the exam easily. She practiced in partnership with him for fifteen years, though it was never a profitable enterprise. After his death, Rae became more and more disorganized and paranoid, which posed a problem for all of us.

The height of the Depression found Ben delivering plate glass for Tyre Brothers. It was strenuous work. One day he joined a strikers' picket line at the plant, which his relatives considered an act of disloyalty. Made uncomfortable by their criticism, Ben left shortly afterward and found a job with Thrifty Drug Company, delivering frozen food products. His constant exposure to the intense cold, going in and out of huge freezers, may have contributed to later health problems.

Ben's first marriage in 1937 had not worked out. Not long after the birth of their daughter, he and his wife divorced. He would visit us in the Bay Area frequently, enabling him to keep in touch with his child, who was living in San Francisco with her mother, who was now remarried.

In 1945, Ben married the beautiful Swiss-born Genya Wirzer, whom he had met through Rae. It was a happy marriage. He started his own business, the Durable Leather Products Company, which supplied large firms like Bell Telephone with belts and tool bags, and also produced mail pouches for the US Post Office. Once successful, Ben was forced to relocate the business from its original site near Angel's Flight, a block from Broadway, to make way for the Los Angeles Freeway. He was then able to set up his factory in a light manufacturing district. He employed mostly Japanese women from Hawaii. Gloria, his forelady, was unusually diligent. Nothing escaped her sharp eye. More demanding than Ben himself, she saw to it that the quality of the finished products was as close to perfection as possible.

Ben's was a rowdy family of three boys, Steve, Eric, and Gary. Living near a pony concession in the Fairfax district—"Ponyland"—all three found recreation and part-time work there. The ponies became an important part of their lives until the concession was zoned out of the city. The older boys graduated to motorcycles, suffering several accidents. During the summers Genya often took the boys to Switzerland to visit her family.

Ben, having inherited some of the stoicism of our immigrant parents, enjoyed peace and quiet, and would frequently "escape" to Berkeley to visit. On these trips, he would buy leather for his business at the Manasse Block Tannery at Gilman and Fourth. Today this area is a collection of artists' lofts and an example of adaptive re-use of the site. Although Ben suffered from a serious and painful dental problem—an incompetent dentist broke off a needle in his jaw—he seldom complained. Unfortunately, he received no compensation for the accident that caused him pain for the rest of his life, and the chronic infection also may have contributed to his early death.

Ben died suddenly of a heart attack at the age of fifty-one, leaving his wife and three young children, Steve (15), Eric (13), and Gary (9). His death occurred not long after Steve's Bar Mitzvah. The boys felt bereft. I arrived in Los Angeles to find Genya in shock. Charlie, Rae, and I were not in much better shape. I wonder if my brother's life might have been saved if there had been a 911 number to call. Following Ben's funeral, as we were leaving the family in mourning, Rae darkly predicted: "I'll be the next to go."

After Ben's death, Charlie hired a manager for his farming operation and moved with his family to Los Angeles. Genya and her boys appreciated his interest—the boys remained devoted to their "cowboy" uncle. Realizing that Genya would have difficulty running the business, Charlie offered to help. With Gloria, keeping matters organized on the factory floor, they were able to expand. Four years later he assisted Genya in arranging the factory's sale to Bell Telephone Company for a good price, securing the financial future of her family. Charlie, Gertie, and their children were then free to return to their home in the Valley.

Phil, their son, became an attorney, although farming was his first love. Dorothy, their daughter, is now a financial secretary and the mother of Karl and Sara. Ben's son Steve has a doctorate in education and is a college counselor. Gary is a commercial airline pilot. Eric, the middle son, handsome and somewhat of a non-conformist, was killed while in his twenties by a hit-and-run driver.

While Charlie was in the L.A. area, he had taken over responsibility for Rae. After his departure, she was on her own for the first time. I received many calls, in which she would invariably complain about her far-ranging problems. Steve, then a graduate student, often stepped in to help. In 1975, I became Rae's conservator, making frequent trips south to extricate her from various crises, picking up the pieces after each eviction. The family was frustrated by her refusal to accept any medical or psychiatric treatment. It was my chore to get her enrolled in Medicare. Upon her final eviction, Rae was homeless. Riding a bus, Eric caught sight of his aunt forlornly seated on a bench, clutching her possessions in plastic bags. After being rescued by her nephew, it was then up to me to find a supervised board and care facility for her. About four years later, Rae suffered a stroke which left her speechless and disoriented. She died not long afterwards, thus ending an unfulfilled and troubled life. She became the fourth member of the family to be interred in the Hollywood Jewish cemetery. Another sad event in my family's saga.

III. From Personal to Political

*"[A. Hamburg] has broad acquaintance among highly placed important people
...it is felt [that] possible embarrassment outweighs potential value of re-interview."*

—Confidential FBI report, 1957

"Hamburg does some writing, not for pay but for 'civic betterment.'"

—Confidential FBI report, 1957

Chapter 20

Shadowed by the FBI

"Pay no attention. Those hearings are a dime a dozen."

—A reassuring comment by a next-door neighbor
during my 1951 appearance before the Burns Committee

I became active in the Henry Wallace Campaign for President on the Independent Progressive Party (IPP) ticket. When asked by "Students for Henry Wallace for President" to host a fundraiser, I agreed. On the day of the event more than one hundred supporters arrived, filling the house. Live music at both the front and rear made it nearly impossible to hear the speakers. It was a party to remember, and a less than auspicious introduction to the neighborhood! I worried that our noisy party might set us at odds with the parents of the children's classmates, several of whom lived nearby. However, we heard no complaints at the time.

In Oakland the IPP office was shared by Jessica (Mitford) Treuhaft, who was raising money for the Civil Rights Congress (CRC). This was the period of the Willie McGee case, a young African American from the South who had been charged with rape. Funds were needed for his legal defense—the still unknown Bella Abzug was his attorney. Marge Frantz and Libby Mines, sharing an office, were managing the Wallace campaign in the East Bay. Libby, newly arrived in the Bay Area, was incredibly efficient and assumed that everyone else was equally so. These three women were dedicated powerhouses who usually exercised their responsibilities with humor. I dropped in from time to time, helping on the campaigns and enjoying their repartee. We remained close friends throughout the troubling years ahead.

Ever on the alert for cases of injustice in the community, we took up the cause of

Barbara Holmes, a local woman who was in a nasty custody battle with her ex-husband. Angered by her marriage to an African American man, he had kidnapped their children. Writing about the case, I became deeply involved. At that time I was also friendly with Robert Kenny, former State Attorney General and judge, whom I consulted about the matter. He was extremely helpful. Perhaps as a result of the publicity, Barbara was reunited with her children.

Although Libby was efficient in the office, her domestic situation was somewhat different. In the absence of childcare, her two boys, Ken and Rick, were left at home while she worked. The younger boy, Rick, had an unfortunate encounter with the kitchen's electric mixer while trying his skill at creating a dessert. His frightened brother called his mother at the Oakland IPP office, but she happened to be out on an errand. Having dropped by, I got the message, and rushed out to the rescue. Failing to extricate his upper arm from the blades, I wound up taking Rick and his attachment to Alta Bates Emergency. He survived unharmed, but the mixer was not so lucky.

By the late 40s the country was in the grips of anti-communist fervor. The entertainment industry was one of the first targets of the House Un-American Activities Committee (HUAC). The Hollywood Ten—a group of actors, writers, producers, and directors—had recently been accused of indoctrinating the public with their radical ideas. Because of the HUAC investigations, many Hollywoodites lost their jobs.

In the Bay Area, I helped organize meetings in support of these talented victims. The Arts, Sciences, and Professions Council (ASP) was actively supporting the Hollywood Ten. I was elected secretary. Our art gallery on the corner of Emerson and Shattuck in downtown Berkeley featured public exhibits of community artists and served as a meeting place. Little did I suspect that my connection with this group would make me a target of the California State Un-American Activities Committee, headed by a Fresno mortician, Senator Hugh Burns.

Feelings against the Hollywood Ten ran so high, we were unable to rent a hall anywhere in Berkeley, and convened instead in Oakland, at the Fellowship of Humanity building. Among those I met at that time were Howard Fast, a well-known writer whose name was eventually dropped from the blacklist, and whose film, *Spartacus*, became a big hit. Gail Sondergaard, an award-winning actress and wife of blacklisted writer Herbert Biberman, stayed with me a number of times, and, on several occasions, I was a guest in her Hollywood Hills home.

That same year, 1949, the California Legislature passed the Levering Act, requiring all state employees, including university professors, to sign a loyalty oath. Some obliged, but many who objected to this encroachment on their civil liberties dropped out or went elsewhere to teach. Thus, many outstanding UC professors were welcomed by prestigious eastern institutions. When Philosophy Professor Joseph Tussman applied to Sarah Lawrence College, he informed them of having refused to sign the Loyalty Oath. To his relief, they replied, "We wouldn't hire you if you *had* signed." There was considerable opposition to the oath in our community. We held the first meeting of the Citizens Committee Against the Loyalty Oath in my home, where Alexander Meiklejohn, the great civil libertarian from the east, was present. Berkeley's Meiklejohn Civil Liberties Institute, founded in 1965 by Ann Fagan Ginger, was named for this outstanding leader.

We were able to mobilize local people against the Loyalty Oath and give as much support as possible to the beleaguered faculty. The struggle went on for several years. My Berkeley Hills address provided the setting for many gatherings during this period—occasionally I now encounter a professor, near-retirement, who reminds me that he had attended meetings at my house decades ago. As one professor noted, "If it was a peoples' cause, your home was available."

These meetings were also cited in a later FBI report about me: "In the 1940s she had been among sponsors of receptions held in honor of Dr. W.E.B. DuBois, Paul Robeson and other well-known communists." What a privilege it was to have been involved with the great men of this century!

Black sociologist W.E.B. DuBois wrote the first definitive history of his people, *The Soul of Black Folk*. Only his strong position at the University of Pennsylvania made it possible for him to continue his important work during this turbulent time. Robeson—tall, commanding, and with an incomparable voice—was a world-renowned singer who was stripped of his passport due to his left-wing affiliations—an infringement on his civil liberties that had devastating effects on his career. At the height of his fame he was unable to perform either here or abroad—a tragic loss for all. In our liberal city of Berkeley, the Board of Education refused to allow him to sing in the newly-completed Community Auditorium. Angered, we demanded a public hearing. Among the speakers in the crowd were several Quakers. Even Republicans were moved to object to this flagrant denial of our right to hear this great artist. Because of our heated protest, his concert went on as planned, with no trouble. Our success in winning the case inspired my article "Berkeley's Example," in the June 7, 1952 *The Nation*.

In 1952, my friends and I planned meetings of the Rosenberg Committee, hoping to save the lives of the principals and their associate, Morton Sobel, who were accused of selling atomic secrets to the Russians—a charge never proven by testimony available at the time. The Rosenbergs were the only individuals ever executed for espionage in peace-time in this country. Because of the war hysteria, efforts to win their lives were to no avail; the couple was executed in June 1953 and Sobel served a long prison term, including years on Alcatraz. In truth, the "secret" of the atomic bomb had already been published in *The Progressive* magazine.

I joined the Women's International League for Peace and Freedom (WILPF) in 1950, attracted by its anti-war activism. Branches of the League existed in Berkeley and San Francisco. WILPF also opposed the illegal wartime internment of Japanese-Americans. My strong feelings about such injustices caused me to intensify my efforts in support of the Hollywood Ten, marking the beginning of my increased dedication to the peace and justice movement. During WILPF's public meetings we planned strategies, mapping out new methods of defiance by which we could support victims of McCarthyism. Peace, I had found, was not enough. We need justice and freedom as well. Although I was aware of the possible dangers of my association with various groups, such as the Rosenberg Committee, I felt it was my responsibility to lend support wherever peoples' rights to free expression were being challenged.

On September 11, 1951, just as school was opening, I received a subpoena to appear before the State Un-American Activities Committee (Burns Committee). Why was I singled out? Why not the ASP president? Several reasons are clear: I was subpoenaed as a supporter of so-called "subversive" causes, because I was hosting meetings in my home. The committee hoped that the public pillorying of a middle-class woman such as myself would frighten and discourage others. Another possibility was that earlier, I had been a witness in Helen Witte's citizenship hearing. Helen, a divorcee, was the daughter of a titled Russian family. What matter that her husband, Gregory Silvermaster, had served as FDR's chief economist? Both were left-wing and since I had been Helen's witness, I was tarred with the same brush!

It was almost impossible to obtain legal representation. Some lawyers, fearful of being subpoenaed themselves, skipped town to avoid the hearing. Anxiously I consulted Ernest Bessig, Executive Director of the Northern California ACLU. I had scarcely finished explaining my case when he asked, "How do we know that some of the organizations you support are *not* communist?" He turned me down flat. The ACLU, now a defender of people of all opinions, was at that time intimidated by the "Red Scare." Later, in 1996, when the ACLU honored Bessig on his 90th birthday, I sent a letter—which appeared in the

ACLU News—recalling the time that he had refused my request for support. When questioned, he claimed to have forgotten about this event. In 1951, I was finally represented by a local attorney, a member of a progressive San Francisco legal practice.

My subpoena was for the first appearance of the Burns Committee in San Francisco. On the morning of the hearing, I was the first to be called and questioned under oath about meetings held for Paul Robeson and members of the Hollywood Ten. Friends who appeared at the same time did not approve of my answering *any* questions, but they had nothing to fear as I was not very communicative.

Following the advice of my attorney, I did not plead the Fifth Amendment, a move for which I later received some criticism. Although a "reluctant" witness, I was the only one allowed to read my complete statement in which I protested and condemned the procedures and purposes of the hearing, calling it "a flagrant violation of the democratic principles which are the very foundation of our great American heritage." To counter their ideas of "subversive," I extended an invitation to the committee to visit our art gallery in Berkeley.

My widely-published statement was picked up by a wire service and even appeared in a New York paper. Sam and his New York relatives were already apprehensive because of the Rosenberg trial. As immigrants, he and his uncle feared repercussions toward Jews. Several recent Holocaust survivors, friends of ours, spoke at that time of the necessity of keeping their passports current. The specter of an angry, anti-Semitic reaction haunted them all.

My co-witnesses in the San Francisco Supervisors' chambers were mostly women, also involved in peace actions, including Edith Jenkins, wife of Dave Jenkins of the California Labor School. Jessica Mitford, humorous and defiant, was the celebrity of the group. Later she would achieve fame with her book, *The American Way of Death*. Many of the witnesses subsequently lost their jobs and there were even some suicides.

Frightened by my appearance before the Burns Committee, Sam considered this the final blow. He accused me of wanting the publicity. "Some of the other people who were in the ASP weren't called, why were you?" He failed to understand that political involvement, no matter how legitimate, could make one a target. I was terrified by his threat to take the children. Fortunately, they supported my right to do what I felt was my duty, although they were not comfortable with the notoriety. Sonya, more or less the spokesperson for the others, maintained, "We may not agree with all of Mother's ideas, but she has the right to express them!"

The twins were at Berkeley High School and Aron in junior high. After suffering through heated political discussions between Sam and me, perhaps they understood our conflicting points of view. In the ongoing strife between us, political issues were the fuel. Although concerned about the effects on the children, there was little I could do. Now I recognize how unpleasant it must have been for them.

Following my Burns Committee appearance, I was asked to resign as secretary of the Garfield PTA. Since I had not been charged with any wrongdoing, much less convicted, I refused. In my letter to the school PTA president, I took issue with the Burns Committee's practice of making unfounded charges against individuals. My letter concluded: "In view of the fact that I have engaged only in constructive activities within my rights as an American citizen, and have worked for many years to build a broader and more effective PTA program, and since tendering my resignation would be construed as an admission of guilt, I have decided against doing so." Not satisfied, a frightened PTA official mounted an unsuccessful campaign for a loyalty oath at the next California state PTA conference. She lost and the PTA survived.

Before my appearance at the committee hearings, I was a middle-class liberal, but I came away from that experience with a fresh—one might even say radical—determination to alert the public to this threat to our fundamental freedoms. During this time, individuals were intimidated and families split. The purpose of the hearings was to immobilize those with idealistic, liberal, or radical thinking, who were working for the public good.

The American Friends Service Committee (AFSC), of which I was a supporter, had begun to deal with the plight of the blacklisted. I was an original member of the Northern California Friends Committee on Legislation (FCL) founded by the AFSC in 1952. Society was permeated with suspicion, even in my own neighborhood. Always friendly with my neighbors, I could hardly believe that one, a prominent Quaker, had been reporting the license plate numbers of visitors to my house, to the FBI.

Eventually, all these committees were discredited. In 1954, after the Senate's censure of McCarthy and Edward R. Murrow's *CBS Reports'* scathing documentary, the committees finally folded. Although the cold war and the effects of redbaiting continued for some time, most of us were able to get on with our lives.

Chapter 21

Gold Mines in Africa

"We must remember that nothing can be woven out of threads that all run the same way. An unchallenged belief or idea is on the way to death and meaninglessness."

—Emily Greene Balch, longtime Secretary to Jane Addams, winner of the 1946 Nobel Peace Prize

Having grown up without grandparents or relatives, with the exception of Uncle Abram, I was eager to explore my roots. Now was the time. I wanted to meet Mother's relatives, some of whom had emigrated from Lithuania to South Africa about the time my parents came to America. I had often wondered how difficult it must have been for my mother to leave her family. My Aunt Hode had lost a son in Russia, and had endured some of the indignities visited on Jews in that country. She was later reunited with her brother in South Africa. Sadly, my mother had not lived to be part of such a reunion.

I flew to Johannesburg in 1952 and was greeted by a large welcoming party. Finally I was able to meet Aunt Hode and Uncle BenZion Shmuelson, my mother's younger brother! My uncle had started a dairy business. He would drive out to the adjoining black township to deliver milk as well as many household items not available in the township. Through this work, he came to know of the hardships suffered under apartheid. Although continents apart, BenZion was engaged in the same enterprise as my father during our early homestead years in the Dakotas; peddling was a common practice among Jews of the Diaspora, wherever they settled. Despite his interest in the blacks, he, like almost every other white South African, could not envision a time when apartheid would end.

Although South African apartheid seemed inevitable to BenZion, he had much higher expectations for the US, and was extremely critical of such institutions as the Central Intelligence Agency and its espionage network. He amazed me with his knowledge of the outside world. I was reminded of Cousin Hannah's remark that although BenZion, her father, was traditionally religious he called himself a *Bolshevik*. He was also a prodigious reader with interests ranging from the Talmud in Hebrew and Aramaic, to Zane Gray. Mostly confined to his bed, BenZion died a few years after my visit.

I enjoyed getting to know BenZion's gracious daughter Hannah, who was married to attorney Saul Burland. Their three lively children reminded me of my own. Staying with Cecil, another cousin, I gleaned an understanding of how native people survived under apartheid. White families generally kept a small lean-to or shack in the back yard which housed their servants. I would wake at dawn each morning to the sound of a woman scrubbing the surrounding walks. For her, each day began with a pot of cornmeal mush, bubbling away on the wood stove.

The highlight of my stay was a visit to the Consolidated Main Reef Diamond Mine. As a white American, I wondered if I might be unwelcome, but the workers were friendly. Since it was Sunday, their day of rest, they were performing their tribal dances. Graciously, they allowed us to watch and take photos. They do the most difficult, dangerous work—such as crushing and sorting many tons of earth to obtain one diamond—and are virtual prisoners, separated from their families except for a yearly visit. The inequities of apartheid left a strong impression on me. Observing the treatment of these native people deepened my resolve to become more informed about race relations in my own country. In South Africa, apartheid was very visible. In this country, racism is less obvious, but equally pernicious.

My relatives planned a number of tours for me, but I was unable to travel to Capetown and other points of interest because of the constraints of time; as much as I enjoyed my stay, my children needed me at home. However, I did visit Pretoria, the capital, where my cousin Skia lived. I was struck by a monumental frieze that decorated one of the main government buildings. This structure depicted the conquest of the native people by the Dutch Afrikaners. Huge statues of early pioneers lined the boulevard.

I have remained close to my cousin Hannah. Her daughter, Sharon, a nurse, left South Africa for Israel after her marriage, joining a *kibbutz* with her family. Hannah's sons, attorneys Jacob (Jack) and Daniel, were frustrated in their attempts to work within the highly prejudicial apartheid court system and in the mid '80s, immigrated to the United States. We were pleased to help them settle in the Bay Area. Hannah, left alone after the death of her husband, is sometimes despondent because of the separation from her children.

Family reunions are infrequent. Her fate echoes that of many Jewish families which have been dispersed throughout the world.

I had also looked forward to visiting Israel for the first time and enjoyed the long but luxurious British Air Lines flight from South Africa to Tel Aviv in 1952—Sam had even arranged for a sleeping berth. Upon landing, I was given VIP treatment since Sam's relatives had been early settlers and comrades of head of state Ben-Gurion and Sam was beginning to make a name for himself in agriculture. This welcome caused me some embarrassment since I was aware of the deep problems plaguing Israel. Government-encouraged Jewish immigration from Russia and elsewhere had resulted in the displacement of Palestinians, causing great resentment on the part of the Arab world.

I found desert *kibbutz* life primitive—a compound of simple cement block houses. Each person was assigned work according to his or her ability. Food was simple, breakfast consisted mainly of onions and cucumbers. I was allowed the luxury of an egg. Since parents labored long hours in the fields, school personnel played an important role in child rearing. Children slept in bunk houses, visiting their families at certain hours. To me, this seemed too austere, and I had a feeling the kibbutz culture was bound to change.

I was also hosted by several of Sam's relatives, including cousin Rachel Katinka and her husband Zev, an army historian. I heard stories of another cousin who had been the chief architect for the luxurious King David Hotel in Jerusalem. I met Sam's Uncle Josef and his daughter Miriam. Their hospitality was overwhelming and I regretted my all-too-short visit.

From my hotel in Tel Aviv, I was driven to the capital city of Jerusalem, a place of longing and religious tradition to Moslems, Christians, and Jews. The stark beauty of this ancient land, and the thought of its centuries-long cultural and religious history, awed me. Large numbers of burned-out tanks and other vehicles still littered the roadside, deliberate reminders of the destructiveness of modern warfare. Unfortunately, conflicts still plague this tiny nation—a landscape torn along Israeli-Palestinian lines.

Chapter 22

Learning the Media Ropes

April 26, 1952

Dear Mr. Sharkey,

I was shocked to read the statement by Mayor Robinson requesting that you deny the use of the Opera House to the great singer Paul Robeson. I believe that we are giving our critics throughout the world an opportunity to say, "The United States preaches democracy, but does not practice it. A world famous singer is denied the right to be heard because some factions do not like his politics..."

—Alice Hamburg, letter to the General Director
of the San Francisco Opera House

In 1953 my daughters graduated from Berkeley High and prepared to enter college that fall, Sonya at Stanford and Tanya at Pomona, in Southern California. During summer vacation, I drove to Yuma, Arizona, to see a friend and former Los Baños teacher. Tanya went with me to visit a boyfriend. In the scorching heat we listened to radio broadcasts of the final appeals of the Rosenberg defense team. Although I had been involved in the Rosenberg struggle, Sam's concern about possible anti-Semitic repercussions prevented me from discussing my feelings about the case with the children. I tried to keep my political life separate from them. On that long drive to Yuma, at this heart-wrenching moment in American history, I could not confide the depths of this tragedy to my daughter. I was overcome with sorrow because the Rosenbergs were being sacrificed to the anticommunist hysteria of the day.

The same year I became active with the California Mental Health Association (CMHA), a broad-based group aimed at improving community mental health. The core members were psychologists and psychiatrists, though a few lay people, former teachers and other professionals like myself also participated. I had been recruited by several of my San Francisco friends, Leona Bayer and political activist Frances Shaskan, wife of the Chief of Psychiatry in the San Francisco Veterans Administration. Despite the title of the organization, our emphasis tended toward education and bringing about a peaceful world.

I served on the planning and publicity committees for the conferences, which were held annually at Asilomar, a splendid center overlooking the ocean in Pacific Grove, near Monterey. Some participants came simply to stroll on the beach and enjoy the tasty food, others were moved to engage in political activity in such a tranquil setting—quite different from our usual venue. The beautiful buildings were designed by famed architect Julia Morgan.

One of our first conferences featured Brock Chisholm, a Canadian physician, the first to head the World Health Organization (WHO). He outlined the complexity of the health problems facing the world's peoples, particularly in the wake of world wars. Dr. Chisholm described the efforts being made by WHO to eradicate smallpox and other scourges.

Other speakers addressed problems of the workplace. A popular book at the time, *Organization Man*, by noted Columbia University sociologist C. Wright Mills, delineated the manner in which major industries were increasing their power and exercising undue influence in our society. Mills warned that people were becoming cogs in corporate machinery, foretelling the globalization of industry and the diminishing importance of the individual.

My volunteer public relations work for the CMHA was a new activity. I had progressed from speaking to women's clubs, the League of Women Voters, and the PTA: Now I was promoting the forthcoming Asilomar conferences in radio interviews. The first time I faced a microphone, during an interview with radio personality Wanda Ramey, I was extremely nervous. My introduction to public relations was to "sell" the attractions of Asilomar's remote, seaside conference grounds as well as to promote our challenging educational programs. With KPFA founder Lew Hill on our planning committee, we had no difficulty arranging pre-conference discussions on Berkeley's listener-supported Free Speech FM radio station KPFA— the first such station to take to the airwaves. Following the conference, fellow committee member Walter Gerstel and I transcribed, edited, and published the proceedings.

Some of the most popular CMHA programs were chaired by Gina Philipsborn, whom I had met shortly after resettling in Berkeley in 1948. This friendly, vivacious woman, with her blonde hair gathered up in a casual knot, was a Berkeley therapist. A Jewish native of Germany, she had been a social worker-therapist in Berlin and a disciple of Alfred Adler, the renowned psychiatrist. Her husband Arthur, a physician, believed the Nazi threat would blow over and refused to leave Germany. Gina made her way with their three small daughters to Bornholm, a tiny island off the coast of Denmark, where she established a camp for the few German-Jewish children who managed to escape the Nazis. She remained there during the war and was eventually joined by her husband. Afterwards they sought asylum in the US and landed in Berkeley.

Gina lived near us on San Mateo Road. Over time, a small group of like-minded women began meeting in her living room. This political discussion group included Esther Zypin, a nurse and full-time Planned Parenthood volunteer; Henrietta Ravenson, a Russian language scholar who at one time counted writer and activist William Mandel among her students; and Esther Gelders Zane, a civil rights activist from a well-to-do Alabama Jewish family who was also a consummate cook. Esther and her husband Joe were close friends of Virginia Durr, one of the most prominent white women leaders of the desegregation movement in the South. Another member of this women's group was fashionable and dramatic Barbara Sicular, a New Yorker and volunteer in the Bay Area Russian War Relief during the war. It was my privilege to view the world through the eyes of these diverse and insightful older women. In trying to justify my political activities in light of my role as a wife and mother, these women provided me with advice about how to deal with my not always sympathetic family.

Esther's younger daughter Blanche was married to Lou Hartman, who, as "Jim Grady," hosted a popular San Francisco CBS radio program. Perhaps his overly enthusiastic reporting of the Russian Sputnik shortly after its 1957 launch caused CBS to remove him from their orbit—he was too partisan. Blanche began a serious study of Zen Buddhism and was eventually chosen Abbess of the San Francisco Zen Center. Marge, the older daughter, became a reentry UC student at age forty-eight, after years of dedicated work at Oakland's Planned Parenthood office.

My friendship with Gina continued to deepen. Through the years, her loving attention came to include my entire family, grandchildren and all. We cherished her warmth and wisdom. On weekends when Sam visited, he would walk over to see her, often staying for hours—no doubt complaining about me and the pain of his separation from the children. Gina lent a sympathetic ear.

Gina also counseled Aron about the difficulties he was having with his father—their temperaments varied widely. Sam's treatment of his son sometimes bordered on cruelty.

Although Aron was steadier and more reliable, he lacked the brilliance, as well as the eccentricities, of his father.

Gina's sudden death in 1968, in the same month as Martin Luther King, Jr.'s assassination, brought great sadness to family, close friends, and to the many individuals whom she had counseled over the years. Several members of her therapy group grieved as if for the loss of a family member. I miss her to this day, especially when confronted with a complex problem.

Chapter 23

Graduation, Marriage, and an International Incident

"Where are you going my little one, little one,
Where are you going, my baby, my own?
Turn around and you're two, turn around and you're four,
Turn around and you're a young girl going out of my door."

—song by Malvina Reynolds and Alan Greene,
"Turn Around"

In 1954 I was asked to lead a weekly senior citizens discussion group at Berkeley's newly completed Temple Beth El. The work was so stimulating that I continued for a number of years. Numerous elders, with an amazing diversity of background and experience, formed the core of the group—European refugees along with native-born Americans, all from a considerable range of class and educational backgrounds. Meetings at Beth El generated many lively discussions and table-thumping arguments. Imagine a room full of elderly, mostly progressive people, almost coming to blows over US foreign policy and local politics!

Many activists were involved in these discussions. Yetta Land, a retired attorney, had represented the Communist Party at the famous Foley Square trial in New York during the McCarthy witchhunt. Extremely well-informed, she was an asset to our group. Rebecca Lubin, a charming, stylish Sacramento widow in her 80s, chaired the meetings. Her father-in-law, Simon Lubin, had owned the Weinstock-Lubin department stores, the largest in Sacramento. Outstanding among civic leaders, he was a widely-known philanthropist who strongly supported the LaFollette Congressional Committee hearings which highlighted the abysmal conditions of the state's farm laborers in the thirties.

Many in the group were German. Anna Strauss was one of the first stenographers to use the turn-of-the-century, "new fangled" typewriter which would free secretaries from endless hours of manual labor. The dignified, carefully groomed Mrs. Stern, aunt of physicist Robert Oppenheimer, stood out in the crowd. Selma Bernstein, a prize-winning weaver noted for her beautiful tapestries, added color and artistic temperament to our assemblies.

The Beth El group distinguished itself as a peace and justice activist organization, making several trips to Sacramento. Members wrote letters to government officials and the press, including U Thant at the UN, Henry Kissinger, and Kurt Waldheim. We circulated petitions, discussed issues, and attracted speakers. Among them was Republican Governor "Goody" Knight, whose policies were not in-sync with the progressive thinking of the majority of the group. Ill-prepared for the sharp interrogation awaiting him, the Governor did not win any votes among our group. On another occasion, to protest cutbacks by Governor Reagan, there were 43 senior citizens standing on the capitol steps, carrying placards that said "Restore Cutbacks!" I continued to commute to Beth El, even though I moved several times during the group's early years.

By 1955, my children were growing up. Sonya and Tanya had graduated from Berkeley High School in 1953 with outstanding grades, and Sam thought that a trip abroad would round out their education. In the summer of 1955, he took the three children to Europe and Israel. They enjoyed the experience enormously, visiting many historic spots. Aron brought back piles of photos. He commented, "You know, Mother, in Italy, 'communism' is really not a bad word like it is here. Even the taxi drivers talk about it."

In order to prepare Aron for college, we arranged for him to take his senior year at the private Menlo School on the Peninsula. To have more time with him, I decided to spend the 1957-58 school year in Menlo Park, commuting to Berkeley every Wednesday for the Beth El senior discussion group. After graduation, Aron was admitted to Claremont College, near Pomona, where Tanya was beginning her senior year.

Life seemed a continuous commute as I became increasingly involved in Peninsula activities. Alice Richards, whom I had met through Gina Philipsborn in Berkeley, was living in the area and introduced me to others involved in the peace movement. Dr. Henry Mayer and his wife Olive, an engineer and textbook writer, became close friends of mine. I joined The Peace Club, a forerunner of Womens International League for Peace and Freedom, and met Valeda Bryant, editor of the club's publication, *The Flashlight*.

I often hiked in the Black Mountain area near Woodside with Ollie, a conservationist, who would later win a Sierra Club award for her work in creating hiking trails in San Mateo County. In describing a trip I had made earlier to Hoover Dam, she surprised me by her general condemnation of dams, which she labeled as harmful to the environment. This shocked me, and I later wondered about the effects of the great Central Valley Project begun in the 50's, which was furnishing irrigation water for our ranch.

With other activists, we organized a *National Guardian* Magazine subscribers group, and sponsored a number of public lectures, where I came to know British anti-war author Felix Greene. With his help, the next spring we set up several meetings in Palo Alto to attract new subscribers to listener-supported radio station KPFA. Under the *National Guardian* auspices we arranged a Bill of Rights Day Celebration in December, 1957. Our featured speaker was the urbane Barrows Dunham, philosopher and author of *Man Against Myth*. Having been fired from Temple University for political activism, he seemed an appropriate speaker for Bill of Rights Day.

Both our daughters were graduating from college on the very same day in 1957, Tanya with a major in International Relations, and Sonya winning honors in Humanities and a Phi Beta Kappa key. I attended Tanya's graduation while Sam celebrated with Sonya at Stanford.

After their graduations, it seemed an excellent time to revisit Europe. Encouraged by their father and Tanya's interest in government and a possible career in the diplomatic service, they decided to visit the USSR. At that time, travel by US citizens was not encouraged. Visas were difficult to obtain and required a stopover in Stockholm, where they were questioned intensely about their reasons for visiting. They replied that their father had come from Poland (which was part of Russia), and their grandparents from Lithuania.

The twins were impressed by the history and physical diversity of Russia. They traveled by train from Leningrad to Moscow, and were dazzled by the ornate architecture of the Kremlin and Red Square. As it happened, they arrived during the celebration of the launching of Sputnik I, planned to coincide with the fortieth anniversary of the Bolshevik Revolution. Shortly before their departure for home, they met two British journalists in Moscow who were extremely frustrated by the blackout imposed by the government, which insisted on "putting its own spin" on the news about this spectacular achievement. Thus, it was impossible for foreign correspondents to cover this breaking news story. Realizing that the young women were about to leave the country, reporters implored them to circumvent the censors and smuggle out their news dispatches. They agreed. They were given secret phone numbers to call after leaving the country. Immediately upon landing, they followed their instructions. They read the dispatches to London editors, who were eagerly awaiting their news. Fortunately for the travelers, their "messenger service" did not trigger an international crisis. Being young and inexperienced, they failed to appreciate fully the danger of breaching Russian security.

The following summer, Tanya enrolled in a statistics course at Stanford, where she met a number of party-minded (non political) students—including Ernest Ruehl. "You should meet my sister!" she suggested, sensing a possible compatibility in their shared farming background, since Ernest's father was a prominent Washington state rancher. To everyone's surprise, the romance blossomed. Not long after, the two announced their engagement. Despite the nuptial plans, Sonya insisted on carrying out an earlier commitment to attend Radcliffe College, where she would earn a graduate degree in Personnel Management.

After graduation, she and Ernest were married in the historic Stanford Chapel, brimming with flowers and well-wishing relatives, family and friends. Sonya's college classmates were bridesmaids, Tanya her maid-of-honor. Sam's friend, Edward Teller, "father of the H Bomb," and his wife were among the guests. In addition to various dignitaries, guests also included the children's former *abuela*, Carmelita Luke, ranch employees, and a number of packing shed workers.

Despite the beauty of the event, Sam and I were disappointed that, although the chapel was non-denominational, the service was not; kneeling at the altar was a Christian ritual not in keeping with the ceremony we anticipated. However, this did not dim the glow of the festivities. As the scent of Amazon lilies wafted through the chapel, I realized that the process of letting go had begun—my first child had left home.

Following the wedding, Sonya and Ernest moved to New York City, where he spent a year as intern at the Francis I. Dupont Investment Company. Sonya found work as secretary to the Mystery Writers of America. I visited the newlyweds in their tiny, old-fashioned apartment in Greenwich Village. This walled building, accessible by steep steps, had uneven floors and poorly-lit, narrow hallways. While there, we attended a number of theater productions, including Kurt Weill's *Threepenny Opera*, my favorite, with Lotte Lenya in the cast. I also enjoyed Thornton Wilder's *Our Town*. The play's powerful wedding scene reminded me of the fleetingness of life and the emotional impact of Sonya's recent wedding and I found myself in tears.

From New York, I stopped in Minneapolis to see Uncle Abram and Aunt Gertrude. I was disappointed to find that Sixth Avenue, where my family had once lived, was now a freeway. I marveled at the new Mall of the Americas in St. Paul, today still the largest in the world.

Spokane, Washington, was my last stop, where I visited Ernest's parents, Lud and Josephine Ruehl. There, I met Dr. Caldwell, Lud's friend who had graduated from the University of South Dakota, where he had known Charlotte Noteboom, my beloved mentor from Hecla, South Dakota. It was from him that I learned that the girls' dormitory at the University had been named in her honor. How ironic, since the school board of our small town had dismissed her.

In 1958, Tanya entered the School of Social Welfare at UCB, a two-year graduate course. Living at home on San Luis Road, she later commuted to her first job for the San Mateo County Child Welfare Department. Imagine my consternation when she was informed by her supervisor that the FBI had paid a visit, asking, "Do you know that the mother of your new employee is under FBI surveillance?" The supervisor informed the agent, in no uncertain terms, that she "didn't give a damn what Ms. Hamburg's mother was involved in," and quickly escorted him to the door. These government practices had often proven disastrous for those under suspicion. Earlier, two agents had come to my Berkeley home, but I refused to talk to them without an attorney. They went away muttering something about "your draft-age son...."

One evening there was a notice about a meeting of Young Democrats on the UC campus. I suggested to Tanya, "Why don't you go? You'll meet people. You might as well get involved in something besides your studies." She followed my advice and there met Ernie Goldsmith—another Ernest! Apparently, the romance began when he escorted her to her parked Citroën. Sam had bought the car for the girls, which had been shipped from Europe. Impressed, he exclaimed, "Is this yours? Could I drive it someday?"

By the time Tanya and Ernie were engaged, ranching was going well and Sam, one for display and splurge, decided on a wedding that would outshine the previous year's event. Wedding plans became more lavish, everyone was caught up in the excitement. My daughters had an avid interest in fashion, which I failed to share. However, on this occasion, I acquiesced and was dragged off to Ransohoff's to select the proper gown.

Tanya and Ernie Goldsmith were married in 1960 at the Mark Hopkins Hotel in San Francisco by the distinguished Rabbi Saul White. Shortly before the wedding, Sonya and Ernest had returned to San Francisco, where a job with the Dupont Company awaited him. Sonya was employed by an investment firm. As Tanya's wedding plans progressed, Sonya became more and more involved. The perfect event both Tanya and Ernie envisioned took place as planned, but with one hitch. Several days before the ceremony, Sonya's old Maxwell's brakes failed at the top of Telegraph Hill. She lost control as the car sped down the hill and crashed into the curb. She was able to bail out. Fortunately, no one was killed. Badly bruised, Sonya appeared at the wedding with knees and elbows bandaged. She feared that her father would be upset, but he never even noticed! He was too excited about the wedding. The San Joaquin Valley attendees included State Senator and Mrs. Cobey from Merced, and Judge and Mrs. Ted Falasco from Los Baños. Happily, we welcomed old friends Paul Taylor and Dorie Lange, Gina Phillipsborn, and the Hassids.

As Tanya stood under the *chuppah* with Ernie, her new husband, surrounded by gladi-oli and roses and beautifully gowned in bridal white, I was deeply happy. Now my daughters would carry the heritage of the past into promising futures. Aglow with expectations, filled with experience gathered through education and family influence, they would lead challenging and productive lives. With horizons broadened through travel, they were now ready to put a lifetime's learning into practice.

During this time, I was renting a flat on Baker street in San Francisco while Sonya and Ernest Ruehl were living nearby on Telegraph Hill. Before Ernie Jr. was born in 1963, Sonya resigned from her job. Although the view from the top of Telegraph Hill was beautiful, their actual quarters were almost as cramped as when they lived in New York City. For a time Junior slept in a tiny, windowless room with scarcely enough space for such an active baby. Later, on walks with me, he would jump up and hang on apartment mailboxes like an urban monkey! I would pick him up, stuff him under my arm, and carry him back up the hill.

At the time, Ernie Goldsmith was attending Stanford Law School, working every sum-mer. Like her sister, Tanya resigned from her job before giving birth, to David in 1964. After graduation, Ernie won a position in the San Francisco District Attorney's Office and the family moved into an apartment on Leavenworth, overlooking Alcatraz Island.

With my daughters both settled in San Francisco, I was able to enjoy my grandchildren, even though I moved back to Berkeley in 1965 and was extremely busy. By chance, Tanya and Ernie rented my former Baker Street flat, while Sonya and her family moved to an apartment around the corner on Green Street. Perhaps they were too close: One day Sonya came to visit her sister, took one look at her swollen, unhappy face and was warned, "Don't come in we've got the mumps!" Nevertheless, Sonya soon succumbed to the same affliction.

Photo of Sachs house in Skopishok,
Lithuania before departure for US

Mother and child - "Jewish Pioneers" -
Brother Charlie with mother Hannah Sachs,
Lithuania, 1904

Main Street - Depot in Wing, North Dakota, ca. 1911

Sister Rachel Sachs,
first child born in Wing, 1912

Sam Hamburg and sister
Rosa, Pinsk, Poland, 1903

Uncle Abram Sachs and Aunt Gertrude
Minneapolis, ca. 1915

Alice's Grammar School class, Hecla, SD, ca. 1918. Alice, standing third from left

Alice, circa 1923, dressed up for college
festival, Aberdeen SD

Brother Ben with father, Herman Sachs, ca. 1925

Alice outside cabin on San Juan Ranch near
Dos Palos, CA, 1926

Graduation with MA Degree at UC
Berkeley, 1929

Alice and Sam in Berkeley, 1931

Alice with twins, Sonya (left) and Tanya, (right) 1935

Twins in stroller visiting Mrs. Segura and her twins on the ranch

Grandpa Herman with Tanya (left) and Sonya (right), 1937

Grandma Hannah with the twins, Los Angeles, 1938

Alice's mother, Hannah Sachs, on Sam Hamburg Farm, ca. 1938

Herman and Hannah Sachs, early 1940s

The family, with the twins and Aron 1944. Photo by Joe Lorber, Lafayette

Aron and Sam with the season's first bale of cotton, 1949

Brother Charlie, Blackie, Aron and dog, and Sam, mid-1950s celebrating the tractor's anniversary

Aron Lee Hamburg in his almond orchard, late 1960s

Alice with gold miners near Johannesburg,South Africa, 1952

In Pretoria capital of South Africa, with the Burland cousins, 1952

Sonya and Ernest Ruehl's wedding, with his family at Stanford Chapel, 1959

Tanya and Ernie Golsmith's wedding, with family at the Fairmont Hotel, 1960

Aron's 21st birthday celebration with the workers' children, at the ranch community room, 1961

Aron with California Governor Pat Brown, ca. 1961

Alice and friends on travels to Armenia, USSR, 1963

Alice with Martin Luther King, Jr., at Oakland Coliseum, Martin Luther King Rally, October 15, 1967

Alice, head of Volunteer Staff, at Temple Beth-El, Berkeley, with David Fogel, Dir. Jewish Community Center and Rebecca Lubin, president of the Senior Discussion Group, 1968

Aron with General Moishe Dyan, 1968

Sonya with SF Mayor Joseph Alioto at KQED auction, early 70s

Charlie's daughter Dorothy and her husband Yev Philopovich and their children,
Karl and Sara, 1970s

Anti-Vietnam War demonstration, ca. 1972, with Alice, a student, and Rabbi Feinberg

Charlie's 70th birthday with Rachel, Charlie, Alice, Gertrude, Genya Sachs
and Gertrude's nieces, 1973

The exuberance of youth! David in the cotton field at Sam Hamburg Farms, early 70s

1976 anti-war coalition billboard campaign in 7 cities including San Francisco

With WILPF Japanese Section President, Dr. Kiyo Tsuji, in Tokyo, 1977

Linus and Ava Helen Pauling at a SF WILPF reception

Nephew Phil Sachs, Santa Cruz, with vintage Ford, 1980s

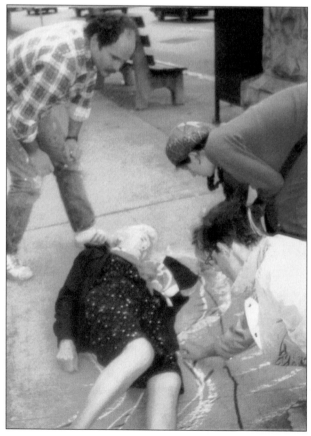

Alice at the Hiroshima Day Die-in, Berkeley, corner of Ashby and College, 1985

Alice with WILPF member Erna P. Harris and Berkeley Mayor Loni Hancock, 1986

Mother's Day Demonstration, Nevada Test Site, May 1987

Brother Ben's sons, Steve and Gary Sachs, with Alice and Charlie Sachs, 1988

Alice with Nobel Laureate Owen Chamberlain at his retirement party, U.C. 1989

Alice at Peace Wall, Berkeley, 1989

Grandson Ernie Ruehl Jr., cousin Albert Sachs, and Alice with daughters Sonya and Tanya at book signing for *Sam Hamburg, Agricultural Pioneer*, 1989

WSP/WILPF demonstration, Oakland, November, 1992

Grandson Ted Ruehl and Claudia's wedding, family members, 1993

Julie and Jose Lopez' wedding, 1995. With Tanya, David and Ernie Goldsmith, and cousin Steve Goldsmith

Ruehl family at cousin Julie's wedding, Berkeley 1995, Ernest and Sonya
with Ted holding Nicholas, Ernie Jr. and Paul

The Military-SANE-WILPF Peace Train, 1996, with Madeline Duckles,
Dale Nesbit, Roberta Brooks, Alice and other activists

Hannah Burland visits sons Dan, Jack and their wives, San Jose, 1996,
joined by Alice and Tanya

Alice honored at JAPA's 5th celebration, 1997

Party at the Ellsberg's honoring Rep. Ron Dellums after his 1998 retirement.
Left to right: Lee Halterman, Ron Dellums, Patricia Ellsberg, Alice, Claire Greensfelder

Alice demonstrates at beginning of the Pacifica-KPFA showdown, 1999

Alice receiving the Berkeley Community Award, Berkeley, 2000

Great grandchildren Henry and Elizabeth Ruehl, carrying on the family tradition, 1999

Great grandchildren Isabel and Nicholas Ruehl, Boston, 2000

Four generations with Ernie Ruehl, Jr. holding Henry, daughter Sonya holding Elizabeth, Orinda, 2000

Four generations including daughter Tanya Goldsmith, granddaughter Julie Goldsmith, and great grandson Samuel Goldsmith-Lopez, born 12/23/2000, named after my deceased husband

Chapter 24

The End of a Dream

"With our parents we bury our past, with our children our future."

—Marie von Ebner-Eschenbach, *Aphorisms* (1893)

With Aron's death the light went out of my life...

Aron was tall, handsome, and broad-shouldered, with a delightful sense of humor. As he grew older, he shared his parents' interests in political and community activity. While I was living in Berkeley, I looked forward to his frequent phone calls from the Los Baños ranch and can still hear his chuckle. People found our son warm and approachable, and he appeared to have a special appeal to women. In Los Baños, he had received an award from the city for his work as Community Chest Drive Co-Chairman, and for heading a successful campaign to establish a town hospital. He was named Outstanding Young Farmer of Merced County in 1967.

Whereas my daughters and I had the usual generational difficulties, Aron and I had few conflicts, outside of the time he left a junky pick-up, which he had acquired as a teenager, in our Berkeley driveway for months, saying, "Oh, I need to make a few repairs."

From the time Aron was born his sisters generally looked after him. They all got along beautifully. In the early years, Sonya played a motherly role, while Tanya and Aron shared similar personalities and enjoyed making mischief. It was she to whom he confided his romantic adventures as well as his disappointments. During her senior year at Pomona College, she was able to help her brother with his studies, smoothing his transition into academic life. In spite of my involvement in peace activities, and my disapproval, Aron signed up for the ROTC program, which earned him a small stipend. He wanted to lessen his financial dependence on his father. We looked forward to his graduation. Sam brought a party from the ranch, all dressed in their Sunday best. With hindsight I recall only one shadow on the celebration. Aron had failed to receive an anticipated special ROTC commendation. Perhaps his mood at that time should have given me a hint of some of the future problems.

After graduation Aron returned to the ranch, which by then was a large and complex operation. Sam hoped that his strong feeling for the land would be shared by his son, since it was simply assumed that Aron would follow in his father's footsteps. If Aron had dreams of his own, we never knew. He did not express them. Sam should have been thrilled with his son's return to the ranch, but being preoccupied with many matters, Sam simply dumped difficult assignments on him, although Aron's only prior ranch experience had been during summer jobs. Inconsistent and moody, Sam provided no professional guidance.

At first, Aron seemed to be getting along pretty well, but as his father became more occupied with his work in Israel, he heaped even more responsibilities on Aron's shoulders. Sam would go off to Israel for the planting of a crop, bringing along the seeds, fertilizer, and whatever else was needed. A few months later, he would return to Israel to see how well his plans had been carried out. Aron's first important job was setting up a system to provide safe drinking water for our ranch. It was necessary to make the "hard" well water drinkable. Until then, good water had been trucked into the camp from the nearby town of South Dos Palos. Without engineering training, the complexity of the task was overwhelming. Nevertheless, Aron plunged in. After several failures and much frustration, he managed to get the job done.

Because of Sam's ability to solve problems quickly, he was intolerant of anyone who failed to function as well as he. This was evident in his dealings with my brother Charlie, as well as with Aron. When Sam gave Aron the task of laying out and planting an almond orchard, instead of calling on professional help, Aron found himself very much on his own. Happily, everything went well, and within a few years, the orchard yielded a top-quality crop of several varieties of almonds. The orchard grew in beauty, its lines of trees covered with delicate blossoms in spring. Bee swarms were brought in to pollinate the trees— even then insecticides and weed sprays were driving bees away from many areas in the country. People would drive from places as distant as the Bay Area to revel in the beauty and fragrance of the Valley almond crops.

At this time, Sam was involved not only with Israeli agriculture, but also with the

US"Point Four "International Aid program, often traveling on behalf of the Israeli government. The purpose of this partnership between the United States and Israel was to teach modern agricultural methods to farmers in several African and Middle Eastern countries. In 1958 Sam was asked by Golda Meir, Israeli Foreign Affairs Minister, to act as an advisor representing Israel in this international program.

Because of his long absences, Sam gradually turned over more and more responsibility to Aron, who then relied on the experience of foreman Walt Lester, and others. Although by now running his own farm, Charlie would often come by to advise Aron. Before departing on one of his trips, Sam made an appointment with a prominent Merced legal firm to review his will. A meeting took place which was to have far-reaching consequences for the family.

There, Sam and Aron met Chris, one of the firm's attorneys. Subsequently, Aron and Chris became close friends. Aron was struggling to operate the ranch during Sam's absence. Chris, after hearing his complaints, offered to help. Aron accepted, having dreamed of doing some farming on his own in order to prove himself to his father. After forming a partnership with Chris, they purchased a small acreage in the area, borrowing against Sam Hamburg Farms, intending to repay the loan with their crop of canning tomatoes. Although the first year was highly successful, the next was a disaster, as an unseasonal rain destroyed their entire harvest. This prompted Aron to experiment with other crops less susceptible to damage. He also envisioned growing produce that was not dependent on chemical fertilizers and pesticides—his interest in organic agriculture was ahead of his time. With the failure of the crop, the mortgage became a powerful tool that Sam used against his son.

The crop loss was humiliating to Aron, but he was not alone. Growers generally finance their farming operations by contracting with large produce companies, such as Heinz, agreeing to repay the loans after the harvest. The loss of a single crop could sometimes result in bankruptcy. Unscrupulous produce companies sometimes made unrealistic loans to farmers with the intention of repossessing their assets in the event of default. Had Aron succeeded in his tomato venture, he might have won his father's respect and approval. But, upon his return, Sam discovered the unauthorized loan, and that his son's enterprise had failed. Unfortunately, that year our farm operations were also less profitable than usual. Sam followed extremely strict business principles and blamed Aron and his partner for the unauthorized loan secured by our ranch. When faced with his role in the poor performance of both ranches, and with Sam's constant, vocal criticisms, Aron was devastated.

Although Chris had offered Aron support and understanding, by his actions it soon became apparent to the rest of us that his true motivation was to alienate his friend from our family. Although he offered friendship, his interests lay in the Sam Hamburg property. My greatest regret was that I was unable to help Aron in this situation. Shortly thereafter, Chris left the ranch to return to the practice of law.

This was the beginning of hard times in agriculture. Large corporations were absorbing small farms in the Valley, as had been the case earlier in the 30s. During the 60s and 70s, many professional people were investing in agri-corporations, primarily as tax shelters with little interest in farming. Also, the growth of agribusiness resulted in the stepped-up use of pesticides and fertilizers. Cotton, the major crop in the San Joaquin Valley area, requires huge amounts of water as well as fertilizer and pesticide applications. Toxins leaching into the ground water resulted in the creation of huge cesspools in the general area of the Kesterson Reservoir, a wildlife refuge on the west side of Merced county. This environmental crisis had come to public attention during duck hunting season. Angry hunters huddled in their duck blinds, shotguns poised, were frustrated by the lack of game in the marshes of the state's most popular duck hunting area. This situation awakened the general public to the dangers caused by farm chemicals. Today, environmentalists and friends of farm labor are working to limit the use of these toxins.

Because of Sam's concern about the land, he would be horrified to witness the problems which beset farmers today. During his lifetime he was forever searching for ways to nurture and enrich the soil. When we first met, he had presented me with a copy of his favorite book, Knut Hamsun's *Growth of the Soil.* The first painting we purchased was the image of a man behind a plow, surveying the rolling, graceful vista of furrowed farmland spreading before him, a timeless scene.

Continuing his mission with the "Point Four" program, Sam traveled to Iran in 1966, then fell ill upon his return. Immediately, the family mobilized. As David, Tanya's son, was still an infant, she called me to take over while she sped to the ranch to join her anxious brother in caring for their father.

Physicians were at a loss to diagnose Sam's ailment, which turned out to be the rare neurological Guillian-Barré affliction, which is similar to polio. After two years, the disease left him almost totally deaf and paralyzed from the waist down. After receiving treatment and undergoing physical therapy at the San Francisco Pacific Medical Center and in a nearby convalescent hospital, he improved, although his hearing loss was permanent and he was never again able to walk unassisted. He remained partially paralyzed through his last years.

We were all deeply involved with Sam's care. Tanya's family now included baby Julie, born in 1966. On many weekends, the Goldsmiths packed up the kids and their golden retriever Daisy and drove down to the ranch to help care for Sam. He was happiest when the grandchildren were around. Although he was a dog lover, he once got into trouble with Daisy. After being rudely awakened by the dog jumping on his bed, he let out a startled cry. In spite of Sam's numerous overtures, he was never forgiven by Daisy.

Aron had a special relationship with Tanya's son, David. Several years earlier Aron had qualified for his pilot's license. On one occasion, he flew to Fresno with his young nephew as passenger. David was most impressed with the deference shown to pilots; he was tremendously proud of his uncle.

Sonya, now the mother of three small boys—Ernie Jr., Ted, and Paul—was able to visit Sam less often. To relieve my daughters and maintain some sense of family unity, I visited whenever possible. I would drive down not only to visit Sam, but also to mediate on behalf of Aron, who was in an emotional state following the failure of his farming enterprise. I tried to buffer Aron from his father's bitter denunciations. In spite of our conflicts, I thought it important to maintain as normal a relationship with Sam as possible. He failed to understand my reasons for wanting a divorce. Over the years I had slowly been asserting myself. Now, I simply wanted the freedom to live my own life. Over his objections, I had finally obtained the divorce in 1961.

In 1968, convinced that he would never walk again, Sam insisted on ending his physical therapy treatments and returning to the ranch. He remained there, almost totally bedridden, for the rest of his life. I vividly recall him propped up in his hospital bed, holding forth to the steady stream of visitors. He read voluminously, and engaged callers on the latest developments in political and world affairs. Always social and in search of constant attention, Sam welcomed my visits. In spite of our past differences, he once again sought my opinion. Several years after the divorce, Sam wrote, asking me to come to Israel to live with him.

Using a wheelchair and accompanied by Aron, Sam managed to take two trips back to Israel. He was consumed by the great desire to see the success of his projects. In a letter to our daughters, Sam described his reception at Ben-Gurion Airport as the "happiest moment" of his life. "Everyone in agriculture was there, from the old ones that started it and set in motion the great drama of returning to the land, to the young ones who are continuing it. Nothing resembling this gathering had ever taken place in Israel before."

Sam needed full-time care, and Aron had recruited the loyal and dependable Tillie Ballez, wife of a farm laborer. She was with Sam daily from the mid-60s until his death in 1976. We compensated Tillie for her devoted care by purchasing a home for her in Los Baños. I continue to be in touch.

With the deterioration of Sam's health and Aron's growing restlessness, the family was concerned about the future. Sonya's husband Ernest, an investment consultant and successful money manager, became closely involved with the business aspects of the ranch. Tanya's husband Ernie, an attorney, was on hand with legal advice. The family decided to employ Dave Dermer, an experienced manager who had been introduced to us by Aron. The new manager carried on with the able assistance of Sam's former secretary, Ana. With Dave's arrival, Aron felt his presence at the ranch was no longer necessary. Deeply troubled by his father's critical attitude and discouraged about the future of independent ranching, he moved to Los Baños, sharing a house with his former business partner, Chris.

With the same energy and dedication he had used in their creation, Sam pursued the sale of his holdings, a difficult task that took several years to complete. Caught up in the emotional trauma, selling the ranch, I was not thinking about my future. Later, I began to wonder how I would support myself?

The ranch was sold in 1972 to Buttes Gas and Oil Company in Oakland, whose owners wished to diversify. To me, this seemed as though we were surrendering to forces which we had so long decried. To what extent would the new management care for the land? Although it was the sad end of an era, change was inevitable. Sam was reassured by the new owners that all loyal ranch workers would retain their jobs. Dave Dermer and the secretary would continue on, and Sam was free to remain on the ranch for the rest of his life.

Ernest Ruehl steered us through a number of difficulties during the sale of the ranch. Through his diligence and hard work, the stock obtained in payment for the ranch was parlayed into securities which provided adequate income for both Sam and me. Thus I was more fortunate than many divorced women in similar situations. For this, I have always been grateful to my family, especially to my son-in-law.

As we drove away from the ranch that last time, it was with a great deal of sadness that we saw the end of Sam's efforts. My thoughts went back to the war years, when he had shipped tons of barley overseas, and had experimented with growing guayule as a replacement for sorely-needed rubber for the World War II war effort. Sam's creative ideas, intelligence, and enterprising spirit, along with Aron's years of dedicated effort, had kept the enterprise functioning through many difficult times. Sam also appreciated the workers for their dedication and often remarked, "Without them there would be no Sam Hamburg Farms."

I recall vividly the early morning of January 6, 1975, when I opened the door to find my daughters and their husbands standing there in the chilly Berkeley fog. I knew immediately that something was terribly wrong. Someone must have died, but who? Earlier that morning, Tillie Ballez, Sam's live-in nurse, had phoned from the ranch but without a hint of tragedy in her voice. Ernest Ruehl put his arm around me as they shared the heartbreaking news: Aron had died in a house fire, just days after his 36th birthday. On that fateful evening, Aron apparently dozed off while watching television. His cigarette ignited the upholstery and he was overcome by smoke.

With Aron's death, a part of my life ended. Nothing could ever affect me the same way. I was utterly grief-stricken. My reaction to this tragedy was different than my feelings when my parents died. After their deaths, I felt alone. I was aware that I was totally responsible for my life. Now came the soul-searching questions. I had brought Aron into the world. What might I have done to save him? Had my concerns about the state of the world overshadowed my responsibilities to him? My daughters attempted to console me, offering their opinion that conflict between father and son was inevitable, and that this tension had contributed, albeit indirectly, to the tragedy.

A memorial fund was established in Aron's name. This scholarship at Fresno State drew contributions from a wide circle of family, friends, and acquaintances. People drove from all over the Valley and elsewhere to our son's service, which was held in the large community room on the ranch—in the same room where we had celebrated his 21st birthday.

The workers with whom Aron had a special relationship were bereft, as if a member of their family had died. I deeply regret not having called upon some of them who might have wanted to express their personal feelings. Tillie Ballez, Sam's nurse, joined us in mourning Aron, asking, "Who's going to take care of me now?" Joel Whitehurst, now a local businessman who named his son after Aron, wrote me in 1980, "I hope my son grows up with the vision, the intelligence and the compassion of the man for whom he is named, my best friend, Aron."

After Aron's death, I determined to involve myself more fully with my daughters and their families. Yet in order to regain my bearings, I needed solitude and turned away friends who attempted to comfort me. I should have been more aware of the difficulties besetting Aron. His malaise had been as much psychological as physical. Under the pressure of dealing with the many vicissitudes of large-scale farming, he began to suffer from insomnia. Even in college, the stress of exams had made him restless. Worried, I sent him what was supposed to have been a non-addictive sleeping pill, Doriden, prescribed by a physician friend. While managing the farm, his anxieties increased. He consulted a prominent San Francisco psychiatrist who, quite unprofessionally, prescribed an unlimited supply of sedatives without any follow-up visit. My son, unfortunately, became dependent on these drugs.

I should have insisted on spending more time with Aron, but sadly, in that last year of his life, his associate did his best to alienate him from us. After taking great pains to guide the development of my children, I had considered myself free to pursue the broader social and political goals to which I was committed. Too late, I struggled with the thought of what I might have done differently.

Sam questioned my protective relationship with Aron. He was inconsistent, at times overwhelming Aron with praise, and at other times voicing strong disapproval when his son did not meet his expectations. Had we been more aware and supportive of Aron's needs, perhaps he would have led a less conflicted life.

After Aron's death, Sam's health took a downward turn. He was in and out of Mercey Hospital in Merced, and finally ended up at UC hospital in San Francisco. At the height of his illness, confined to a wheelchair and totally deaf, he had a tracheotomy to assist his breathing. UC hospital's Dr. Atchley consulted the family about continuing treatment. He did not receive a definitive reply. When asked directly whether Sam wanted to end his suffering, the answer was "No." He wanted to hang on! Tanya was with her father when he died on the morning in May 26, 1976.

Sam had fulfilled more of his dreams than most of us ever will, yet he remained unhappy. He had never lived his early fantasies of farming on the vast steppes of the Ukraine. He had not seen the fruition of his work in the Middle East and Africa. He was aware, finally, that his hard-driving style had estranged many people along the way. His greatest unhappiness, however, was that his son would not continue to work the soil. One could only imagine his deep sorrow. Nothing is more tragic than to live to bury your own child.

When I think of Sam, I recall the quote from the livestock and land baron Henry Miller, in Edward Treadwell's *The Cattle King:*

He saw the great levees, dams and reservoirs he had constructed to hold and control the forces of nature. He saw the alfalfa, rice and cotton which he had introduced on a large scale into the industries of his state...But he saw no son to perpetuate his work...

Thus ended a tumultuous and fascinating life, not an easy one for him, nor for those closest to him. Sam was buried in the plot adjoining Aron in the Los Banos cemetery on Center Street. Both he and Aron had been close to the soil, and they now rest in adjoining graves overlooked by the foothills and close to the land both had loved and cultivated.

Political Life: 1948-2000

"For veteran peace activists like Alice Hamburg, taking a stand is as natural as taking a breath.."

—Karen Gellen, Executive Director, Jane Addams Peace Association (JAPA), 1997

IV. The Women's Peace Movement

We in the peace movement continue to be dedicated to informing ourselves and educating others, challenging the wrongs we see and fighting the anti-human legislation coming out of Congress. The ultimate aim of the peace movement has always been to settle disputes using the tools of communication, non-violence, negotiation, and diplomacy.

Chapter 25

Witch Hunts and White Roses

"Women need no longer be made a party to proceedings which fill the globe with grief and horror."

—Julia Ward Howe, head of Women's International Association, introduced the idea of Mothers' Day, 1872

Although in close touch with my family, the thread of their story remains in the first book. In Book II, I will now concentrate on the political and public aspects of my life, attempting to record the important events and the individuals with whom I have been involved. This is the story of the second half of this century.

The two most important organizations in which I have been involved are the Women's International League for Peace and Freedom (WILPF) and Women Strike for Peace (WSP). We work together for the abolition of war, the peaceful settlement of conflicts through a strengthened United Nations, racial equality, and a more equitable distribution of our national resources.

In *Pioneers for Peace*, 1965, Gertrude Bussey and Margaret Tims have written about WILPF:

This is the story of an unusual group of women during an unusual period of history. In a time of violence they dared to envision and strive for a world free from the ultimate violence of war and oppression. Never numerous, they have exerted an influence well beyond their numbers. They anticipated by 60 years the world's recognition of the importance of women's work in achieving equality, development, and peace.

WILPF, the world's oldest international peace organization, has chapters in thirty-nine countries on all five continents, and more than 120 branches in the US including national headquarters in Philadelphia and the International Office in Geneva. We participate in international symposia throughout the world and enjoy UN Non-Governmental Organization (NGO) status. Since 1945, we have worked ceaselessly against the nuclear threat, social injustice, and environmental degradation. In order to broaden our message, wherever possible, we work with local schools to develop peace-related curricula.

Jane Addams, the founder of WILPF, was a social visionary who started one of the first settlement houses in this country, in Chicago, before the turn of the century. Hull House, as this enterprise was called, functioned as a neighborhood center whose purpose was primarily to serve immigrant and native poor populations; but it soon became embattled in the struggles for immigrant rights, child labor laws, child care, and trade unions. She believed firmly that there could be no peace—domestic or international—without social and economic justice.

In 1915, during World War I, Jane Addams led a group of women on a mission to the Hague, appealing directly to leaders on both sides for an end to the fighting. Unfortunately, their mission was unsuccessful. Later, meeting with President Wilson, Jane Addams was able to convince him of the importance of a number of principles, which came to be known as the "Fourteen Points," which were incorporated in the UN Charter.

When the Democratic National Convention was held in Chicago in August 1996, the name of Jane Addams was invoked several times, yet little effort was made by the delegates to visit the still vital Hull House Center, a short distance away. Hillary Rodham Clinton spoke of parallels between Hull House and the premise of her book, *It Takes a Village*. Both point to the need for community involvement. When Oprah Winfrey started a program to help Chicago families get off welfare, she asked Hull House to administer the project. Our founder's vision is still alive today.

Between the several moves to and from the Valley to the Bay Area, I maintained my contacts with the San Francisco Labor School circle. My friend Peggy Sarasohn, school secretary, had wide social connections. Through her, I came to know avant garde artists and theater people, several of whom would become my friends. Among them were Emmy Lou Packard, protégée of artists Diego Rivera and Frida Kahlo, and Mara Alexander, a leading actress with San Francisco's American Conservatory Theater.

I also learned about the case of Al Naukana, a disabled young Hawaiian member of the International Longshore & Warehouse Union (ILWU), whom noted Bay Area jazz composer Dave Brubeck had met when both were hospitalized on the island. Learning that Al, a paraplegic, had won a college scholarship but lacked funds to take advantage of the award, Brubeck offered to give a benefit concert for him. I chaired the committee that organized the very successful event which enabled Al to fulfill his dream. *San Francisco Chronicle* reporter Jack Foisie wrote that Al was "deserving of any consideration given." I remained in touch with Al for some time, and through this participation, I became well acquainted with Henry Schmidt who, along with Harry Bridges, was one of the founders of the ILWU.

I became more active in WILPF after 1961, when I moved to an upstairs flat on Baker Street, close to San Francisco's Presidio. Hazel Grossman, with whom I would work closely for many decades, had taught at the Labor School. Earlier, she and her husband Aubrey had defied the US State Department by attending the left-wing World Peace Conference in New Delhi, India. One of our initial cooperative efforts was to organize the first Bay Area commemoration of Hiroshima Day, August 6, 1961, with a candlelight vigil held in Aquatic Park. I have participated in every annual Hiroshima commemoration since then.

At this time, there was a great deal of organizing against the dangers of nuclear testing. Leading scientists throughout the world met together in May 1961, at the Oslo Conference Against the Spread of Nuclear Weapons. Noted physicist Linus Pauling, a professor at the California Institute of Technology in Pasadena, was one of the conference conveners. He enjoys the rare distinction of having received two Nobel Prizes, one for Science in 1954, and one for Peace in 1962. He credited his wife, Ava Helen, a WILPF member, for involving him in the anti-war struggle. A WILPF member, Frances Herring, had worked closely with the Paulings to organize the Oslo Conference.

In 1950, the Stockholm Peace Pledge had been formulated calling for a ban on atomic weapons. Locally, Hazel and others, including popular folk singer Barbara Dane, vigorously circulated the Stockholm Peace Pledge, gathering signatures and support. Although millions of names were collected worldwide, this effort did not bring us closer to ending the nuclear arms race. Unfortunately, this appeal was thought to be advanced by socialists, and was ignored by government leaders. Frances had taught philosophy at Vassar College before joining the Institute for Governmental Studies at UCB. While there, she was one of the first faculty to decry the use of nuclear generation for domestic power. She opposed Eisenhower's propaganda about the benefits of the "peaceful atom," and stressed the dangers of *all* nuclear development in her writing.

In 1961, the WILPF organization was proceeding at its usual pace pursuing its goal of a world without war. However, some members felt that since dangers from nuclear testing were mounting, a more immediate response was needed. In September, WILPF member Dagmar Wilson, a well-known children's book illustrator in Washington, DC, convened a handful of women to plan a national strike. They were protesting the resumption of atmospheric nuclear testing, and the inevitable fallout, both literal and figurative. Participants were told that it would be a one-day strike, but eventually this ad-hoc group of activists became Women Strike for Peace (WSP). Demonstrating unusual militancy, they demanded a ban on all testing. They wrote to friends around the country. Among those activated was the fiery New York civil rights attorney Bella Abzug. Others included Ava Helen Pauling and Mary Clarke in Los Angeles. Ethel Taylor was asked to start a group in Philadelphia.

We also began organizing in the Bay Area. Among those who responded to the call were Frances Herring, Elsie Coggins, Frances Shaskan, Hazel Grossman, Leona Bayer, Lenore Job, and myself. Our plan was to stage a national women's march to persuade the heads of local governments to join our test ban campaign. "End the Arms Race not the Human Race" was our call.

On November 1, 1961 60,000 women in sixty cities came out of their kitchens, left their jobs, and descended on city halls and federal buildings throughout the country. This highly-motivated group was comprised mostly of women, many pushing baby carriages. We feared for our children's health, since scientists had tested baby teeth and found traces of radioactive Strontium 90. Breast milk was also under suspicion. We had become shockingly aware of previously unsuspected dangers in milk production. In "hot spot" mid-western states, 160 million residents, including children, were drinking milk containing up to 100 rads of iodine 131 from nuclear fallout. This level—equal to fifty mammograms—was ten times the normal exposure for children, and led to countless cases of thyroid cancer.

About fifty women in San Francisco joined our crusade, calling on a surprised and flustered Mayor George Christopher. Before this event, the nuclear issue had not yet penetrated the public consciousness. *San Francisco Chronicle* columnist Art Hoppe came along on the march and dedicated his next column to us. Later on, he was proud of having been nominated for an honorary membership in Women Strike for Peace.

In the East Bay, women targeted the Berkeley Public Health Department to protest the growing levels of Strontium 90 in the local dairy supply. Activist Dorothy Benson's husband created graphic flyers, including some milk bottle images to illustrate the danger. Following the strike a public meeting was held at Willard Junior High School auditorium, where one of the speakers, Jessica Mitford—Oakland author of the soon to be published book, *The American Way of Death*—wryly commented that "Nuclear fallout would greatly increase the profit potential of the mortuary industry."

At the beginning, WSP was a movement demanding an immediate end to nuclear testing. Although we wanted quick action, it became increasingly clear that this would be a long-term project. Many felt impatient about working through a structured organization such as WILPF, which required some consultation with national headquarters for approval of local actions.

When we decided to form an ongoing organization in the Bay Area, the term, "Women's Strike," seemed a bit too militant to some, and we settled on "Women for Peace," although it is the same organization. In these pages, WSP is synonymous with Women for Peace.

For the first fifteen years, WSP functioned without an official membership list in order to confuse would-be investigators. In spite of this strategy, convener Dagmar Wilson was summoned before the House Un-American Activities Committee in Washington, DC in December 1962. As Amy Swerdlow describes in her history "Women Strike for Peace" the strategies followed by the witnesses ended in turning the spotlight on the investigators and making them a laughingstock. Their forthrightness, their bravado and sincerity made it apparent WSP was not out to overthrow the government; their aim was to end nuclear testing which was threatening their children's health.

A popular cartoon by Herblock inquired "I came in late, which was it that was Un-American—women or peace?" Clearly there was nothing to investigate. We had helped bury them! Not long after, the red-baiting committees died and WSP prevailed.

Concerned about California's increasing dependence on war-related industry, the San Francisco WILPF branch sponsored a conference on Disarmament and the Abundant Life in 1963. As chair of the Program Committee, I signed up a representative from Governor Pat Brown's office and a delegate from the ILWU as well as former Oregon Congressman Charles Porter. A PG&E spokesman withdrew, threatened with the loss of his job—disarmament was a taboo topic. California was protective of its "defense industry," and America was still in the grip of Cold War psychology.

Members of the arch-conservative John Birch Society picketed the event, and a number paid admission to come in and disrupt. "Where's the American flag?" one heckled. A WILPF member brought one forward and the Birchers quieted down. The disarmament issue focused public attention on our group. We were attacked in the Hearst press as a "Communist-front" organization. Subsequently, we organized a delegation, including Ben Seaver, head of the Pacific Mountain Region American Friends Service Committee, and WILPF leader Laurie Sisson, which called on the editor of the *San Francisco Examiner* to complain about the paper's red-baiting policies. One of their writers dashed up to his office, triumphantly returning with the evidence: Jane Addams was listed as a "red" in *Red Channels*, a notorious far-right publication. Luckily, the Nobel Committee, which awarded her the Peace Prize in 1931, had consulted neither the *Examiner* nor Hoover's FBI. We were assured by the editor that we would be advised in advance of any future coverage of our organization.

WILPF women were among the first to point out the dangers in California's heavy reliance on military contracts, which constituted approximately twenty-five percent of the state's total economy. In order to publicize this imbalance, WILPF joined WSP in organizing the first statewide women's peace delegation to Sacramento in 1962. These combined actions continued for several years. We spoke to the governor and to legislators against the "defense industry," which was claiming its large share of government tax revenues. We insisted that funds be directed to preparing industry and training workers for the inevitable shift from the war-related economy to peacetime production. Had our advice been taken, our state might have been better prepared to handle the massive lay-offs and attendant social ills that resulted from base closures and the restructuring of industry.

On a later visit, we found Governor Reagan equally unreceptive. After refusing to see us, he changed his mind when informed of the size of our delegation. Quickly applying makeup for the TV cameras, he made his appearance. Madeline Duckles and Mary Clarke argued with him about our state's role in the military effort. Neither side was swayed—we had failed to pierce the governor's "teflon shield."

That year, 1963, I was a delegate to the WSP conference in Bryn Mawr, Pennsylvania. During this three-day gathering, we worked to establish the group's policy, considering dilemmas such as whether we should struggle against the war which was heating up in Vietnam or confine our activities to halting nuclear testing. We decided to do both.

On a visit to New York City for another WSP conference, I ran into Bella Abzug in the lobby of the Chelsea Hotel. I joked with her: "Well, I guess you're not entirely satisfied with the proceedings of the WSP conference?" She responded, "I'm never satisfied. We need to do more!" That was Bella. Unhappy with some of the restrained debate which had taken place, Bella visualized a group of full-blown radicals, ready to take to the streets.

That same year, we demonstrated at the Palace Hotel in San Francisco against the visit of the notorious Madame Nhu, sister-in-law of US ally President Diem of South Vietnam. At this event, we were reinforced by a number of Young Democrats, a sign that more middle-of-the-roaders were climbing on the anti-war bandwagon. I was at the head of the picket line when a man confronted me: "Why aren't you home taking care of your children?"

A flattering comment, since by then, my children were quite old enough to take care of themselves.

WSP's efforts were acknowledged by President Kennedy in 1963, two years after the one-day strike. As he observed the rain-drenched WSP women marching by the White House he commented, "I get their message." WSP's dramatic flair had paid off. Shortly thereafter, he signed the Partial Test Ban Treaty with the Soviet Union. Science Advisor Jerome Weisner credited WSP, the Committee for a Sane Nuclear Policy, and Linus Pauling with having had the most influence on the president in his decision to sign the treaty, more than the arms controllers within the government. Tragically, that same year witnessed the president's assassination.

Over the years, the lines between WSP and WILPF have blurred. In the Bay Area we work closely together and a number of women, including myself, are active members of both. For four decades, we have walked, talked, demonstrated, lobbied, petitioned, written, voted and acted. During the Vietnam War, starting in the early days of the movement, our women's peace groups sent delegations to Geneva, Vancouver, NATO headquarters, Djkarta, Accra, and North Vietnam, where our members met with the women of other countries to discuss ways to stop the fighting. Many of the original WSP branches no longer exist, as members have gone on to other organizations. Although WILPF has maintained its presence in San Francisco, the WSP activity has been continued through the National Legislative Office in Washington, DC. The organization's newsletter, *Legislative Alert*, is sent to branches and individual subscribers, recommending action on hot issues and procedures for contacting our national and state representatives on peace, environmental, and justice concerns. The WILPF legislative office works closely with WSP on issues of common concern.

Chapter 26

Black Panthers and People's Temple

"There was nothing too bizarre...[we were] always trying to think of something that would arouse the people to what was going on."

—ASH, interviewed by Tom Wells in *The War Within*, 1994

By the mid-sixties, the war against Vietnam was heating up. The fifth floor of the International Building at 50 Oak Street in San Francisco served as the combined headquarters for WSP and WILPF. By this time, we were cooperating in all our activities under the aegis of the Womens Peace Office, which became a center of planning for various anti-war mobilizations, marches, demonstrations, and sit-ins. Hazel generally managed the office, assisted by Eleanor Ohman, and was responsible for the monthly *WSP Newsletter* which kept members informed of all activities and helped attract new people. The task of spokesperson fell to me.

To raise funds for both WSP and WILPF, we published frequent appeals. Since Hazel was primarily interested in building the WSP organization, and I was concerned in keeping the WILPF membership up-to-date, I pounded away at my Smith-Corona, working on its newsletter. I was able to persuade my neighbor, "Bo" Bogardus, to duplicate it on his trusty mimeograph—cranking out copies by hand. We were continuously answering telephone inquiries, and staging demonstrations. Events included nighttime marches, candlelight processions, and church memorials, where we read the growing lists of war casualties from Vietnam.

Nothing was too extreme for us. We were always trying to think of something that would motivate more people. For us, civil action was like breathing or feeding our children. There was no alternative. However, many members felt family pressures; younger women were tied to their children's schedules and volunteer time was precious. Hazel and I were in the fortunate position of being able to dedicate ourselves full time to these efforts, since our children were grown.

Times were changing. In the beginning, there were some attempts to portray WSP as an organization of *young* women, which pushed aside the older members. Over the years, we have managed to counter such efforts by "hanging in there," while many of the younger women left in pursuit of other interests. The non-working mother was a typical, white middle-class phenomenon. They could organize their community activities around family responsibilities while their husbands were at work. Single mothers and working-class women did not enjoy such freedom.

I addressed businessmen's groups, Sproul Plaza audiences at UCB, and various school assemblies, including several in the Catholic Archdiocese of San Francisco. At one time I followed the Archbishop to the podium. I was heard frequently on radio station KPFA, and presented public service messages on various San Francisco radio and television stations. Billboards throughout the Bay Area carried the now famous WSP slogan, *End the Arms Race, Not the Human Race*. Billboards at freeway entrances and city off-ramps confronted drivers with our message. Starting in 1963, we also collected funds for newspaper ads and bus displays, raising thousands of dollars for this campaign against the Vietnam War. Local East Bay buses accepted our ads only after our successful legal battle against the AC Transit District.

We organized demonstrations at the Concord Naval Weapons Station at nearby Port Chicago where bombs and other weaponry were being shipped out to war zones. This Bay Area port was a den of activism, drawing demonstrators from around the world.

We even extended our struggle to shopping centers. In 1964, our "No More War Toys Committee" was influential in stopping Sears, Macy's, and the Emporium from featuring guns and other war toys in San Francisco stores. That year, anti-war activity was heating up at the university. Mario Savio made his historic "Free Speech" proclamation protesting the corporatization of the university in his famous admonition delivered from the top of a police car, "There's a time when the operation of the machine becomes so odious, it makes you sick at heart...You've got to put your bodies on the gears...You've got to make it stop." I felt drawn to return to the scene of such activity, and in mid-1965, moved back to Berkeley, with its tree-lined streets and abundance of flowers. However, I continued to commute, since the locus of my major activities remained in San Francisco. In the First International Days of Protest, on October 15, 1965, we marched, fourteen thousand strong, from Berkeley toward the Oakland Army Terminal. We were attacked by the police at the Oakland border and there were many arrests. Later, some protesters lay on the railroad tracks in an attempt to stop the trains loaded with troops traveling north to the training camps. Fortunately, no one was killed.

In 1965, our Women's Peace Office played an important role in forming an early anti-war coalition in the Bay Area: The Committee to End American Intervention in Vietnam. The same year, Helen Rand Miller, a retired college teacher and WILPF member, initiated a national letter-writing campaign to the Johnson administration and Congress which lasted until the end of the war. The National Committee organized the first big anti-war march on Washington, April 17, 1965.

In San Francisco, WILPF conducted anti-war vigils and began weekly Saturday afternoon leafleting at Union Square—a ritual that continued from 1966 through 1972. On June 19, 1970, Beverly Koch published a full-page story about us in the *San Francisco Chronicle* entitled "The 55-Year Drive for Peace."

"The women," she wrote, "ranged from their early 20s to their early 80s." There were young teachers and students, as well as the recently retired physicians Leona Bayer and Ernst Wolff. We engaged many shoppers and tourists, and occasionally military people from the US as well as other countries in spirited conversation. Many passers-by accepted our leaflets and signed petitions which called for an end to the war. International travelers were amazed to discover this degree of public dissent in America.

As the Vietnam War escalated, young men were refusing to register for the draft. We raised funds for Hazel's husband, Aubrey, who helped young men in their efforts to avoid the draft. Since the preponderance of those drafted were from disadvantaged, mainly minority, segments of the population, several of us pressed for the inclusion of civil rights issues in our agenda. We were able to win support from some African American mothers, thus broadening our appeal.

Hazel and I represented the San Francisco women's peace movement in all the anti-Vietnam War activities, including the planning of large events.

Anti-war sentiment continued to grow. Ever responsive to the marches and demonstrations on the East Coast, and seeking new allies, a core group of several dozen people kept busy planning corresponding events in Berkeley and San Francisco: "Stop the Draft Week," the "Nuclear Freeze," the "Mobilization to End the War," the "Spring Mobilization," and others.

We kept close tabs on everything. Our determination to help end the senseless, cruel war was what saved us from total exhaustion. We hired Marylouise Lovett, to help with the huge work load involved in planning the marches.

May 1966 heralded the first Vietnam Day Teach-In at the University of California at Berkeley (UCB). It was thrilling to see Sproul Plaza filled with eager participants. Every available inch of space was occupied all day. I remember an attractive young mother with a baby carriage—she would later become Berkeley's popular mayor, Loni Hancock. In a newspaper interview some years later, Loni credited WSP with having inspired her political involvement. There was a tremendous feeling of solidarity among the crowd.

In San Francisco, we helped plan the "First International Days of Protest," which was well-attended. In the effort to understand the interconnectedness of war and racial repression, we invited speakers like Ralph Abernathy, a Southern Christian Leadership Conference associate of Dr. Martin Luther King, Jr., and Fannie Lou Hamer, a member of the "Alternate" Mississippi Delegation to the 1968 Democratic Party Convention. A humble timekeeper, Hamer had been beaten and jailed in her efforts to register fellow sharecroppers (to vote); she ended up as a strong national leader.

Whenever major events were planned in Washington or New York, we would coordinate local efforts for same-day actions. Joining us at this time was the American Friends Service Committee (AFSC), and other groups. As pacifists, the Friends had been loath to engage with political activist groups, but after some hesitation, they were finally willing to work with us. We were pleased when Trevor Thomas, then employed by the Friends Committee on Legislation (FCL), began attending our meetings. He often served as a moderating influence. We were also joined by labor delegates, including members of the ILWU, which broadened the movement. The Young Democrats, unlike the Democratic Party, were willing participants, in spite of President Johnson's hawkish official policy.

The women's peace movement opposed the use of napalm bombs, which leave a highly flammable petroleum residue, causing horrible burns. In some of our campaigns, gas masks, coffins, and the graphic representation of injured children were used to inform the public about the terrible reality of war. In 1967 we took a delegation, including several community people, to call on the chairman of Dow Chemical Company in San Francisco. In answer to our protests, the reply was, "Dow is simply filling government orders."

Did Dow ever consider the victims?

Madeline Duckles, one of our most active WILPF members, was involved with the Committee of Responsibility. COR, created in 1967 to bring war-injured Vietnamese children—many of them victims of napalm attacks—to this country for medical treatment, including plastic surgery. Physicians donated their time and expertise, and money was raised to cover other expenses. Madeline arranged transportation and helped to locate homes for the injured children during the course of treatment. In 1968, she took a young Vietnamese girl, Thuy Nyugen, into her own household. Thuy had suffered severe facial injuries during a rocket attack. She returned to Vietnam as stipulated by the agreement that the children would be sent home after recovery. However, some host families were reluctant to part with their charges. After twenty years and a great deal of correspondence in both English and Vietnamese, Thuy returned to Berkeley to live in the Duckles home. She has since married and is currently employed in Berkeley and considers Madeline her mother.

During "Stop the Draft Week," Oct. 16-20, 1967, there was a march and sit-in at the Oakland Induction Center. Joan Baez and her mother, and Kay Boyle, a WILPF member and a leader of the San Francisco State strike, were among those arrested and sent to Santa Rita Detention Center. Kay, a well-known writer, won the admiration of the students for her confrontation with San Francisco State College President Sessue I. Hayakawa, who became a US senator. Kay also distinguished herself with a unique protest against the war, maintaining a lonely vigil outside the local mortuary, where body bags with servicemen's remains were being pieced together for shipment home. Dressed completely in black, she drew intense media attention. Her act recalled the Women in Black demonstration at the Pentagon in 1965, organized by WSP and WILPF, when hundreds of women from the peace movement were arrested.

In April, 1967, fifty thousand people turned out for a San Francisco march, filling Market Street from the Embarcadero to Civic Center. Coretta Scott King and Rita Moreno, the Hollywood peace activist, were among the speakers. Abraham Feinberg, formerly the rabbi at Holy Blossom Temple in Toronto, Canada, also took the podium. He accentuated his points by waving a beautifully carved walking stick, given to him by North Vietnamese President Ho Chi Minh when he was on an unauthorized mission to North Vietnam.

On the East Coast, controversy surrounded the choice of black militant Stokely Carmichael as a speaker at the big march in New York. Dr. Martin Luther King, Jr. was the spokesman featured at the New York event. I first heard Dr. King in the mid-50s when he spoke at UCB's Wheeler Hall. I was impressed, even though he had not yet become the commanding figure who would "transform America from an apartheid state into a true democracy of all hues." The Montgomery, Alabama Bus Strike had begun and he was the newly-ordained minister at the Dexter Avenue Baptist Church in that city, where his father had also preached.

Speaking at New York's Riverside Church in 1967, Dr. King warned, "The bombs we drop in Vietnam are exploding on the streets of America." The effects were palpable. Some liberal groups as well as many African American church people criticized him severely for stepping out of his civil rights role. He was questioned: "If you're leading the bus boycott and trying to help your brothers and sisters, why are you going on about the war, why muddy the waters?" Nevertheless, King courageously persisted in combining the anti-war and civil rights struggles. This speech is thought to have triggered the conspiracy which led to his assassination.

Although large public anti-war meetings had been taking place in San Francisco and other cities in the 60s, there was a feeling that it was imperative to enlist more communities in the effort, especially African Americans. Since Dr. King was planning a National Poor People's March on Washington, we decided to conduct a rally in the Oakland Coliseum, to generate support, featuring him as speaker. I joined Joan Baez and her sister, Mimi Fariña, as well as several African American leaders, on the *ad hoc* planning committee. In addition to Dr. King, the tall, charismatic Harry Belafonte, and the popular singer Sammy Davis, Jr., were headlined. These two performers were dedicated to King and the Civil Rights cause. We were somewhat disappointed that the crowd, although enthusiastic, did not quite fill the huge coliseum. Support for the march on Washington was developing but a great deal more effort would be required to turn the tide toward peace.

Nineteen sixty-eight was a frantic year. At first, we felt as though we were making progress, as more and more people were joining the peace movement. But the war was not over. In April we were stunned by the news of Martin Luther King, Jr.'s assassination. Ever involved in the struggle to improve the lot of the most exploited, he had turned his attention to the poorly-paid sanitation workers in Memphis, Tennessee. They were experiencing difficulty in organizing and King was there to intercede on their behalf. After checking into his hotel room, he walked out on the porch for a breath of air. Suddenly, an assassin's bullet from across the street cut him down. His death sparked riots all over the country. Cities were burning. This great leader had lived and died for the cause of peace and justice for all people. Who knows what he might have accomplished, had he lived. I feel privileged to have had close contact with such a warm, humane individual. A photograph of the two of us is among my prized possessions.

Another tragedy took place that year. In June, while campaigning for the Democratic presidential nomination, Bobby Kennedy was shot down in a Los Angeles hotel. The younger brother of then-deceased President Kennedy, had been demonstrating a deepening awareness of the inequities in our society, involving himself in Cesar Chavez' struggle for the farmworkers in our state. In my opinion, Bobby would have surpassed his brother in achievement, had he lived.

1968 was also the year of the Democratic Convention in Chicago, a bloody affair in which Mayor Daley's police viciously attacked the demonstrators outside, mostly young people. Frustrated at the willingness of party leaders to maintain the status quo, the protesters were representative of the country's rising disapproval of the government's involvement in the Vietnam War. Television images of the violence stirred the entire nation, and Richard Nixon was elected over Hubert Humphrey on his promise to end the war. However, the conflict dragged on for six more years.

Our peace coalition, ever on the lookout for new activists, enlisted young stockbrokers on a "No Business as Usual" day in downtown San Francisco. We staffed tables and collected signatures to our petitions demanding an end to the fighting. It was essential to attract new members, since many of our "old timers" were aging and becoming less involved. Anci Koppel—the original organizer of Seattle Women Act for Peace—humorously wrote about the "slowing down syndrome affecting us all." Many potential recruits—young women and some not so young, were responding instead to the lure of feminist, environmental, and other political action groups.

With regional, ideological, and other differences among people in the peace coalition, it was inevitable that problems would arise. For example, planners of the New York events had an approach somewhat different from ours. Throughout the 70s, they sent representatives to attempt to influence the direction of our campaigns. In the Bay Area the moderates prevailed and concentrated on ending the devastating war. More radical groups agitated for the North Vietnamese to *keep fighting* against US intervention. Infiltrating our meetings, they did their best to gain control, pressing for speakers who represented their more doctrinaire, leftist approach. They argued against such slogans as "Negotiate Now," and were willing to see the fighting continue in the hopes that Communist North Vietnamese could win. There was a real struggle to keep this faction out of our executive meetings; at one of these, the effort to exclude them almost led to blows.

Among the *ad hoc* leaders of the anti-war effort was attorney-activist Terence "Kayo" Hallinan, currently the San Francisco District Attorney. To broaden our appeal, he suggested that we involve the militant Black Panthers. Karen Talbot, recently returned to the East Bay from Helsinki, Finland, where she had served as secretary of the World Peace Council, was our liaison with the Panthers organization. In spite of some opposition, she was able to gain approval for one of their leaders, David Hilliard, as speaker at the next rally. The selection of spokespeople for public programs always involved a tug-of-war between the factions.

Despite its growing pains, the peace movement continued to attract a changing and colorful cast of characters, including celebrities Jane Fonda and her husband, Tom Hayden, former Students for Democratic Society (SDS) leader. Jane, forthright and very approachable, was at times referred to as "Hanoi Jane" by the popular press and was castigated for her anti-war activities. Tom was goal-driven and efficient. Together, they were a persuasive anti-war force. They helped raise funds by lending their considerable celebrity to the cause. Later, they participated in a billboard campaign, traveling from Los Angeles with their infant, Troy. I remember holding the baby at some of our meetings.

By 1971 the movement was joined in larger numbers by religious groups, and meetings were held in churches and synagogues. Thus, we encountered the enigmatic Jim Jones of People's Temple in San Francisco. The Alliance for Survival, one of the many variations of our ongoing anti-war activities, held a big meeting at Glide Memorial Church that year. Jim Jones had become a strong supporter of our peace coalition, and brought busloads of followers from his Northern California commune in Redwood Valley. We were pleased to have a crowd, but noticed that the Temple members, including entire families, seemed oddly regimented and disciplined. They marched directly in, filling up the front rows, scarcely looking from left to right.

I was in charge of the collection and remember that Jones later thrust a wad of large denomination bills into my hand with the comment, "Well, they're going to take it away from me anyway, so you might as well use it for a good cause." Stunned by the gesture, I wondered how he might have accumulated that much money from his low-income congregation? Not only did he attract poor African American families, but also some non-minority, educated professionals. Retired people among them willingly turned over their social security checks. This was my first encounter with Jones' growing paranoia, which he would eventually direct at his own followers.

In the early days, Jones was well-received in The City, yet disturbing reports began to circulate in the press, hinting at his instability. Not long after the Glide meeting, we were shocked at the news that he had moved his flock to Guyana, a remote location in South America—the beginning of a long and terrifying ordeal for them. Temple members wrote home about hardships, restraints on their freedom, and Jones' increasingly autocratic and paternalistic behavior.

A congressional committee headed by the Bay Area's Leo Ryan and his secretary Jackie Speier, now a member of the State Legislature, flew to Guyana to investigate. Shockingly, Congressman Ryan was murdered, his secretary and several others wounded, and a mass suicide followed, engineered by Jim Jones. Imagine the kind of power that could coerce mothers to force poison-laced Kool-aid on their children?

The People's Temple story was particularly poignant to me because of the involvement of my former Berkeley neighbor Lisa Layton, who had joined along with her daughter and son. The incident had tragic consequences for Lisa's family. Her son Larry, one of Jones' bodyguards, was charged with Ryan's shooting and the wounding of his aide and remains in prison today. Lisa died of cancer ten days before the massacre. Her daughter, Deborah, absent from the compound that fateful day, now lives in the Bay Area. Her book, *Seductive Poison, a Jonestown Survivor's Story,* published in 1998, offers insights into the frightening manner in which Jones exercised control.

I believe this kind of event occurred because of the strong need people have for a sense of community, especially during politically turbulent times. This tragedy is just an indication of how vulnerable people are to insidious influences. Many of the poor in Jones' church had recently lost their homes in a massive redevelopment program in San Francisco's Fillmore District. Uprooted and unhappy, they were looking for something, or someone, to believe in.

In contrast to cult influence, we in the peace movement have been sustained by our concern for all humanity and respect for differences. We are working to create a society where individual rights are preserved. Despite our diverse points of view, we are learning to work together. In the words of WILPF'er Leona Bayer, "Surprisingly I discover that happiness is a sort of habit learned [by] sharing...Another habit is to join with others in seeking non-violent ways to build a global society which is saner, cheerier, more just and promising. May we succeed!"

Chapter 27

The War Finally Ends

"The ultimate weakness of violence is that it is a descending spiral, begetting the very thing it seeks to destroy. Instead of diminishing evil, it multiplies it. Returning violence for violence multiplies violence...Darkness cannot drive out darkness; only light can do that. Hate cannot drive out hate; only love can do that."

—Rev. Martin Luther King, Jr.

On March 8, 1968, WILPF celebrated International Women's Day by launching "Feed the Cities, Not the Pentagon" program. In the effort to bring about a change in national priorities, we gave out catchy, oversized, "Feed the Cities" buttons which always elicited comments and questions. The culmination of the "Feed the Cities" plan was a march on the nation's capitol. On January 15, 1968, five thousand women trudged silently through the snow to the White House, carrying our message. Dressed in black, they were led by Jeannette Rankin, an eighty-seven-year-old former Montana legislator, the first woman elected to Congress. An anti-war activist, she had voted against US participation in both world wars.

San Francisco WILPF leader Vivian Hallinan traveled to the east coast to help organize the national campaign. A civil-rights activist, she along with her sons, had been arrested at a sit-in during the "Cadillac Row" demonstrations of the 60s. As a result, San Francisco's auto dealers were forced to break the "color line" and employ African Americans as sales representatives.

Women were attracted to the Jeannette Rankin Brigade because it consciously united the issues of war and poverty, reaching across race and class issues. Rankin, a former suffragist, served as the link between the earlier pacifist-feminist-suffragist generation and younger women. Using the Rankin Brigade march to insert feminist demands into the struggle for peace, we tried to build a mass movement. We wanted our sisters to become more politically active. We wanted to convince government leaders to fund social programs. Following the Brigade march, we realized that more concentrated efforts were needed to bring a change in national priorities.

In August 1970, we marked the 25th Anniversary of the bombing of Hiroshima. This was the first of an ongoing series of demonstrations and protests at the Lawrence Livermore Lab, where nuclear weaponry research was continuing under the aegis of the University of California at Berkeley. Should our university serve as an arm of the military? We said "No!" and leafleted Lab workers to that effect. In this, we were joined by environmentalists and several UC physicists. One of them, Nobel Laureate Owen Chamberlain, had helped build the bomb. But years later, realizing its awesome, destructive potential, he joined our forces, making his expertise on nuclear issues available. Chamberlain accompanied us to Sacramento on a lobbying trip, where he gave testimony that backed up our opposition to increased "defense" spending and echoed the dangers of nuclear development.

We relished the success that came with the signing of the Anti-Ballistic Missile (ABM) treaty in 1972, to protect the US against long range guided missiles. Our office had campaigned extensively in its favor. Unfortunately, this treaty would be threatened years later by Reagan's "Star Wars" fantasy. As often happens, unenlightened schemes can enjoy a life of their own. Although impractical, every Congressional session hears proposals for some version of "this perfect defense," which, unfortunately, our representatives insist on continuing to fund.

When a US-Vietnam peace agreement was signed in Paris in 1973, WILPF women, including US Section President Marii Hasegawa, were invited to Saigon by the Vietnamese Women's Union to celebrate the event, as the war continued to wind down. Nixon finally admitted defeat in the face of massive protests and street demonstrations. Threatened with impeachment over the Watergate break-in scandal, he resigned in 1974. Two years after the peace treaty was signed, the war finally drew to a close. Congress cut off funding and the last Americans were run out of Saigon.

In 1974, the San Francisco's Women's Peace Office decided to form the Coalition to Cut Military Spending. We planned a large community meeting at Marina Junior High School in November with Jack Massen as chair. He and his wife Minerva were Bay Area peace activists involved with the UN. Our main speaker was Rear Admiral Gene LaRocque, former Navy Commander of the Pacific Fifth Fleet, who had just started the Center for

Defense Information (CDI) in Washington, DC. The CDI, an active Pentagon watchdog group, now includes other retired generals and admirals alarmed at the escalating arms race. The Center produces a weekly TV program on the US military and publishes *The Defense Monitor.*

At the same time, a number of Japanese activists were visiting San Francisco on their way home from a UN conference. These members of the Japan Council Against the A and H Bombs were a left-leaning peace group headed by the eccentric Reverend Sato, a former Kamikaze pilot who defied authorities by taking up residence in a pagoda at the busy Tokyo airport. I felt they would add interest to our meeting and wanted to introduce them to the audience. But the Admiral warned that his Advisory Board prohibited his appearance on the same platform as the "radical" Japanese. Since the visitors ended up in our auditorium, I felt it was only courteous to introduce them. To my amazement, I discovered later that, far from being enemies, Reverend Sato and Admiral LaRocque were actually old friends. After the meeting, these "enemies" spent several cordial evenings together discussing their wartime experiences.

In 1974, Michael Klare—a leader in the Columbia University anti-war movement of the 60's and a Bay Area writer/activist—and I demonstrated outside the Federal Building in San Francisco, protesting the treatment of the Viet Cong by the South Vietnamese Army. These prisoners were confined in tiny bamboo "tiger cages," too small for them to stand. Michael would later be appointed to lead the Peace and World Security Studies program at Hampshire College. He is an authority on the US military arsenal, as well as defense contributor to *The Nation* magazine, and has appeared on the *MacNeal/Lehrer NewsHour.* On Michael's visit to the Bay Area, I had the pleasure of presenting him with a memento of our collaboration, a "tiger cage" photo. He chuckled at the thought of sharing it with his son, Alex. "This is what your Dad looked like with long hair." During the early days of the Mobilization to End the War ('The Mobe'), Daniel Ellsberg, of "Pentagon Papers" fame, helped us strategize. Later, he traveled east to set up the Manhattan II Project, developed under the aegis of Physicians for Social Responsibility (PSR). The purpose was to concentrate the same effort into eliminating *all* nuclear weapons as had been directed toward the creation of the original bomb.

At an anniversary celebration of the San Francisco Women's Peace office, Frances Herring called for a "joyous, visible, national action" to recharge the movement with the same spirit which helped end the Vietnam War. It was clear that the peace movement would now need to develop new strategies. With the end of the war in Vietnam, we could now concentrate on eliminating the nuclear threat.

In 1975 I was elected to the WILPF National Board and represented them at the White House Public Forum on Domestic Policy chaired by Vice-President Nelson Rockefeller and held in Los Angeles. I protested our overspending on the military at the expense of society's deepest needs. In response, Rockefeller wrote: "It is encouraging to hear incisive proposals from people all across the nation as we have done in these forums...Your comments are being given full consideration...[Thank you] for your important contribution to our domestic policy review." As with so many of these hearings, the reality is in the carrying out. It is obvious that although we helped bring an end to the war we have not brought an end to the militarization of our government.

In 1976, WSP conducted a national drive, installing large billboards with the message "The Nuclear Arms Race Can Make This the Last Generation." The campaign aroused much interest in the Bay Area, New York, Chicago, and other cities. Locally, we worked hard to raise funds to blanket the Bay Area with our message. To further publicize the horrors of nuclear warfare, we obtained permission to exhibit Hiroshima/Nagasaki murals by Japanese artists. These murals, depicting the destructiveness of the bomb, were displayed at San Francisco City Hall and won considerable press attention.

The anti-nuclear movement continued to gather steam, at that time under the banner of "The Nuclear Freeze," a 1979 campaign initiated by SANE—the nation's largest peace organization, which included prestigious groups such as the Conference of Catholic Bishops. The Freeze was supported by a number of celebrities including Hollywood actor Ed Asner, who played an active role. According to *The Nation* correspondent John Tirman, the "Freeze" was the catalyst which brought about the end of the decades-long cold war. A number of us took advantage of the opportunity to promote our programs by presenting "free speech" messages on Bay Area TV and radio stations. My son Aron, who was living in Los Baños, was delighted to see his mother on TV.

On August 6, 1979, at the West Gate of UCB, we joined dedicated Quaker leader Margaret Olney and others in a silent vigil to recall the awesome event at Hiroshima. These one-hour vigils, called the "Circle of Concern," have continued at this location every Thursday and Sunday, a remarkable achievement. One year, vigilers were so numerous that we ringed the entire campus. From the beginning, WSP, WILPF, and religious activists have supported the vigils. We provide colorful signs for demonstrators and form a "silent billboard" for peace. Invariably, passers-by indicate support by honking their car horns. Volunteers are recruited, information is exchanged, petitions are circulated, and signatures are gathered on special commemorative days.

In the East Bay, our next effort was to organize Survival Summer, which included women's groups, environmentalists, and minorities. Our slogans were "Stop the Arms Race," and "Stop Nuclear Production and Testing." We were demonstrating the lethal connections between the military budget, inflation, and unemployment.

In 1980 I spoke before the UC Regents against the University's role in the operation of the Livermore Lab. In spite of all the protests, nuclear work continues at the Lab under the direction of the University. In 1984 several hundred protesters were arrested and confined for two weeks, the women segregated in a large tent at the Santa Rita Detention Center. Among the detainees were WILPF members Ethel Sanjines and Marge Frantz. Marge had taken time from her Women's Studies teaching at UC Santa Cruz to organize lectures and discussions on women's and civil rights issues. These arrests coincided with the 1984 San Francisco celebration of Hazel Grossman's seventieth birthday, planned by Ethel and me. We had no idea that so many of those invited would be incarcerated, including Ethel herself, but we were delighted when Hazel received a birthday telegram from Santa Rita signed by Ethel and others. The "inmates" were released after several weeks.

Another mutation of our anti-nuclear coalition was the Alliance for Survival. As chair of an Alliance meeting in Oakland in 1986, I had the privilege of introducing Dr. Helen Caldicott to our community. Dr. Caldicott, a pediatrician and Australian peace leader, had alerted her government to the dangers of ships transporting nuclear materials in offshore waters. When this beautiful young woman, looking more like a student than a medical specialist, took a seat at the front of the room, I cautioned, "These chairs are for the speakers." Imagine my chagrin when the "student" rose and, with her pronounced Australian accent, began her talk. She so inspired the group that the Bay Area physicians present, led by Leona Bayer: Peter Joseph and Phil Shapiro, decided to reactivate the local Physicians for Social Responsibility (PSR) chapter. This prestigious group lent medical as well as social credibility to the anti-nuclear campaign. This East Bay meeting helped launch Dr. Caldicott's career as a spokesperson against all nuclear development, for which she is known throughout the world. She was elected National President of PSR. Currently, she is a National WILPF Sponsor.

Demonstrations against the Livermore Lab, the Concord Weapons Station, and the Nevada Test Site continued. In 1987 WSP member Evelyn Velson and I helped coordinate the East Bay contingent of the huge Mother's Day demonstration at the Nevada site, which drew several thousand. Native Americans participated in significant numbers. Patricia Ellsberg, wife of Daniel Ellsberg, joined their impassioned protests against the defiling of "Mother Earth" by continuing nuclear explosions.

After the Vietnam War, peace activists began paying more attention to our government's intervention in Central America, particularly Guatemala, El Salvador, and Nicaragua, after the leftist Sandinistas overthrew the corrupt Somoza dictatorship in 1979. In the 1980s we joined with other groups, such as The Committee for Health Rights in Central America, which were working against US efforts to destabilize the new regime. We erected thirty-three billboards on El Salvador, eight of them in the Bay Area. We also supported the Sanctuary Movement, headed by Berkeley's Bishop Gus Schultz, of the University Lutheran Chapel. This effort provided safe haven for many who were fleeing persecution in Central American countries.

During this period, there were protests at Port Chicago against the shipment of weapons to Central America. At the height of the demonstrations one of the protesters, Vietnam War veteran Brian Willson, lay down on the tracks hoping to stop the train. Instead, his legs were amputated—another tragedy of the war. Willson, a former army pilot, continues his anti-war activities.

In reflecting on the series of anti-nuclear demonstrations, the one I am most pleased to recall took place in 1982 in New York City. A million people spilled into the streets in the largest demonstration ever, ending up in Central Park. My daughter Tanya, who was visiting there with her children, David and Julie, reported the thrill they experienced in joining this flood of protesters. It seemed my daughter was beginning to interest herself in the movements about which I cared so passionately.

Chapter 28

China to Babi Yar

"Since wars begin in the minds of men, it is in the minds of men that the defenses of peace must be built..."

—The Charter of United Nations Educational Scientific
and Cultural Organization (UNESCO)

As the child of immigrants, I had a desire to see the land of my parents. I had already traveled to South Africa to visit my mother's relatives but I was interested in understanding social conditions in other countries and garnering a sense of how US influence is manifested worldwide. Beginning in the fifties, I managed to visit Israel, Europe, China, the USSR, Japan, Thailand, India, Malaysia, Mexico, and Cuba. During my travels, I have attempted to connect with peace forces in those countries.

While visiting my friends Henry and Olive Mayer of Woodside, California, I learned that they had undertaken a project in citizen diplomacy, which would result in exchange visits with women from the Soviet Union. In 1961, I joined them in forming the Committee for Friendly International Visits (CFIV). After lengthy negotiations with the State Department, we won approval for eight Soviet women to visit this country as our guests. I helped arrange homestays for them. Members of San Francisco society responded warmly, eager to sign up as hosts.

One of our committee members, a Monterey restaurateur, obtained the cooperation of the St. Francis Hotel in hosting a gala reception for our guests. Five hundred people attended, many prominent and influential individuals among them. A *San Francisco Chronicle* editor called, asking to bring his Russian-born parents. One of the hotel owners invited our party for a day-long yacht cruise on the Bay.

In 1962, the Soviet Women's Committee reciprocated, inviting several of us to visit the USSR. En route, I joined a tour group traveling through France and Italy. When I divulged my final destination as the USSR, they were incredulous, but promised to pray for my safe return. They did not trust the Russians. These tourists also insisted on visiting every cathedral along our route. After viewing hundreds of religious icons, I longed for a more contemporary art experience.

Our delegation spent over two weeks in the USSR, traveling to different regions, including Armenia, Moscow, and Riga. Leningrad, which we visited, had been under German siege for three years during WW II, and the population had suffered terrible starvation and widespread death. Somber moments were spent at their famous war cemetery. Fortunately, the Russians had protected their wonderful art treasures, which we were able to enjoy. Members of the delegation whom we had hosted on their trip to the US met us. Maria Ovsyennikova, Editor-in-Chief of *Soviet Woman*, and one of our hosts, had fought in the war, in which her husband was killed. We visited her and her daughter, Vera, in their homes.

The trip was not without its disappointments. People were extremely rigid in their thinking. As staunch supporters of the government, they saw no weaknesses either in communism or the Soviet system. Few women sat in the Russian parliament, the Duma. The most prominent female in the government was the Minister of Culture, Madame Ekaterina Furtseva, a close friend of Kruschev.

One of our members, Grace McClatchy, was born in Russia while her father, George Kennan, served as US ambassador. He was the author of the State Department's Containment Program, an important feature of our Cold War policy. Gracious and attractive, she had joined our group as interpreter but appeared more interested in improving her Russian than attempting to translate for us.

I wanted to get as close as possible to my mother's birthplace in Lithuania, but had to settle for Riga, Latvia, where I met some interesting people. One was a young Jew, an employee of the radio station where members of our delegation were interviewed. Later, he and I spoke in Yiddish, which often serves as a universal language for Jews. I was shocked to hear of the extreme repression under which local Jews were suffering. He risked his job to talk with me; the government forbade such frank discussion about social matters with foreigners.

We also traveled to Yerevan, the capital of Armenia. Each place we stopped was different. There was an unusual routine in the hotels: every time we came in, our room keys had to be retrieved from a caretaker seated on every floor. Was this surveillance or service?

By coincidence, we met Lionel Steinberg, a friend of my husband's from the San Joaquin Valley, who was leading a group of California ranchers through the Soviet Union. Also in his plans was a trip to China with some American farmers. He invited me to come along, but that trip never materialized. I did not get to China until several years later.

After leaving the Soviet Union, Olive Mayer, now joined by her fourteen-year- old daughter Judy, and I continued on our travels around the world. Ollie had arranged meetings with several peace groups along the way. In India, we were welcomed by people from the peace movement. As a result of my complaints about the spicy hotel food, we were given the opportunity of sampling some home-cooked meals. To my dismay, I found them equally spicy to my mid-western taste buds. We toured locally with our Indian hosts, and were captivated by the beauty of the Taj Mahal. The destitute people begging in the streets provided an unhappy contrast to this exquisite, world-famous structure. Although social stratification exists in America, theoretically our public education system offers children of the poor an opportunity to improve their lot. In India, it was virtually impossible for lower-caste individuals to change their situation.

Thailand was next on our itinerary, a country of many temples, resplendent with glittering, tile-covered walls which I photographed avidly. In contrast, Bangkok's main streets overflowed with noisy traffic and pollution, the results of too-rapid industrialization. Ollie, the conservationist, pointed out the effects of runaway industry on the people's health.

In Japan, we were hosted by a number of anti-nuclear activists. We held conversations with labor representatives, mainly women, and with Tokyo University faculty, including a leading legal scholar, Professor Yasui. Intensely interested in fostering peace, the group engaged us in many lively discussions. The dangers of war, particularly nuclear attacks, were close to the surface in that country. Later, we enjoyed a tour of the bustling, overgrown city of Tokyo. The following year, when Yasui was denied a visa to the US because of his membership in a left-wing peace group, we interceded with the State Department and were able to bring him here for a visit with peace groups.

We rested in Hawaii, where we stayed on the garden island of Kauai, one of the most lush spots I had ever visited. Famed as the real-life location of the filming of *South Pacific*, its "Bali Hai" presented a sharp contrast to the heavily-industrialized main island, Hawaii. No wonder this is a favorite cinematic site. While in Hawaii, I contacted William Reich, a former California community activist, whose modest home was disturbingly close to an active volcano. Shortly after settling, he had resumed his peace and labor activities.

As we circumnavigated the globe, Ollie, taller and more assertive, and I seemed an "odd couple." I worried that some of the normal aggravations of a lengthy trip would affect our friendship. Yet Ollie and I must have gotten along, judging from a note received from her almost fifty years later, in which she fondly recalled our travels together. We had been away a number of weeks, during which time I had only limited communication with my children and was eager to be reunited with them. After our return, Ollie reminded members of the USSR delegation of our commitment to share our Soviet experiences in print with the American public. I wrote several articles about the trip for the *Liberal Democrat,* and for Dr. Carlton Goodlett's *Sun-Reporter,* San Francisco's black newspaper. Ten years later, Dr. Goodlet headed up a delegation to the World Peace Council meeting in Moscow. Among the delegates were Enola Maxwell of the Potrero Hill Neighborhood House, Jack Massen, Karen Talbot and myself.

On a number of my travels, I was accompanied by my long-time friend, Walter Gillen. Walter had attended UC Berkeley on the GI Bill. After graduation, he was so conflicted about accepting state employment because of the loyalty oath requirement, that he consulted a therapist. We had met at Garfield Jr. High PTA, where our sons were in school together. He and his artist wife, Margaret, had been staunch supporters during my appearance before the Burns Committee in 1951 and my difficulties with the PTA. Ardent conservationists, they were also active WILPF members. After Margaret's death, my friendship with Walter continued. A firm opponent of Hitler's Germany before the US entered the war, he had enlisted in the Canadian Air Force, later transferring to US military service. He was stationed in Kunming, China, and flew in the Burma Theater.

Walter loved to travel and shared my interest in people. Having recently retired and settled in Nevada City, he was free to accompany me on a number of trips. An anti-war activist, he joined me in attending WILPF's International Triennial Conference in Tokyo in August 1977. This event was planned to coincide with the Hiroshima and Nagasaki memorial observances that year.

We were greeted at the Hotel Tokyo by a huge banner proclaiming "Welcome Womens International League for Peace and Freedom." The conference proceedings were featured in the local media—I could not imagine receiving the same amount of publicity in the US. I was also pleased to see a Japanese WILPF "pen pal," Kora, with whom I had corresponded. She had been hosted by our San Francisco branch some years earlier.

In Hiroshima, the entire city turned out for a day-long observance. We visited the Memorial Shrine, the Atomic Age Museum, and the Atomic Survivors Hospital, where the suffering of unfortunate patients bore testimony to the devastation caused by the first and second nuclear bomb explosions at the end of World War II. We brought home the message from Hiroshima and Nagasaki, which we also visited. I did my best to spread the word, sending out press releases and writing articles for a local newspaper.

Later in 1977, Walter accompanied me on a trip to China where we joined one of the first "unofficial" groups of visitors from the US. We cruised to Canton, one of the country's largest cities, and spent time in the surrounding agricultural communes. Each commune had its own medical clinic. We were surprised to find that China, the world's leader in "alternative medicine," had standards of hygiene that would be unacceptable in the Western world. I'll never forget the mysteries of the squat toilet.

Since I enjoy probing into other cultures, I had several discussions with Ying, one of our bright young women guides. She was shocked to hear that, in our country, we elect our leaders and criticize them freely when they fail to keep their campaign promises. Totally indoctrinated in the Communist-Maoist "party line," she was amazed. From her perspective, they had the perfect system. Yet I may have raised some questions in her mind. We, in turn, learned a few things about China, including the fact that tipping was strictly forbidden. On a shopping foray during which I bought gifts for my grandchildren, we asked Ying if she would like something for herself. Walter noticed that she was not wearing socks; perhaps she would like a pair? No! She had everything she needed.

In 1978 I went to Cuba with Women Strike for Peace as a guest of the Cuban Women's Federation. As in our travels to the Soviet Union, we were constantly reminded of the benefits of socialism, with its universal education and health care. We traveled the entire length of the island by bus, stopping at historic revolutionary spots. In this cooperative society, we could see new buildings rising everywhere, as well as old ones being renovated, mostly by volunteer labor. Earlier, some of our tour members had traveled to Cuba to help during the sugar cane harvest season.

We met American émigrés who accepted the shortages and inconveniences of life on the island, made more difficult because of the US embargo. They spoke enthusiastically about the spirit of the Cuban people. Of the many Americans drawn to settle in Cuba, one woman we met comes to mind. Her husband had been an editor of the New York *National Guardian* and she served frequently as Castro's interpreter. Despite the differences between her past and present lives, I found her generally satisfied with their very minimal possessions, which included an old icebox on the porch.

In Havana, we met the daughter of a Bay Area Unitarian minister, married to a Cuban, who was benefiting, by virtue of her residence in Cuba, from the free medical training offered there. We learned later that after graduation she moved to Canada with her children to pursue a career in medicine.

We also met a young man, the son of a prominent San Francisco political activist, who had hijacked a US plane to Cuba. Not welcomed there as a hero, he had served time in Cuban jails and was now subsisting on government handouts. When he encountered me in the hotel and learned that I was from the Bay Area, he asked me to relay a message for help to his mother. Upon returning home, I contacted her, and was disappointed with her rather chilly response. Apparently she had severed all ties with her son.

Confident in the belief that their government was striving to improve conditions, Cubans were willing to endure privation and discomfort. At long, probing sessions with the Cuban Women's Federation, most of our group were favorably impressed. However, several questions were raised concerning race relations and freedom of religion. To some, it seemed that there was still lingering evidence of racial discrimination.

We learned of the existence of a Jewish community in Cuba. After a number of inquiries, Libby Mines—a fellow WSP traveler—and I were able to locate an old Jewish synagogue, only to find it dilapidated and abandoned. Recently, I've learned that Havana is witnessing a vigorous revival of Jewish community life, including religious observances and holiday celebrations. Such efforts are assisted by groups in Miami and the Bay Area, whose members make frequent trips to the island to deliver ritual goods. They also take powdered milk and medical supplies, which are distributed to hospitals and the general population.

My travels continued. In 1979 Walter and I visited Israel on a trip organized by an Israeli labor group, *G'vat Haviva*. There, I met Ruth Markovetzky, director of the Israeli Cotton Institute, and a close friend of my late husband. We met at the Hilton Hotel and I was struck by its elegance, in contrast to our Spartan quarters in a Tel Aviv suburb.

During this trip we heard many complimentary remarks about Sam, who had been described by Israel's first Prime-Minister Ben-Gurion as a "visionary who knew how to achieve things," and an agricultural genius who had taught his methods to many in that country. Even schoolchildren knew him as "the father of Israeli agriculture." His mechanized farming innovations had contributed a great deal to Israel's agricultural and industrial independence, and were absolutely essential to its survival. Walter had known Sam, and was very impressed with his celebrity there.

I enjoyed this trip more than my earlier "VIP" visit, even though much had changed since then. The Jewish encroachment upon territory claimed by Palestinians continues to be the source of mounting anger and armed clashes between the two peoples. Unrestrained growth of the Jewish population has impeded the faltering peace process.

In 1983 I was presented with an opportunity to revisit the USSR. A Connecticut peace group, Promoting Enduring Peace, co-sponsored the Volga Peace Cruise with WILPF. On this cruise, we avoided most major cities, stopped in a number of small towns, and participated in festive village ceremonies and picnics. Many friendly locals came on board for seminars, during which we argued the relative merits of our different economic systems.

On my insistence our group visited the shrine at Babi Yar. It is just outside Kiev, the capital of the Ukraine, and one of Russia's most beautiful cities. Most of the Americans on this trip were unaware that this was the site of the massacre of more than 30,000 Jews by the Germans. Locals were unwilling to recount its full history; they preferred to think that Ukrainians were the only victims of the war. I later discovered that, in the minds of the guides, Jews were not regarded as citizens even though they had lived in the Ukraine for many generations. I hope that we left them with some questions about their own history. We solemnly placed wreaths at the foot of the shrine.

After the trip, I was interviewed by Sovietologist William Mandel on KPFA. I also wrote articles for the *Berkeley Daily Gazette,* which provoked a running argument in the Op Ed section. One correspondent wrote about the militarization of Russian schoolchildren as an example of the "pro-war" mentality of the people. In reply, letters supported my account of the universal Russian yearning for peace. After suffering the loss of twenty million people in World War II, is it any wonder there should be a deep longing for stability and peace? Nevertheless, the Russians feared a possible attack by the "Great Super Power" across the Atlantic.

V. Oral Histories, Free Speech Radio, and the Future: 1984-2000

Dr. Bonnie Hardwick, Chief Curator of the UC Bancroft Collection, upon receiving the Women's Peace Office collection in 1986, informed me that students organizing campus anti-apartheid activities studied our methods—clear evidence that our archiving as well as our activism has proven worthwhile.

Chapter 29

Peace Pioneers and Holocaust Survivors

"Pat Cody, Her Contribution in Health, Peace and Politics by Alice Hamburg is a fine history of [Pat Cody's] work on peace, politics, and especially, about Fred Cody and Cody's Books...[as well as] so many events of importance in the last fifty years."

    —Willa Baum, Director of the UC Berkeley Regional Oral
        History Office

My oral history and archival work began in 1984 with a request from the Union of Vietnamese Women for documentation about US women who had actively opposed the Vietnam War. The Vietnamese wished to honor us with an exhibit in the war museum they were planning in Hanoi City. That spring, internationally recognized WSP leader Cora Weiss received the communication, and conveyed the request to the San Francisco Women's Peace Office.

Eager to respond to their request, Hazel Grossman and I sent a representative collection of our papers, fliers, and posters. We wished the Vietnamese women "peace and speedy recovery" in their beautiful country and sent warm regards. The Union's request sparked our own interest in recapturing the stories of American women who have contributed greatly to the history of the peace and human rights movements in our time. We have continued our cultural contacts with the Vietnamese during a number of reciprocal visits, and we have hosted Madame Binh, who was one of the chief negotiators at the 1973 Paris Peace talks.

In 1985, I signed up for my first oral history course from Elaine Dorfman of the UC Bancroft Library and chief oral historian of the Western Jewish History Center at the Judah

L. Magnes Museum. What a challenge! Little did I realize, when I joined the Oral History Association, that this would be the beginning of a major chapter in my life.

In 1986, the San Francisco Women's Peace Office was approached by Judy Adams, director of Stanford University's Oral History Project, who was recording the stories of older women involved in lifelong peace work. Here was a chance to honor Bay Area women whose lives might inspire others. Judy and I held a number of oral history training sessions in my home.

My first interviewee was Betty Segal. She and her husband, Meyer, were the former publishers of the East Bay weekly *Freedom News*. Next, I interviewed German-born Augusta Trumpler, then in her 99th year. This "Grand Dame of the Co-op movement" was honored as one of its founders. She was also a long-time WILPF member. I recorded the stories of WILPF members Hazel Grossman, Frances Herring, Frieda Wolff, Vivian Hallinan, Leona Bayer, and others.

One of my most memorable projects was the life story of Pat Cody of Cody's Books, a Berkeley institution and one of the last successful independent bookstores. She and her late husband, Fred, had been mediators in the student/hippie confrontations of the 1960s and were founders of the Berkeley Free Clinic. Their store provided a refuge for tear gas victims in those turbulent times. In fact, they deliberately designed the bookstore with a frontage space for public demonstrations. For Pat, there was a point when "we were running the store almost as a sideline." As a long time writer for *The Economist* and an original member of Berkeley WSP, Pat also led the campaign for health and other services for the transient student population in Berkeley.

My 1986 oral history, *Pat Cody, Her Contribution in Health, Peace and Politics*, can be found in Bay Area libraries and the Berkeley Historical Society. Pat's example continues to inspire peace activists and students in health and women's studies.

This, and the aforementioned WILPF histories, are filed in the archives of the Bancroft Library and Stanford University. Unfortunately, it was too late to obtain the stories of a number of our most effective and colorful early activists, namely the Peninsula's Anne Peabody Brown, and the East Bay's Peggy Calder Hayes, the sister of artist Alexander Calder.

Although we were not able to interview noted cellist Margaret Rowell, the Bancroft Library recorded her oral history. After her death in 1993, I received the following note from her son, Galen, the renowned nature photographer and author. In answer to my question, "Is there any relation between your work in the arts and the peace movement?" he answered. "Of course! For artists... it's simply natural...to be involved. I think that my mother's involvement with the world peace movement and WILPF definitely affected my own work by osmosis..."

At about the same time, I was organizing the papers of Frances Herring for the UC Bancroft Library. Frances, one of the WSP founders, had worked closely with the Paulings and was one of the first to point out the environmental dangers of nuclear power, despite President Eisenhower's lauding the benefits of the "peaceful atom." She had taught philosophy at Vassar and later joined the Institute for Governmental Studies at UC Berkeley, where she worked until her retirement. Her death in 1993 was a great loss. At that time, Hazel and I were mounting an exhibit of Vietnam War newsletters, pamphlets and other items collected between 1961 and 1986, to be exhibited at the San Francisco International Center.

The San Francisco WILPF office received a request from the curator of the Peace Archives at Swarthmore College for current WILPF material to include in their Jane Addams Peace Collection. Hazel and I spent months gathering and organizing the files, a contribution that was gratefully acknowledged. Since then, Barbara George has archived later materials for the Bancroft.

During the Vietnam War years, The Committee of Responsibility (COR) had shared our Berkeley WSP office. When Florence Forrest, their former secretary, heard of my archival work, she mentioned several boxes stored in her leaky garage. These contained items documenting COR's work, including photographs portraying the stages of reconstructive surgery involved in treating young Vietnamese napalm victims.

I contacted Dr. Fred Epstein, a member of the local Physicians for Social Responsibility (PSR) and a colleague in the anti-war struggle. He was elated to hear that the materials had been preserved, and encouraged me to call the UC San Francisco Medical School Library, whose director welcomed the collection. The physicians—who had earlier offered their services *gratis* to help these young, disfigured war victims—were pleased to learn that this documentation was now available to others. Our efforts have made Woman's Peace Office material and COR memorabilia available on microfilm for research by historians, as well as students, at libraries throughout this country.

In 1987 Eleanor Salkind introduced local artist Carolyna Marks at a WSP meeting. She won our support for her proposal to build a "Peace Wall" in downtown Berkeley's Martin Luther King Jr., Park, a busy area directly opposite the high school. Each tile would be hand-painted by children and adults, fired in the artist's kiln, and permanently embedded in the wall, a reminder to all passers-by of our yearnings for lasting peace.

As a result of worldwide publicity, Carolyna was later invited to the Soviet Union to spend a year creating peace walls there. Before her departure, I was asked by Therese Pipe of the Berkeley Historical Society to record the artist's story. In the interview, she recounted her hopes and aspirations for spreading peace by building many such walls. In her words:

"Together we will create a wall that will, lasting for centuries, tell of our desire to see our lives continue in the beauty, harmony and brotherhood we all cherish…The expression of peace goes beyond all spiritual, political and psychological boundaries."

Creating peace walls throughout the world has become Carolyna's lifelong mission. She has since constructed walls in San Francisco, Oakland, and Atlanta, Georgia, in conjunction with the Olympic games. Recognized internationally as a good-will ambassador for peace, she has erected walls in Japan and even in the troubled Middle East, including some in Israel. One is at the Jerusalem YMCA and a second at *Neve Shalom*, a community jointly inhabited by Israelis and Palestinians. The tiles, created by youths from both sides, bear hopeful messages and vivid images of peace and understanding. In 1991, while Carolyna was in the Soviet Union, she asked me to accept, on her behalf, the Mal Warwick Berkeley Peace Award, presented at the City Council meeting. She continues her peace wall efforts to this day.

That year I was interviewed by Joan Levinson of KPFA's Women's Magazine *Peacemongers Program*. Later, when the station's Linda Spector asked me to appear on the *Heritage Program*, I suggested that we include several other older women of different backgrounds with unusual stories to tell. The resulting program proved interesting because of the wide range of experience represented: Suse Moyal and Nelda Cassuto were victims of the reign of fascism under Hitler and Mussolini. Mildred Schoenberger, a lifelong teacher, had been affected by the witchhunts conducted in the New York public schools in the 30s and 40s. I was the catalyst. I had come up with the idea of documenting the lives of women who inspire us by their lifelong struggles for a peaceful, just, and more humane world. This is a project I hope to pursue further.

Chapter 30

Man of the Soil: Writing Sam's Life Story

"I will never forget what you have done for our country, which is no less your country."

—David Ben-Gurion, first Prime Minister of Israel, 1955

"Like many who possess a spark of genius, Hamburg tended to be more accurate about the future than the past."

—Steven R. Goldsmith, journalist,
Western States Jewish Historical Quarterly, Jan. 1978

In the mid 1970s, Willa Baum, the UC Berkeley Bancroft Library's director of the Regional Oral History Office, expressed interest in Sam's life story. She contacted our mutual friends Paul Taylor and Dorothea Lange, who conveyed her message to Sam. Even at his best, he was not one to sit quietly, particularly while undergoing lengthy questioning. "At this point," he said, toward the end of his life, "I don't know if I can sift out the truth of what really happened." Confined to his ranch home and disabled, he asked the Taylors to communicate his regrets—a missed opportunity!

In 1986, ten years after Sam's death, the Western Jewish History Department of the Judah L. Magnes Museum in Berkeley requested the papers, photographs and memorabilia of this "genius on a tractor" for an exhibit. Earlier, I could never have told Sam's story because of the heartbreak of our son's death. How do you disclose details of a family tragedy? We were all aware that Sam's relationship with Aron had been deeply upsetting and had contributed to Aron's depressed condition at the time of his death. Ten years later we were still grieving. In our hearts it was difficult not to question whether a greater attempt on our part to understand Aron's difficulties might have changed the outcome.

As I went through the captions of each photograph, I realized that Sam's was an unusual tale waiting to be told. I had to sort out the most significant photos, letters, articles, tributes, and other documents in English, Yiddish, and Hebrew, from various parts of the world. I turned to my typewriter, completed the captions, and kept on writing.

After approval by Seymour Fromer, head of the Judah L. Magnes Museum, and Professor Moses Rischin, Director of the Western Jewish History Center of the Magnes Museum, the project started in earnest. Thus began *Sam Hamburg, Agricultural Pioneer in California and Israel*, published in 1989 by the Magnes Museum and partially funded by the California Council for the Humanities. The book was the main attraction at the "Ethnicity in California Agriculture" symposium at UC's Clark Kerr Campus held that year.

One of the symposium speakers was Lionel Steinberg. In 1970, he had been the first large grower to sign a contract with the United Farm Workers Organizing Committee (UFWOC changed to UFW in 1973). In 1952 he was Agricultural Advisor to the Democratic Party's presidential candidate Adlai Stevenson. Lionel had grown up in Fresno, managing his stepfather's extensive grape-growing acreage. Later, his farming operations extended to the Imperial Valley. His involvement with the UFW marked a turning point in the history of that organization. Once he had signed the contract, other growers followed suit, thus bringing an end to the six-year consumers' grape boycott. Lionel remembered Sam as his mentor and "a man of indomitable courage and great ingenuity with unlimited enthusiasm for farming, art, music, and people." He noted Sam's "wisdom and zeal in improving farming methods and irrigation practices," as well as his "keen personal interest in the well-being of his farm workers."

While writing Sam's biography, I also worked with the Holocaust Oral History Project, in San Francisco, directed by former San Francisco State's Women's Studies instructor Lani Silver. The group has conducted well over a thousand interviews of Bay Area survivors from Germany, Greece, Holland, Italy, Poland, and France, and continues to record remaining stories. On several occasions I was able to interview victims myself. A number of these unforgettable sessions took place at my Berkeley home, with cameras and recording equipment taking up almost the entire living room.

I joined Tanya in a trip East in the fall of 1986 to visit her children. David was at the Landmark School in Putney, Vermont. Our next stop was Yale, where we would celebrate

Parents' Week with Julie. As a course requirement, she had decided to record my life story. In doing this she asked many questions. In my single-minded approach to peace issues and the day-to-day activities, I had been fairly oblivious to evidences of male chauvinism. Julie's probing questions helped me view these past issues through the lens of a young feminist. Ten years later she would again interview me, providing several tapes that have helped me in the writing of this memoir.

Julie's interview caused me to think further about oral histories. I Recalled the two hundred members of Sam's family who had perished in the Holocaust. In New York I took the opportunity to find out if his second cousin, Anita Rubinstein, who was a native of Poland, would tell her story. Although she had survived physically, she bore deep psychological scars. Her tale was particularly poignant. Anita stopped by our hotel. Since I had brought my tape recorder, we were able to start an effort which proved therapeutic for her. Over the course of several hours she spoke of the uncertainties and tragedies that had marked her childhood. The resulting transcription exceeded my expectations. In my mind, Anita was a symbol of the lost generation of youth whose talents the world would never know. I still can hear her statement: "My father suggested to my mother initially that she give us both up to a priest." And my mother responded, 'No, I do not give birth to Jewish children for them to grow up to be Christian'."

Anita and I were pleased when the Oral History Project in San Francisco and the YIVO Institute for Jewish Research in New York both were interested in adding her history to their archives.

Chapter 31

Pacifica and KPFA: The Battle for Free Speech Radio

"Why settle for crumbs from Pacifica's leadership...? Why let Wall Street and Madison Avenue have unchallenged control over our journalism and culture? The point is not just to democratize the margins but to battle for the very heart and soul of our whole nation."

—Robert McChesney, *The Nation*, October 18, 1999

"This is Nicole, and I've just been fired." The voice on my answering machine was that of KPFA General Manager Nicole Sawaya, and her call to me in early March 1999 marked the beginning of the listener-supported, free-speech radio station's greatest crisis in its fifty year history.

Earlier, when Nicole asked me to join KPFA's 50th Anniversary Capital Campaign, I had agreed. Among the numerous organizations I support, the station has been at the top of my agenda, because of its role in providing the "news behind the news," and furnishing information to enable listeners to place other more mainstream media coverage in context. Since I work at home, I regularly plan my schedule around the station's daily programming. How would I keep informed without its excellent, freewheeling, in-depth coverage of local, national, and international news as well as cultural events?

In 1989, as a member of the KPFA Capital Campaign Committee, I had helped raise funds for a new building, which would make possible a move from the dingy, inadequate, rented space they had occupied since 1949. Following the successful effort on the part of many supporters, a groundbreaking ceremony was held in 1991—a fit celebration for the station's 40th anniversary!

The wedge of land on Martin Luther King, Jr. Way, near University Avenue, seemed so minuscule. It was difficult to imagine that a plot so small could house an entire complex of studios. It was barely large enough for the Native American dancers to perform their consecrating ceremony. Yet the results were gratifying. Many months later, a beautiful, state-of-the-art building was completed.

KPFA was founded in 1949 by a group of conscientious objectors, who, in 1946, had established the Pacifica Foundation, the first nonprofit FM radio network in the United States. Many of the founders had chosen prison rather than register for the WW II draft. Headed by Lewis Hill, their philosophy leaned toward socialism, and the station's motive was to promote issues of world peace and social justice. A totally new concept in communication, KPFA required years of trial and error to establish its identity and to become viable. It was to provide in-depth discussion of the vital issues of war and peace, and, in general, take on the serious problems of our time.

KPFA struggled for funds. In 1951, a Ford Foundation Grant of $150,000 rescued the station temporarily. Differences arose between volunteers who flocked to the station, some with their own agendas, and the more permanent management. To what extent would the station serve particular intellectual interests, or would it appeal to a wider audience? Zen interpreter Alan Watts and book store owner Roy Kepler were among a dissenting group, whose ideas about the future of the station varied from those of Hill. Even among pacifists, differences can arise.

In 1953, the controversy between Hill and the others was exacerbated, causing Hill to resign. He returned, but disagreements continued. In 1957, suffering from severe back pain and unwilling to continue the struggle, he took his own life at the age of thirty-eight. The community was shocked. His death marked a break with the station's historical emphasis on pacifism. At that pivotal juncture, a new generation aligned itself with radical, 'unpopular' ideas, not limiting itself to strict pacifism.

In spite of the early turmoil, Pacifica managed to survive, offering commentators of every stripe. Poets, including the Beat legends Ginsburg and Ferlinghetti, were regular contributors. KPFA even welcomed the voices of extreme conservatives to be heard, such as Casper Weinberger, who later became Defense Secretary under President Reagan. Diversity became the *sine qua non* of the station, which continues to bring people together in its sponsorship of teach-ins, lectures, training and apprenticeship programs, as well as concerts, festivals, and other community events. It provides a voice for at-risk high-schoolers in "Youth In Control," aired on its repeater station, KPFB. Community groups are invited to broadcast their announcements on the air.

One of the early programmers was William Mandel, a political commentator specializing in the Soviet Union. It was he who initiated the popular "call-in" format, now used almost universally by radio. The social humorist and folksinger Malvina Reynolds achieved her fame as a result of her frequent appearances on the station.

There was no lack of news to appeal to the KPFA audience. Listeners themselves were often part of the events. When the House Un-American Activities Committee held hearings in San Francisco City Hall in 1960, station supporters were among the demonstrators washed down the marble main staircase by water hoses, and KPFA was there with microphones. The station was also in the forefront of the Civil Rights Movement. Local students brought back stories of harassment at the hands of Southern law enforcement. I participated in fundraisers to support volunteers, sent by the womens' peace movement, to join other young people during "Mississippi Summer."

KPFA also proved a great asset to the free speech movement on the UC Berkeley campus in the 60s, covering student demonstrations and airing their appeals to the public. We were pleased when Jackie Goldberg, a student member of Women Strike for Peace and currently a Los Angeles City Council member, circulated our anti-war, anti-nuke literature, thus helping to break the administration's ban on the distribution of protest literature and soliciting funds in Sproul Plaza. In May 1966, the station aired the first "Vietnam War Day" Teach-in at UCB, which filled the entire Sproul Plaza for most of the day. One may re-live those historic events by obtaining copies of tapes from the Pacifica Archives, which continues to be a priceless resource for historians.

In the 70s, following a turbulent period, including a hard-fought strike, the staff was unionized. There was also a push for greater diversity in programming and staffing, including the addition of women's and Third World departments. KPFA continued as a voice of dissent in the political arena. Nineteen eighty witnessed the Stop the War Teach-In at UC's Wheeler Hall, protesting escalating military spending and a possible return of the draft. I was chosen to represent the women's peace movement, joining a number of male speakers. For once, our role was being recognized, and I was pleased to see my photograph in the *Oakland Tribune's* report. It was next to that of fellow speaker, Harry Bridges, president of the International Longshore and Warehouse Union (ILWU).

In spite of the expanding Pacifica network, with sister stations in Los Angeles, New York, Houston, and Washington DC, and KPFA's auxiliary, KFCF in Fresno—local membership growth was not fulfilling expectations. There was also little turnover in local governing board membership. In the mid-'90s, management, in its attempt to enlarge the listenership, gambled on laying off long-term commentators to make way for new staff.

In response to these firings, a "Take Back KPFA" movement sprang up among some supporters. Pacifica was accused of imitating the Public Broadcasting System (PBS) in giving precedence to national news programs at the expense of local issues, and of abandoning the original emphasis on free listener access and wide-open discussion. A shocking rumor that Pacifica was trying to sell the KPFA franchise began to circulate.

In early 1999, at the Pacifica National Board meeting held in Berkeley, a decision was made to 'centralize' the network's governing structure by separating local and national advisory boards, thus eliminating representation from the Local Advisory Board. KPFA could no longer be represented on the Pacifica National Board, thus preventing stations and listeners from participating in the important decisions concerning the network.

Following the distressing news of Nicole Sawaya's firing, and reacting to these changes, I decided that I could no longer participate in the 50th Anniversary Committee. Despite her outstanding success in fundraising and her ability to bring all elements together, Ms. Sawaya's contract was not renewed because, according to Pacifica Executive Director Lynn Chadwick, she was "not a good fit." All other members of the Anniversary Committee agreed with me, thus bringing our fund raising activities to a halt.

The controversy quickly turned into a standoff. Sawaya's departure was followed by a string of other firings and reprimands. Some staff members were terminated because they broke the gag rule by on-air discussion of internal matters—an ironic twist to the notion of free speech in Berkeley. Pacifica's interim general manager ordered the closing down of the station, placing armed guards around the building and boarding up the windows. A news commentator was pulled off the air. KPFA's union staff was placed on paid administrative leave. Demonstrations mounted. An around-the-clock vigil in front of the boarded-up station was maintained. More than a hundred arrests took place, including staff members as well as supporters.

Community and national support for the station continued to grow, demanding the reinstatement of the manager and the dismissed staff. A benefit concert featuring famed folksinger Joan Baez filled the large Berkeley Community Theater to overflowing, and raised over $60,000 for the struggle. At the end of July, an illegal tent city, "Camp KPFA," attracted hundreds of protesters, who continued the round-the-clock vigil at the site. Observers have commented on the restraint exercised by demonstrators, who were obviously trained in the principles of non-violence. The outpouring of concern about the possible loss of this free-speech beacon inspired many young people, who turned out regularly in huge numbers.

The strong stand taken by Berkeley Mayor Shirley Dean and the City Council at a special meeting in late summer, resulted in a vote to contribute funds to assist the staff in its struggle. The Council expressed criticism of Pacifica's handling of the dispute and called for the resignation of the Pacifica Governing Board and the Executive Director. At the end of the month, over ten thousand people turned out for one of the largest demonstrations in the history of this free-speech-conscious city.

Several months of controversy resulted in widespread condemnation of Pacifica's labor practices by the California State Labor Federation, as well as by those of Alameda, San Francisco, and Contra Costa counties. In early August, due to intense community pressure, the lockout officially ended and the KPFA staff resumed broadcasting. The Pacifica Foundation and KPFA entered into mediation in the attempt to settle the impasse. However, many issues remain unresolved. The staff returned to find $30,000 damage to broadcasting equipment, which occurred while the security guards were in charge. And they were confronted with a hiring freeze. The on-air gag rule was lifted, and as part of the settlement, total control of the station was returned to the local staff for the time being.

Dion Aroner, Berkeley Assemblywoman, won support among fellow legislators for an inquiry into Pacifica's management of KPFA. The all-day hearing before the legislature's Joint Audit Committee, chaired by Assemblyman Scott Wildman, was held in late August at the State Building in Oakland. Questions were raised as to whether Pacifica was living up to its charter, and if the non-profit organization was continuing to qualify for tax exempt status. In spite of warnings from Pacifica, many employees eloquently aired their complaints against the foundation. Although notified, Pacifica's chair Dr. Mary Frances Berry and Executive Director Lynn Chadwick refused to appear. The committee served Dr. Berry with a request for answers to questions raised by the shutting down of the station and a full financial accounting. In answer to the demand of the committee, Pacifica has furnished incomplete information on the more than $500,000 spent during the lockout, some for armed security guards and a public relations firm. The dispute is far from settled. KPFA's future as an independent voice remains uncertain.

In my fifty years of involvement with the station, I have seen turmoil unleashed time and again. Free speech is still under siege. We must exercise eternal vigilance in order to prevent the corporate takeover of local media and the challenge to the people's interests. Yet what is happening in Berkeley and the Bay Area gives some reassurance that democracy is not dead. Power is still in the hands of the people.

Chapter 32

Still Making a Difference!

"Your heart knows no borders...You have saved us 100s of hours of hard research. We are so grateful for your [ballot measure] work."

—Father Bill O'Donnell of St. Joseph the Worker Church,
November, 1998

When Tom Wells, author of *The War Within*, 1994, interviewed me, he wondered about the lack of credit given women for their work in the peace movement, noting that several of them, disturbed by chauvinist male attitudes, had left our organizations. "How do you feel about your role?" he asked. Response was difficult. Gender issues had not been a special concern of mine, although I had noticed some ageism within our groups.

I recall a time in early 1982 when, representing the women's peace groups, I was being interviewed on a San Francisco television station along with Alan George, a young UC Berkeley physics graduate student. Although I was equally well informed on the issues in the Nuclear Weapons Freeze Campaign, the male moderator invariably turned to Alan with all the pertinent questions, an extremely frustrating experience for me.

We were not deterred. Nothing could keep us from our work. In looking back, I recall the continued and valuable efforts of Hazel Grossman, who, as reported in Chapter 26, played a preeminent role in the San Francisco's Women's Peace Office since the beginning of the antiwar activities in the 60s. In 1995, with fewer members attending regular meetings, it was decided to close the San Francisco Peace Office. At the same time, Hazel, who was experiencing health problems, decided to gather the remaining newsletters, leaflets and other documentation of the Peace Office, including many of her own writings, to complete the collections which had been sent earlier to the Bancroft Library and to Swarthmore College. Whenever world events call for action, Hazel continues to send out her now-celebrated newsletter to the members who remain on the WILPF mailing list.

On October 1998, we took the occasion to honor Hazel at the Potrero Hill Neighborhood House. The event brought forth outpourings of appreciation and affection for this tireless activist for her dedication to the women's peace movement. Friends came from all around the Bay Area to pay tribute. Rhoda Norman served as chair and Enola Maxwell gave the welcoming address. As coordinator of the event, I introduced the many friends who gave testimonials about the honoree, including Ann Spake, one of the original members of Womens Strike for Peace (WSP) in 1961. The daughter of two prominent San Francisco peace activists, she was then a young mother with small children and worried, as we all were, about the dangers of nuclear fallout. She spoke eloquently of Hazel's role as her mentor.

Hazel gave an impassioned talk, offering an overview of the years of dedicated peace efforts on the part of so many. "I call for a dynamic women's movement to end and restrain the arrogant superpower, the US. I am tremendously encouraged by this wonderful turnout. It raises hopes that despite my limitations, I could still be of some use to the women's peace movement. I decry the most genocidal century in known history and look toward a new generation of women and men which hopefully will build a much stronger peace movement than any achieved in our time, and will bring about a peaceful United States and a peaceful planet."

A special feature of the event was the display of Hazel's collection of newspaper articles, letters, flyers, photographs and more, arranged by Ethel Sanjines and her husband, Carl. Barbara Stack videotaped the event. We were entertained by singer Barbara Dane, another icon of the movement who is still very much in demand after so many years, and whose nostalgic musical tributes to Hazel brought tears to our eyes. We were family.

A Personal Musing

An item on the front page of the Sunday *San Francisco Examiner* of November 14, 1999, has caused me to look back in time. I was one of the interviewees for the article, "Red Scare Files Detail Lives Left in Ruin: Transcripts reveal how those who defied the panel were ostracized." The article recalled my appearance before the California State Committee on Un-American Activities (the Burns Committee) in September 1951. In reading it, I reflected on how times change, and how this once red-baiting newspaper is now interested in giving the "real" story behind the hearings.

Reading my FBI "dossier," upon which the Committee undoubtedly relied for information, I found:...*the subject [is] an individual with a definite potential for subversive activity in the event of a national emergency."* I find it ironic that in the fifty year interim, I have received *awards* for the same kind of community involvement which had caused me to be called before the committee.

What would the Burns Committee have to say about my being honored by the San Francisco Board of Supervisors for "Outstanding Service to the People of the City & County of San Francisco" in 1991? The committee might have been surprised at its "subversive" having received the Berkeley Commission on the Status of Women Award in recognition of Women's History Month in 1993, and the Jane Addams Peace Association Award for "Fifty Years on the Front Lines" in 1997. JAPA is the educational arm of the national and international WILPF organizations.

What would the committee have thought of my nomination, in 1999, by women's peace groups for the Sixth Annual Berkeley Community Fund Award, which I received for "a lifetime of activism and leadership in social justice and world peace"? Fund president Narsai David wrote, "Having the names Alice Hamburg, Women for Peace and Women's International League for Peace and Freedom prominently displayed in the program at the awards dinner added to the "wonderful community feeling of this event."

In my acceptance speech I lauded all those responsible for carrying on the everyday activities of our organizations. I congratulated the fund for offering the opportunity to bring together representatives of so many groups involved in efforts to solve the problems of homelessness, violence and injustice in our community, among them the Women's Daytime Drop-in Center, the Emergency Food and Housing Project, and the Ecumenical Chaplaincy to the Homeless.

What would they have thought of Congressmember Ron Dellums' tribute that was entered into the Congressional Record in 1997: "She has been on the forefront of progressive activism in the Bay Area for a half-century." He commends "her decades of work on behalf of world peace and disarmament...and the veritable laundry list of activities that the Framers protected in the First Amendment to our Constitution."

Most memorable was the JAPA event:

Berkeley's historic, century-old Spenger's Fish Grotto was the scene of the festive occasion. In the wood-paneled dining room, filled with a wonderful aroma of seafood and a colorful display of memorabilia, photos, letters and placards, I greeted 150 people—family members, friends, and associates of long standing—some of whom had traveled from various parts of the state for the event. Congratulatory messages arrived from former

International WILPF president Katherine Camp and retired JAPA director Ruth Chalmers.

My good friend Madeline Duckles, former National WILPF Board Member, who chaired the event, commented on the wonderful spirit pervading the occasion, and with her fine sense of humor, made everyone feel at home. National WILPF President Betty Burkes, a striking African American woman who has enlivened the US section, came to our event after making a presentation at the Oakland Conference of Abolition 2000, calling for the end of all nuclear testing. She was followed by Berkeley's Dolores Taller, JAPA President, who for decades has spoken for us at international conferences and public demonstrations. No other member is as dedicated to the cause of Mideast peace.

Berkeley Vice-Mayor Maudelle Shirek read a tribute, a Proclamation from the City Council. Attorney Peter Franck, who has carried on the tradition of free speech in his work for independent radio, wrote that he was "honoring Alice as well as his grandmother, Selma Bernstein," whose membership in WILPF dated back to pre-Hitler Germany. He credits Selma for his own ongoing dedication to peace issues.

Once again I was delighted by the warm presence of Barbara Dane, vocalist, composer, master blues interpreter, activist, and our crowd's favorite entertainer who thrilled the audience, singing movement songs by request. Her published works, the Paredon Record label, have been donated to the Smithsonian.

What would the Burns Committee have thought?

How times change.

Chapter 33

Peacework from the Ground Up

"Where growing numbers of people are being marginalized, impoverished, scapegoated and beleaguered, I don't feel I can accept an award from the government that is pursuing these policies."

—Poet and activist Adrienne Rich, upon rejecting the National medal for the Arts from President Clinton, 1998

As a longtime member of WILPF, I take seriously its goals of "equality, development, and peace for all women everywhere and in the interest of humanity." Through WILPF I feel connected to others, in this country and throughout the world.

I believe that one of the most significant events of the past decade was the Fourth UN Women's Conference held in Beijing in late 1995, in which WILPF was a leading participant. The conference focused on *human*-based rather than *military*-based security issues, and adopted an International Bill of Rights for Women covering education, healthcare, inheritance rights, business opportunities, and the elimination of all forms of discrimination.

In June 2000, at a special follow-up session of "Beijing Plus Five" entitled "Women 2000, Gender Equality, Development, and Peace for the Twenty-First Century," there was much discussion but, to date, little progress in implementing the commitments made in 1995. Patterns of discrimination against and disenfranchisement of women persist worldwide.

WILPF members continue to work toward the goal of changing our national priorities: We demand that our abundant national resources be used toward fulfilling the needs of people, rather than for funding impractical, unworkable, complex missile defense systems against enemies which no longer exist.

We in WILPF join women's organizations around the world in Abolition 2000, the international grassroots network pressuring governments to abolish all nuclear weapons. Because military expenditures consume such a large part of our government's budget, we have seen a decline in the incomes of most families during the past two decades, while those of the wealthy have increased dramatically. Over twelve million jobs were lost in the 80s following corporate restructuring. These losses are speeded up by the largest banking and industrial mergers in history, the result of the internationalization of capital.

Closer to home, in the desire to inform myself and others on state and local measures which confront the voter, for years I have summarized and condensed information from the complicated initiative and referendum issues at each election. I make recommendations based on data from the League of Women Voters, the Friends Committee on Legislation, the California Council of Churches, the ACLU, the Sierra Club, the Data Center, the Tax Reform Association, labor groups and others. The demand for my analysis continues to grow. During elections the phones in the Berkeley WSP office ring off the hook with urgent requests from as far north as Mendocino. The recommendations have been translated into Spanish and also published in the parish bulletin of St. Joseph the Worker Catholic Church in Berkeley. Several organizations distribute these summaries with their newsletters, and they are sent out on email lists. As part of this voter education project, I also present discussion programs on election issues to members of Gray Panthers, Liberty Hill Baptist Church, the Berkeley/Richmond Jewish Community Center, Finn Hall, and retirement centers: Claremont House, Albany Senior Citizens, Piedmont Gardens, Redwood Gardens, and Strawberry Creek Lodge.

I join others in leafleting the local post offices on Income Tax Day, hoping to alert taxpayers to the disparity between the government's military and domestic priorities. We dress as "living sign boards" along the evening commute route, wearing placards asking, "Do you know where your tax dollars go?" We are generally greeted with approving honks and toots.

I take heart in the history of past struggles that have made a difference. We in the peace movement worked to stop the Vietnam War. We went on day after day, year after year, feeling it would never end, yet we succeeded. Today we all need to redouble our efforts.

Our goal, from the beginning, to educate the public, and our decades-long efforts to achieve that goal, must continue. As part of our outreach, we organize and speak at public gatherings, issue press releases, make radio and TV appearances, distribute literature, and lobby our elected representatives.

We must have universal, high-quality public education, housing, nutrition and health-care. Free speech and access to media for all points of view are equally critical. We need to foster a broader knowledge of history, especially working people's history, which is rarely taught in schools. We need more peace and conflict studies and less military research and ROTC training. Young people must learn how to unite in order to create change in the world.

The World Bank and the closely-connected International Monetary Fund, which have been the target of a number of international protests, promote large loans which often prove beyond the ability of poor countries to handle. In contrast, in Bangladesh, Muhammad Yunus established the Grameen Bank, an innovative program to furnish mini-credit and small loans, primarily to women. The aim is to fight poverty around the world. The program has been highly successful, and has grown to several million dollars a year, with a remarkable repayment rate of ninety-six percent. The Grameen Bank concept is spreading to other countries, even including several US inner cities, marking the beginning of a grassroots economic revolution.

And there are other signs of hope, I have been impressed by the strategies of many organizations that move us toward our goal of a just and humane society. (Many of them are included in the Appendix.) The range of these initiatives varies from international to local. This upsurge in activism has rallied growing numbers among the younger generation of trained personnel.

Doctors Without Borders sends 2,500 volunteers to 80 countries wherever human rights are being violated or lives endangered by war or natural catastrophe. This group, which was awarded the 1999 Nobel Prize for courage, assists victims, speaks out on abuses, and insists on total independence.

After years of declining membership, the AFL–CIO is experiencing a moderate upsurge and has been able to win the passage of some bills aimed at abuses in the garment industry. "The labor movement needs to return to class consciousness." This phrase has rarely been heard among union leaders since the 30s, but labor's image is changing and professionals, including medical doctors and graduate student instructors, are in the process of unionization. In the past, organized labor has not been supportive of the estimated 5 or 6 million workers who have temporary status, or have entered the US illegally. To quote John Wilhelm of the AFL–CIO, "This system doesn't work and is used as a weapon against workers." Union leaders have recently called for amnesty for undocumented workers. The potential of increased membership will add to labor's clout. Labor as a social movement, an idea whose time once came, now seems to have come around again.

In more than 30 cities, the Campaign for a Living Wage has succeeded in bringing together unions, churches, and community groups, including Oakland's Association of Community Organizations for Reform Network (ACORN). These campaigns demonstrate labor's concern about improving the lot of the nation's thirty million working poor.

In the Bay Area, *Street Spirit* is a publication by the homeless, sponsored by the American Friends Service Committee (AFSC), which permits the seller to keep the dollar received. Paul Boden, of the San Francisco Coalition on Homelessness, says, "They see help and charity as simply the decent thing for a just society to do, not a handout."

WILPF is celebrating its 85th year. To emphasize the organization's ongoing commitment to the redistribution of power, women from across the country continue to visit congress, pushing peace issues by meeting with representatives, attending briefings, and listening in on committee hearings.

Locally, Claire Greensfelder, an early anti-nuclear activist, was greatly inspired during her work at the Jane Addams Hull House in Chicago in the late 70s. Later she launched the Rainbow Serpent Plutonium Free Future project, a liaison with anti-nuclear activists in other countries. Currently, as director of the City of Oakland's Martin Luther King, Jr. Freedom Center, she coordinates programs for youth in non-violence, equality, and ecology. In this she is giving practical application to the ideals of WILPF founder Jane Addams, and setting an example for the kinds of citizenship we should encourage.

Schools are enlisting millions of students in volunteer efforts in community service, as part of graduation requirements. Americorps, City Year, National Youth Service Day, and more, offer young people the opportunity to improve their communities. The lifelong efforts of older activists like me are meaningless unless they are continued and built upon by future generations.

After the many years I have dedicated to these issues, I sometimes wonder what keeps me going? I'm not foolhardy enough to think that world peace depends solely on WILPF and WSP, yet our contributions have been substantial.

Since we helped bring an end to the Vietnam War, it is my hope that with real dedication, and by working in coalitions, we may unite peace, justice, women's and environmental organizations to accomplish our goals. We're not going to have real improvement in the world until more people become active. Women in the peace movement can be only *one* instrument in a greater challenge to the status quo.

By working together, we can alter the way our government relates to the rest of the world. We must change its image from that of the most powerful military leader in the world to one of preeminence in peace, justice, science, education, health, the environment, and the arts. I envision a world without war and without the threat of nuclear disaster as well as a stronger and more effective UN. I dream of a world without want, and can only hope for an end to racial and religious fanaticism.

Chapter 34

Welcoming the New Millennium

*The love of one's country is a natural thing, but why should love stop
at the border? We are all leaves of a tree, and the tree is humanity."*

—Pablo Casals, master cellist

Our family had stabilized after the wrenching events of the 70s—the deaths of Aron and Sam. In 1989 I had published *Sam Hamburg: Agricultural Pioneer in California and Israel*. Was his experience unique? I reflected on the fact that other branches of our expanding family had arrived in this country under somewhat similar circumstances. I spoke to Sonya's husband, Ernest, about recapturing the story of his forbears. His great grandfather had emigrated from Germany, settling in the Spokane, Washington area. He and his son did some farming, eventually branching out into what became one of the largest ranches in the state.

Then came the shattering news of my son-in-law's prostate cancer diagnosis, postponing my dream of recording his story. After a valiant, ten-year struggle, he died in his Orinda home on Easter Sunday, 1997, with his loved ones at his bedside. The family established the Ernest H. Ruehl Scholarship at Princeton University, his alma mater, from which his sons had also graduated.

Following in his father's tradition, Ernest Jr., with an MBA from Stanford, is a managing director of the investment banking division of a prominent New York banking firm, working in the San Francisco office. His wife Jennifer Lowry is an MBA graduate from the UC Berkeley Haas School of Business. Ted works for a leading Boston law firm. He and his wife, Claudia Svoboda, both earned doctorates from Harvard where she became an instructor. Paul pursues a career as a screenwriter in Hollywood and New York. Perhaps someday he will write about one of his pioneer forebears?

Tanya's husband, Ernie Goldsmith, also comes from immigrant stock. His grandparents arrived from Romania in the early part of the century. The presence of his grandmother in his childhood home insured the continuation of old-world Jewish traditions. Of scholarly bent, his standing in the legal profession earned him a 1997 appointment to a California Superior Court judgeship.

David Goldsmith majored in physics at American University in Washington, DC. In the Bay Area, he works as a computer troubleshooter. His sister Julie, with a Ph.D. from the University of Pennsylvania, is a senior policy analyst with the San Francisco Department of Human Services. Her husband, Jose Lopez, a fellow Ph.D. and a specialist in econometrics, works for a leading San Francisco banking establishment. His parents, who emigrated from Spain in the mid-30s, currently divide their time between that country and New York.

The fourth American generation of our family is making its debut as I write this story. Ted and Claudia have two children, Nicholas, who arrived in 1995, and Isabel in 1998. Ernest Jr. and Jennifer are the parents of Henry, born in 1997, and have also welcomed a daughter, Elizabeth Emerson Ruehl, who made her appearance just in time to be included here. She is named for a great-grandmother, a descendant of the Ralph Waldo Emerson family. Julie and Jose have also welcomed their first child, following Jewish custom named after Julie's deceased grandfather, Samuel.

As I look back on the many years of hard work and achievement by sucessive generations in building the "house of tomorrow," I can only hope that our legacy will empower future generations in their struggles for a better and more peaceful world.

Chapter 35

Epilogue: Letter to My Grandchildren

Your children are not your children...
They are the sons and daughters of life's longing for itself,
You may give them your love but not your thoughts
For they have their own thoughts.
You may house their bodies but not their souls
For their souls dwell in the house of tomorrow

—Selected lines from
Kahlil Gibran, The Prophet

Dear Grandchildren,

In this story, I have written about change. It is important that young people understand how quickly a situation can be altered, and that only education can prepare them for what lies ahead.

In my lifetime I have seen America come nearly full circle. In a brief, ninety-plus-year period, we have moved from rural hardship and limited education to massive industrialization, the explosion of higher education, multinational corporations, and then back again to increasing poverty and an educational system that has failed to keep up with the times.

When immigrants like my father arrived in this country, many were fleeing the tyranny of dictators. They came here with the hopes of enjoying freedom. Yet once again, the world community faces dictatorial leaders. An economic elite presides over multinational economies, while most people face a deteriorating standard of living.

How quickly things change.

We activists wanted to abolish war, and thought our voices were being heard. We believed that US leadership had been transformed by the lessons of the Vietnam War. Yet government has overseen the greatest escalation in military spending since Reagan's "Star Wars" campaigns even though the cold war is long since past.

My family came to this land seeking opportunity. America offered new hope, a living to all who could work, and the freedom to make choices. Yet now my anger rises when I see the quickening pace of corporate consolidation and offshore relocation of industry, low wages paid to exploitable, third world labor, and the increase of temporary employment without benefits. As poverty sets in, families break up, children are lost, and despair begins to pervade society. Consequently, race-baiting, intolerance, and hate attacks toward synagogues and churches continue to escalate.

We in the peace movement work for more than peace. We struggle to support workers. We strive to maintain our idealism, which keeps the movement going. According to the UN Human Development Report, a new concept of human security is needed, "One that focuses on the security of people in their homes, in their jobs, in their communities, and in their environment."

In the last century, we have witnessed the greatest upheavals, the cruelest battles, and the most tragic suffering on the part of millions through racial and religious warfare. As an expression of reconciliation toward the Jewish people who have suffered unremitting persecution throughout history, New York Catholic Cardinal John O'Connor issued "a call of repentance" on *Yom Kippur* of last year, on the Jewish Day of Atonement. In a full-page ad in the *New York Times*, he wrote, "working together, I ask that you understand my own abject sorrow for any member of the Catholic Church, high or low, including myself, who may have harmed you or any of your forbears in any way."

I hoped that this declaration would be the first of similar statements of reconciliation between peoples of all cultures, beliefs and backgrounds. Several months later, I was gratified to read German president Johannes Rau's emotional apology for the Nazi genocide in World War II. "With the people of Israel watching, I bow in humility before those murdered, before those who don't have graves where I could ask them for forgiveness. I ask...for myself and my generation, for the sake of our children and grandchildren, whose future I would like to see alongside the children of Israel."

In the words of Stephen Vincent Benet:

Our earth is but a small star in the great
universe, yet of it
we can make,
if we choose, a planet
unvexed by war,
untroubled by hunger or fear,
undivided by senseless distinctions of
race, color or theory.

Today, peace workers are needed more than ever. We must continue to act in coalition with other peace, justice, women's and environmental organizations. Our mission has not yet been accomplished, however Jane Addams and our foremothers have left us a legacy of courage and steadfastness. From them we inherited great tools, structures, and principles that we will need in order to reach out and reforge our methods for the 21st century and beyond. As Nobel Peace Prize winner Linus Pauling, says "Our strength must grow so that future generations may not have to sacrifice their security or lives."

With love,
Your grandmother,

Berkeley, California
November 2000

Appendices

Taking Stock:

Essays on Local, National, and Global Concerns

"Every country that opposes US Policy or refuses to accept corporate free-market globalization will be at risk...As the Roman historian Tacitus said, 'Where they make a desert, they call it peace'."

—Douglas Mattern, head of the Association of World
Citizens, warns of the US-NATO war machine,
Letter to the Editor, San Francisco Chronicle, June 22,1999

From Welfare to Work

"The eighth and most meritorious degree of charity is to anticipate charity by preventing poverty."

—Maimonides

"Everyone has the right to a standard of living, adequate for the health and wellbeing of himself and family."

—Article 25 of *The United Nations Universal Declaration of Human Rights*, 1948

The years 1998 and 1999 witnessed the worst layoffs since the Depression. Unfortunately, the trend accelerates into 2000 in the midst of the booming economy. The new century is greeted with the following: "Chevron Profits Rise 63% But Oil Giant Still Plans to Cut 3,500 Jobs," and "Coca-Cola Cuts 6,000 Jobs [Reducing] Staff by Half." Where is the voice of compassion for the thousands of Americans who are being thrown out of work each day? Why is no one in a leadership position calling a halt to this gutting of our labor force? As thousands of workers are discharged by almost every industry, who will buy the flood of new products coming off the assembly lines? Where are the unemployed to turn?

Even in a period of economic expansion, two or three unemployed go uncounted for every one surveyed. Secure jobs are a thing of the past, as statistics indicate that only thirty-three percent of the state's labor force has traditional employment of one full-time, year-round job, while the rest of the workforce is largely without benefits. The number of temporary employees, not including migrant farm workers, is steadily growing. Workers are threatened with plant closures and the shifting of production overseas. Minimum wages hover below the point of subsistence while Americans work longer hours in their jobs than do their counterparts in other industrialized nations.

The problem with America's acceptance of the "information economy" is that it creates an unbalanced mix of jobs, an abundance for a few highly intelligent workers and virtually none for anyone else. We are becoming a nation divided. The doors of affirmative action are being slammed shut. I find it shocking that more than a million children in the US between five and fourteen work full time illegally, for less than the minimum wage. Roughly one quarter of American children live in poverty, more than in any other advanced nation. We are the only industrialized society without universal health care. Minimum wage salaries do not support families. Almost seven million Californians live without access to health care, among them many immigrant families. And the number is growing.

An April 1998 survey in twelve California counties revealed high hunger rates, even among households receiving emergency food. Because of the vagaries of welfare requirements, many immigrant families are going hungry because they are no longer eligible for government assistance, such as food stamps. Rick Mockler of San Francisco Catholic Charities commented, "Whether...soup kitchens or food banks, what we provide is just a drop in the bucket..."

In 1996, President Clinton shredded the sixty-year old safety net when he signed the Federal Welfare Restructuring Act, placing a five-year lifetime limit on welfare. Although some attempt has been made to maintain prior levels of assistance through various programs, many recipients, particularly those with children, have been unable to take advantage of them because of complexities of the system.

California grants an average of $565 a month for a family of three. Welfare-to-work programs have had questionable results. Former welfare recipients who find themselves unemployed, often become ineligible for public assistance because of welfare reform time limits. US firms are slow to hire from the welfare rolls, and will select only the most employable people, leaving behind those with the fewest skills and the worst problems. In California, sixty percent of adult welfare recipients lack even the most basic skills. Although numbers of welfare recipients have found jobs, far fewer are able to keep them. According to several California state studies, between one-third and one-half of those placed in jobs lose their employment within the year. In addition, the welfare-to-work folks—who receive low wages, no benefits, and inadequate training—compete with current employees, sometimes leaving *them* displaced and jobless.

The minimum wage, $5.15 an hour, is not a living wage, and as a result, most people are back on welfare within six months. It is difficult to track where former welfare recipients have landed, although we can note the growing numbers of homeless—including many children—in food lines. Every night more than a million children face the dark with no place to call home. Experts claim there are more homeless children now than at any time since the Great Depression. Some forty percent of the homeless are now women and children, the fastest growing group. Housing costs are skyrocketing in the Bay Area. Cities vary in their handling of the problems. Thousands are turned away nightly from San Francisco shelters, where only two thousand beds are available. The City's policy of confiscating homeless peoples' clothing and property, including medications, is inexcusable. No other industrial nation accepts such conditions. We pay a high price in hopelessness, despair, crime and violence.

California's prison system is approaching two hundred percent occupancy—with two million people behind bars—even though crime has dropped considerably in the past several years. Our state spends far more on prisons than on schools. Americans continue to favor incarceration with little attempt at rehabilitation. A bill that would toughen sentences for violent youth is under consideration. This would allow fourteen-year-olds to be tried as adults and sent to prison, where they often face sexual attacks, sometimes leading to suicide. In its 1999 annual report, the Coalition for Juvenile Justice criticized the practice of locking up juveniles at earlier ages for a wider range of misdemeanors, with inadequate drug treatment or training. Why do we imprison more people than any other developed country? Prison construction is a thriving industry. According to David Doi, executive director of the Coalition, "When centers that confine juveniles are safe, humane, and rehabilitative...both the public and children benefit." In California, 'Three Strikes' legislation passed in 1994 has drastically stepped up teen prosecutions. The state now tries nearly 1000 minors a year in adult court, and sends the majority of them to the state penitentiary for lengthy sentences, including life.

The future of our civilization depends on a good educational system, particularly in the primary grades, where every child should be encouraged to blossom. And yet US education is falling behind the rest of the developed world, devoting a smaller percentage of the national income to teachers' salaries than in other "first-world" countries. California's public educational system is no longer the envy of the nation; our schools are now the most crowded in history. We rank *last* in the number of teachers, counselors, and librarians per pupil. In the next ten years California schools will need a substantial investment in the education infrastructure as well as thousands of new teachers. So called "Solutions" such as vouchers, charter schools, and corporate-run schools, have the potential to destroy our system of free public education.

It is natural for parents to be dissatisfied with the public schools, but setting up charter schools—which can exclude children with special needs while at the same time draining money away from public schools which must accept *all* children—does not solve the problems. These schools are not required to meet the State Board of Education standards for teacher certification and are not accountable to local school boards. Studies reveal that charter school students are doing no better than those in public schools.

We must improve the entire educational system instead of relying on simple solutions. We must stop ignoring the needs of the young and give all of them a chance to develop their talents. Society needs them as future leaders as well as skilled and productive workers. Our survival depends upon an educated citizenry. In the words of Rabbi Hillel, "If not now, when?"

Policeman of the World

"Making weapons of mass destruction in the name of peace, and possessing nuclear weapons, is nothing but an act of murder waiting to happen."

—Andreas Toupadakis, former chemist at the Lawrence Livermore National Laboratory, who quit his job in protest, *San Francisco Chronicle*, February 17, 2000

I feel strongly about the role of the military in this country and what I perceive to be the militarization of our society. Far from having achieved universal disarmament and the peaceful settlement of disputes through the United Nations and the World Court, the planet bristles with deadly weaponry. The US continues to be the driving force in escalating the technology of warfare. With the end of the Cold War, what justification is there for maintaining our own nuclear stockpiles? According to General Lee Butler, Retired, Strategic Air Command, "There is no security in nuclear weapons...it's a fool's game. The stakes of nuclear war engage not just the survival of the antagonists, but the fate of mankind."

Why, after two world wars and the creation of the UN, which was meant to end the "scourge of war," are we confronted with so many crises? The Middle East, Yugoslavia, the Congo, North Korea, and the former Soviet Union, among others, constitute a potential threat to world peace that could involve the US as the self-appointed policeman of the world. At the end of 2000, surveys indicate that sixty-five nations are mired in some form of conflict.

Rarely is the true reason given for the use of force between nations. When the US, with NATO support, attacked Iraq in 1991, it was in retaliation for that country's invasion of Kuwait. There was no mention of its importance as a supplier of oil to the western world.

241

Following the end of the Gulf War, the US with the support of its allies, instituted sanctions against Iraq. The embargo has been maintained with the aim of toppling its leader, Saddam Hussein, whom they have demonized, accusing him of continuing the development of weapons of mass destruction. This policy has caused untold suffering of the Iraqi population, with a high death rate among their children.

The US policy of supporting Israel in its military build-up is the cause of great concern among its neighbors in the Middle East. Arab states deeply resent US favoritism toward Israel. A small country without natural borders, Israel could be wiped out easily. Its presence has never been welcome in that part of the world. Unfortunately, we do not yet have a functioning international peace force or a structure for the resolution of territorial and other disputes, especially those rooted in religious and cultural differences. Thus Israel justifies maintaining its strong defense.

After years of foot-dragging by the Israelis, Israeli prime minister Barak has indicated in his dealings with Palestinian leader Arafat that he is willing to consider seriously the return of some of the displaced Palestinians to their former homes. The return of additional territory is being discussed. There is also the problem of East Jerusalem, which Palestinians wish to establish as the capital of their future state, a demand which Israel steadfastly opposes. Ongoing negotiations will help determine Israel's size, and its future as a secure or threatened state.

Despite this history, and the advocacy of peaceworkers throughout the world, military spending at cold war levels continues with the 2000 Pentagon Budget of $289 billion, a substantial increase over the previous year. In spite of the eloquent arguments of generals, diplomats, and scientists, the US is forging ahead with the development of dozens of new nuclear weapons programs through "subcritical" testing of old weapons as well as the development of new ones.

The National Ignition Facility (NIF) is part of the Stockpile Stewardship program, which involves work at Livermore and Sandia Labs as well as testing on the Nevada desert. These programs are in violation of the Comprehensive Test Ban Treaty (CTBT) which one hundred and fifty other countries have signed. Instead of the "peace dividend" promised at the end of the Vietnam War, prospects for the future are not good. According to the Center for Defense Information (CDI), the failure of the US Senate to ratify the CTBT and the pursuit of the National Missile Defense System (also known as "Star Wars") indicates that the US is willing to return to the worst days of the Cold War nuclear arms race.

To add to the nightmare, the US will resume production of tritium gas as fuel for thermonuclear weapons. Even worse, the Department of Energy has ordered the tritium to be produced in *civilian* power reactors operated by the Tennessee Valley Authority (TVA). Mixing the military with the domestic will set a bad precedent for other governments. According to the CDI, "The US is engaged in a costly, dangerous effort to perpetuate its nuclear dominance at a level which is higher than any rational military or political justification." Those of us dedicated to a peaceful world must accelerate our efforts to stop these programs.

It is crucial for the U.S government to support the United Nations and rely upon it, as well as on the regional security organizations established for the settlement of international disputes. The US refusal to pay its full UN dues jeopardizes the survival of the very institution which should serve as the world's greatest safeguard, our best hope for lasting global peace.

So far, the peace movement has been unable to stop the military from engaging in disastrous, no-win operations, whether in Iraq, Kosovo, Colombia, or Indonesia. A worst case scenario is the $1.6 billion allocation toward fighting the drug war in Colombia, a program which will displace 10,000 *campesinos*. These funds may result in our troops being mired down in a decades-long civil war there, fueled largely by America's insatiable demand for illicit drugs.

Global Warming or Global Warning?

"I turn to the outdoor experiences where I have had a one-on-one relationship with the natural world without having it first judged or controlled by others. The relation of the environmental movement to the peace movement is very strong. Both seek to preserve conditions on the planet in a way that is most suitable to human life."

—photographer Galen Rowell, in letter to ASH

"Ours is a tiny planet in a small galaxy at the edge of an incomprehensibly boundless universe...We are but transient passengers on this planet Earth. It does not belong to us. We are not free to doom generations yet unborn. We are not at liberty to erase humanity's past nor dim its future..."

—Bernard Lown, MD, and Evangueni Chazov, MD, members of
International Physicians for the Prevention of Nuclear War (IPPNW)

Many military problems eventually become environmental concerns. For example, one million deadly landmines have been planted around the world and the number is growing. As some of the most devastating and deadly weapons of modern warfare, landmines maim or kill 26,000 people every year. Many injuries occur long after a conflict has ended. The 1998 Nobel Peace Prize was awarded to the International Campaign to Ban Landmines and its American leader, Jody Williams. Although 130 nations have endorsed the Landmines Elimination Act, the US has refused to sign. Likewise, cluster bombs dropped during the Kosovo war, containing depleted uranium, are a great threat to the environment.

It is unconscionable that twenty percent of the world's people consume eighty percent of its resources, causing extreme damage to the environment in the process. While nations squander their capital on methods of destruction in order to protect their wealth, one fifth of the world's population does not have access to safe drinking water. Continuing environmental erosion affects all of us, threatening life and livelihood from pollution and toxic wastes, large scale deforestation, desertification, drought, and soil depletion. Health problems related to the environment are increasing. In my own case, I made a conscious decision, when I moved to an area with access to the post office, the library, and public transportation, not to be dependent on my automobile. For myself, giving up the freedom to move about freely has been a sacrifice, but as I walk or take a bus, in a small way, I feel that I am doing my part for a pollution-free atmosphere.

Poor and minority communities have long protested the presence of toxics in their neighborhoods. It was not until 1998 that the Environmental Protection Agency (EPA) recognized "environmental justice" as a criterion for reviewing new development. This policy has been attacked by industry as well as state and local governments which claim that these restrictions endanger jobs so desperately needed in poor and minority communities. Lana Pollack, President of the Michigan Environmental Council, responds, "I think it's a shameful argument that says poor people have to choose between jobs and protecting their children." A complete reform of US nuclear waste policy is badly needed. There is *no safe method* for disposal of nuclear waste.

A coalition of Native Americans and environmentalists, including the women's peace movement, is close to success in the long struggle to stop the nuclear power industry's plan to build a huge waste dump at Ward Valley in the Mojave Desert. This victory will result in cleaning up the residues of fifty years of nuclear weapons production. The Western States Legal Foundation, led by the indefatigable Jackie Cabasso, has won a $6.25 million settlement which will be used to conduct scientific reviews of the Department of Energy (DOE) cleanup activities. A real victory in an ongoing war.

We must develop environmentally safe methods of energy generation. Nuclear production, whether for energy or for military purposes, should be ended. The recent tragic accident at a nuclear plant in Japan, which obtains one-third of its power from nuclear sources, has raised questions about the future of this method of power generation. At least one of the plant workers has died and others are seriously ill from high radiation doses. Although the government had invested billions of yen in nuclear facilities, a senior government official is quoted as saying, "The accident was serious enough to press Japan to reconsider its nuclear power policy in the future." All nuclear plants produce waste that contaminates water and soil; and they provide raw materials for building nuclear weapons. All governments need to experiment with alternative methods of power generation, including wind and solar energy.

It is estimated that by 2040 the California population will double—to 60 million people—causing a greater demand for housing, transportation, schools, and other services, especially water. Population growth results in loss of the best farmlands as well as increased use of the automobile. Emissions of carbon dioxide (CO_2) and other greenhouse gases continue, causing global warming and endangering the health of all. We hear predictions of greater flooding and water shortages, landslides, and the outbreak of new diseases.

As a follow-up to the 1997 Kyoto Conference on global warming, 160 nations met in Buenos Aires in the fall of 1998 to discuss ways to reduce emissions of CO_2 and other heat-trapping gases. The US agreed to cut its emissions by seven percent over the next ten to fifteen years, depending upon its ability to purchase "credits to pollute" from less developed countries—a highly questionable policy. Is our health more sacred than that of poor people? The US has finally signed the Kyoto treaty, but it still awaits ratification by the Senate. Science should be used to benefit *all* people, rather than to create profits for corporations. It is important that we act for the good of the planet and not only for our own narrow interests.

Why Bigger Is Not Better

"...The processes of deregulation and globalization have removed governments and labor unions as effective restraints...Corporations are surpassing governments in power..."

—David Korten, *When Corporations Rule the World*, 1995

I see some hopeful signs as we enter the year 2000. A brief review is necessary in order to understand what happened in the "Battle in Seattle," and the events leading to it. The globalization of trade and capital has not proceeded entirely according to the plans of world leaders. In reality, globalization has resulted in increasing poverty and a general deterioration in conditions among the less-developed world.

The 1994 North American Free Trade Association (NAFTA) reduced or eliminated tariffs, creating a free flow of goods and capital through Mexico, the US and Canada. Thousands of workers from this country have lost their jobs as companies continue to relocate south of the border in pursuit of cheap labor. The three thousand shabbily built border factories, the *maquiladoras*, lack proper sanitation or other amenities. Mexicans have also lost jobs, especially farm workers, as cheaper US subsidized corn enters the market. Poor farmers in some areas have turned to coca and poppy growing as the best land has been taken for export crops, and they are sometimes forced to cultivate unstable hillsides with serious ecological consequences.

A recent UN report states that "...global inequalities in income and living standards have reached unbelievable levels." A UNICEF study reveals that malnutrition is killing seven million children every year, at a rate comparable to the bubonic plague.

Deplorable labor conditions in offshore US factories were first brought to public attention by Charles Kernaghan of the International Labor Committee (ILC) and San Francisco's Global Exchange. The UN International Labor Office (UNILO) charges that 250 million youngsters between ages five and fourteen work in developing countries, many of them in hazardous jobs. In Pakistan, India, and other countries where child labor exists under the worst conditions, children are part of a grassroots movement demanding rights similar to those of unionized adult workers. They want job training, time off for school, and the elimination of dangerous work conditions.

In the US, a broad coalition of religious, human rights, labor, women's, and student organizations is circulating a petition to the President and the US Congress to end child labor and sweatshops. Many college students nationwide are reacting to a powerful anti-sweatshop movement with sit-ins and teach-ins, protesting companies that use a college logo on sweatshop merchandise. The energy generated by the movement reminds me of the early days of the suffragist struggle, as it attracts a large number of dedicated young people.

Although globalization is the term now being applied, the movement among leading governments to increase the free flow of trade by removing barriers began with the General Agreement on Tariffs and Trade (GATT), in 1947. Its successor, the World Trade Organization (WTO), currently includes 135 countries.

A full page ad placed in the *New York Times*, November 22, 1999 was sponsored by the Sierra Club, Greenpeace USA, and the United Steelworkers of America among others, stating: "The WTO is already among the most powerful, secretive, undemocratic and *unelected* bodies on earth. It has been granted unprecedented powers including the right to rule on whether laws of nations, concerning public health, food safety, small business, labor standards, culture, and human rights, or *anything*...are 'barriers to trade' by WTO standards."

The December 1999 ministerial meeting of the WTO in Seattle drew the largest protests since the anti-Vietnam War demonstrations of the 60s. Sixty thousand marchers, from youths to the elderly, demanded an immediate stop to WTO expansion and a reassessment of its policies. Ten thousand activists—including a coalition of hard hats, longshoremen, environmentalists, miners, farmers, even sea turtle impersonators—called for guarantees of labor rights and environmental protection.

The discipline maintained by the thousands of young people trained in nonviolence was remarkable. Over six hundred people were arrested for peaceful protest. Through the clouds of tear gas and the forest of picket signs and banners, one could at last glimpse the rough outlines of a future progressive coalition. The ILWU cooperated with the anti-WTO marchers by closing down every West Coast port for that day.

The WTO demonstrations were the result of many months of communication via the

Internet, which has made it possible for a new generation of activists to function. Mobilized through various networks operating on an international level, organizers sent out email and put up web sites, posting graphics and slogans for the grassroots movement. According to columnist Walter Truett Anderson in the *SF Examiner*, December 5, 1999, the most powerful aspect of internet communication is "an ongoing expansion of our mental maps, as we come to see the whole world, not just our neighborhood or nation, as the space we inhabit."

As a result of the outpouring of protest, the WTO delegates left Seattle without having reached agreement on any of the outstanding issues. At a follow-up meeting of the WTO's governing board in Geneva early in 2000, deep differences over Seattle's issues remained unresolved, including internal reforms, labor rights, and certain exemptions for poor nations. The old rules have expired and there is no consensus on dealing with new ones. The WTO remains deadlocked. To quote Daniel Singer in an article in *The Nation*, January 3, 2000, "The protesters in Seattle...have revived the forgotten belief that people can shape things through collective action. They have set the agenda for the coming millennium by reminding us that there are many people...ready to struggle against their own governments and corporations for a different world."

There is *strength in numbers.*

Tributes to Alice

"In a more spiritual sense, I am certain of what I inherited from my grandmother: my concern for others, my desire to understand social inequality, and the commitment to work toward its eradication," wrote Julie Goldsmith, Alice's granddaughter, in her Ph.D. dissertation

The Sonoma State University Women's Studies Program, on September 26, 1986, thanked Alice for "sharing experiences." They were particularly heartened to "realize that not everyone burns out doing social change work—some persist through a lifetime."

Nobel Peace Prize winner Linus Pauling wrote, "I've been aware of and inspired by Alice's strong commitment and contributions to world peace and justice." Nobel Laureate Owen Chamberlain, has commented on Alice's "tireless work for peace...and excellent judgment. [She has] been able to mobilize the resources of our community."

San Francisco Chronicle Columnist Art Hoppe, writing in 1969, noted that, "As always, you have my admiration." Later, he remarked, "I am interested that you are still active in politics." In 1983 *San Francisco Chronicle* Columnist Herb Caen wrote that, "As usual...Alice made nothing but sense and enlightenment...you have never been more needed."

Organizations have also voiced their praise and support for Alice's work. The Berkeley Gray Panthers cited Alice for "annual, in-depth descriptions of the ballot measures," which have "helped legions of Berkeley residents cast more informed votes." East Bay Women for Peace honored Alice at a dinner in December 1982, stating "She, in no small way, helped end the Vietnam War."

Linda Lazzareschi, director of the Women's Daytime Drop-in Center (WDDC), thanked Alice for being "a supporter of the center for as long as anyone can remember...The list of community organizations [you] support must read like the 'Big Blue Book' of Alameda County." To Global Exchange Director Medea Benjamin, Alice is "a great role model."

On International Women's Day in 1993, upon presentation of the Certificate of Recognition as an Outstanding Berkeley Woman by the Commission on the Status of

Women, Berkeley Mayor Loni Hancock wrote, "You inspire others to help make a difference."In 1999, the Berkeley Community Fund Award was presented to Alice for "A lifetime of activism and leadership for social and economic justice and world peace."

Alice Sachs Hamburg: A Chronology

1870	Father Herman Sachs is born in Skopishok, Lithuania.
1880s	Herman attends *yeshiva*, apprentice tinsmith.
1892	Herman apprentices in Finland.
1893-98	Herman joins and serves in Russian Army.
1899	Sam Hamburg born.
1901	Herman marries Hannah Shmuelson.
1902	Charlie Sachs born in Pokroi, Lithuania; Father Herman Sachs immigrates from Lithuania with brother Abram.
1903	Father works in several cities including Chicago and Denver.
1904	Mother Hannah and brother Charlie, two years old, join father in Wilton, ND; Father applies for homestead in Burleigh County, ND; Uncle Abe learns plumbing at Fort Lincoln Indian Reservation near Bismarck, ND.
1905	Alice born in Wilton coal mining company hospital, November 25.
1906	Family moves onto homestead sixteen miles out of town.
1907	Rachel Sachs born, first birth registered in Wing, ND; terrible drought.
1908	Herman Sachs becomes a US citizen.
1909	Family receives land title, leaves farm and moves to what would become Wing ND.
1910	Herman and Abram raise first building in Wing, the Sachs General Store & Post Office, operate store through 1914.
1911	Northern Pacific Railroad comes to Wing; Mother and Alice visit Chicago on train.
1911-13	Birth and death of baby sister and brother; store fails, years of hardship and drought.
1914	Ben Sachs born; family moves to Minneapolis; Alice starts first grade; First World War breaks out.
1915	Family moves to Annandale, MN, then to Hecla, SD, where they live four years.
1916	Excellent fifth grade teacher Mrs. King lends books to Alice.

1918	Flu epidemic hits Hecla.
1919	Principal Miss Noteboom arranges for Alice to skip 8th grade and enter high school.
1920	Family moves to Aberdeen, SD.
1921	Betty Kraft is third year high school English teacher; introduction to poetry.
1923	Herman and Charlie depart for California; Alice graduates from high school, enters Northern State Teachers College in Aberdeen.
1924	Charlie returns and drives family to Fresno, CA; Alice enters Fresno State as sophomore and meets Sam Hamburg; Sam graduates UCB and starts farming in Chowchilla, CA.
1925	Alice has summer jobs in Fresno at Wilson's Restaurant; a dry goods store, and in office of Krasner Fruit Co.; Sam becomes tenant farmer on Miller & Lux land, the San Juan Ranch, between Los Baños and Dos Palos.
1926	Family, except Rae, moves to Los Angeles; Alice enters UCLA as a junior; Alice and Sam elope to San Francisco at end of spring semester, live in a tent on Sam's ranch near Los Baños that summer; Alice enrolls at UC Berkeley.
1927	Alice elected Phi Beta Kappa and graduates from UCB with Highest Honors in Economics; Mother attends graduation; summer job at American Trust Co. in San Francisco; Alice enters graduate program in economics.
1928	Summer job at American Trust Co. bank branch in Los Baños.
1929	Alice earns M.A. in economics from UC Berkeley, dissertation on Economic Policies of the Soviet Government 1920-27; also earns general education and special "lifetime" adult education teaching credentials, begins teaching in ungraded school for migrant children on the ranch.
1930s	Cotton picking machine comes to ranch.
1930	Alice and Sam move to Dos Palos; Alice teaches high school history until 1932.
1931	Alice is chair of Youth Conservation Section of California Federation of Womens' Clubs, attends conferences and gives first speeches; Jane Addams, founder of WILPF, is awarded Nobel Peace Prize.
1932	Alice and Sam move to a larger ranch near Los Baños in foothills of Santa Cruz Mountains; Charlie moves to Tucson, AZ & starts business; Roosevelt elected on "New Deal" platform.
1933	Cotton strike in San Joaquin Valley; New Deal legislation passes ("National Industrial Recovery Act").
1934-37	Charlie's business fails, he comes to help out on ranch, mediates conflicts between dust bowl victims and *braceros*.

1934	ILWU strike in San Francisco starts in May; General Strike in July; Upton Sinclair, of End Poverty in California (EPIC) wins Democratic Primary for Governor; Social Security legislation passes.
1935	Sonya and Tanya born in Los Angeles; hailstorm on Memorial Day ruins barley crop; family engages Carmelita Luke ("KuKu") as nanny.
1936	Franklin Roosevelt reelected.
1937	Charlie marries and starts his own ranch nearby.
1938	Sam visits his family in Poland; Culbert Olson elected governor.
1939	Steinbeck publishes *Grapes of Wrath;* Carey McWilliams writes *Factories in the Fields.*
1939	Aron born in Fresno, twins start school; Alice engages Jenny Allen as nanny.
1940	Alice starts backyard playground in Los Baños; member, Merced County Recreation Commission.
1942	Alice leads Brownies and Girl Scouts in Los Baños.
1944	Alice organizes former professor's congressional campaign in Merced County; Alice and children move to Berkeley; Alice works on desegregation in Berkeley schools.
1945	Father Herman dies; brother Ben remarries; United Nations founded.
1946	Mother Hannah dies. Alice works with intercultural programs of PTA; joins League of Women Voters; gives benefit for Oakland Labor School which Sam co-hosts; Alice and Gordon Williams called before Alcohol Control Board; first family vacation in New York.
1947	Alice moves back to Los Baños.
1948	Alice and children return to Berkeley, settle on San Luis Road; writes recommendations on ballot measures; Henry Wallace for President campaign; Secretary of "Arts, Sciences and Professions Council."
1949	First meeting of "Citizens Against the Loyalty Oath" held at Alice's house; becomes original subscriber to KPFA; works with National Council of Jewish Women.
1950	Secretary of Garfield Jr. High School PTA; Robeson concert; Alice joins WILPF; Nixon elected to US Senate; Rosenbergs arrested.
1951	Alice subpoenaed by State Committee on Un-American Activities (Burns Committee); Rosenbergs convicted; construction of cotton gin on ranch and Central Valley Water Project completed; Sam's first trip to Israel.
1952	Alice travels to South Africa to meet Mother's relatives, visits Israel; Robeson concert in May; *The Nation* publishes Alice's article, "Berkeley's Example."

1953	Alice works on CA State Mental Health Association conference at Asilomar, Alice's first radio interview publicizing conference; Rosenbergs executed; Sonya and Tanya graduate from Berkeley High, enroll at Stanford and Pomona, respectively.
1955	Sam and children make trip to Europe and Israel; Alice meets Martin Luther King, Jr.
1957	Twins graduate; Sonya, Phi Beta Kappa, they visit Europe; Alice starts Senior Discussion Group at Temple Beth El, Berkeley.
1957-58	Alice and Aron live in Menlo Park where he attends Menlo School; activities on Peninsula: Bill of Rights Day, Palo Alto Peace Club.
1958	Aron graduates from high school and enrolls at Claremont College.
1959	Sonya marries Ernest Ruehl.
1960	Tanya marries Ernie Goldsmith. HUAC hearings; police wash demonstrators down steps at San Francisco City Hall
1961	Alice moves to San Francisco; Nov. 1, One Day Women's Strike for Peace (WSP) groups start in San Francisco and East Bay; Linus and Ava Pauling and Frances Herring organize Oslo conference against nuclear weapons; Aron's 21st birthday barbecue on ranch.
1962	WILPF and WSP send annual delegations to Sacramento to lobby governor and legislature about fallout shelters; California dependence on military contracts; Russian cosmonaut Titov reception organized by Labor School; Alice helps organize first visit of Soviet women and Committee for Friendly International Visits; WILPF holds first candlelight vigil against Vietnam War in Aquatic Park, San Francisco; Aron graduates from Claremont and returns to ranch.
1963	Grandson Ernie Ruehl, Jr. born; Conference on Disarmament and the Abundant Life held at Palace Hotel; John Birchers picket and *SF Examiner* attacks WILPF; Madame Nhu (Vietnam President's sister-in-law, known as the "Dragon Lady") at San Francisco's Palace Hotel; Young Democrats join protest march outside; Alice travels with Olive Mayer to Soviet Union as guest of Women's Committee, meets with peace groups in Japan and India, visits Thailand; WSP National Conference at Bryn Mawr; Dagmar Wilson called before Senate Internal Subversion Committee Hearings in DC; Test Ban Treaty signed between US & USSR.
1963-75	Opposition to the Vietnam War: campus activities, support of draft resisters, teach-ins, mobilizations, moratoriums, marches, weekly vigils, tax day demonstrations, billboards, Central America activism; Martin Luther King, Jr. leads March on Washington.

1964   Grandson David Goldsmith born; first Christmas Eve Vigil held at Union
        Square, San Francisco; Civil Rights Act passes.

1965   Alice moves back to Berkeley; attends first Vietnam Day teach-in at UCB;
        International Days of Protest for Peace; March to Oakland Army Terminal with
        ILWU; San Francisco WILPF holds First International Day of Protest for Peace
        in Vietnam and Justice in Selma; Port Chicago vigil; Helen Rand Miller initi-
        ates anti-war letter writing campaign lasting until end of war; Women in Black
        demonstration at Pentagon, hundreds arrested; Dr. Martin Luther King, Jr.
        speaks at 50th anniversary banquet of WILPF in Philadelphia, demands an end
        to the war in Vietnam; Voting Rights Act passes; Brother Ben dies.

1966   WILPF holds anti-war vigils in Union Square every Saturday until 1972; grand-
        daughter Julie and Grandson Ted born; Sam falls ill with Guillian-Barré disease.

1967   "Spring Mobilization to End the War" 67,000 march in San Francisco with a
        rally at Kezar Stadium, speakers: Coretta Scott King, Rita Moreno, Rabbi
        Abraham Feinberg; WILPF organizes boycott of Dow Chemical Co; Committee
        of Responsibility (COR) concerned with treatment of young Vietnamese war vic-
        tims; Martin Luther King, Jr. delivers anti-war speech at Riverside Church, NY.

1968   Jeannette Rankin brigade: 5000 women march on the White House; "Feed the
        Cities" Campaign launched on International Womens Day; WILPF and WSP
        open Women's Peace Office on Oak Street in San Francisco; Rally at Oakland
        Coliseum, speakers: MLK, Jr., Joan Baez, Mimi Fariña, Harry Belafonte and
        Sammy Davis, Jr.; WSP delegation to Gov. Reagan; WILPF joins Poor Peoples'
        Campaign; MLK, Jr. assassinated.

1969   "March Against Death in San Francisco;" speakers: Ralph Abernathy and Black
        Panther David Hilliard; WILPF, joined by Americans for Democratic Action,
        begins moratoriums on 15th of each month to initiate "No Business as Usual"
        campaign and concentrates on ending the war; Grandson Paul born.

1970   Citizens "Anti-Ballistic Missiles" coalition formed; Ron Dellums runs for
        Congress in California's 7th CD, speaks at Berkeley Community Theater,
        defeats Jefferey Cohelan.

1972   Mass march and rally at Kezar; ABM Treaty signed; San Joaquin Valley ranch
        sold to Buttes Gas & Oil Co.

1973   Alice attends World Peace Council in Moscow; Enola Maxwell chairs Domestic Action Coalition, Enola and Karen Talbot organize community meeting on "Urgent Domestic Priorities"; US WILPF delegation, headed by US Section President Marii Hasegawa, invited to Hanoi to celebrate signing of official peace accords.

1974   "Coalition to Cut Military Spending" formed, one of first activities is community meeting at Marina Junior High with Admiral LaRocque; "tiger cages" demonstration at Civic Center.

1975   Son Aron dies on Jan 6; Alice elected to National Board of WILPF; Vietnam War ends in May; Alice represents WILPF at the "White House Public Forum on Domestic Policy," held in Los Angeles; UFW recognized by Valley grape growers.

1976   Sam dies May 26.

1977   Alice attends WILPF Triennial and A&H Bomb Conference in Japan; Takes cruise to China, Singapore, Malaysia; Visits Great Britain; publishes article about Hiroshima in *Grassroots*.

1978   Trip to Cuba with WSP; Oakland demonstration against the military; murals from Hiroshima displayed at San Francisco City Hall; People's Temple members mass suicide at Jonestown.

1979   Trip to Israel and Egypt arranged by Israeli labor group G'vat Haviva; Nuclear Weapons Freeze Campaign begins.

1980   Sister Rachel dies; Alice elected to Agape Foundation Board of Trustees; speaks to UC Regents requesting that the University cancel its contract for management of Livermore and Los Alamos Nuclear Research Laboratories.

1981   Billboard campaign against US intervention in El Salvador.

1982   Alice speaks at "Right to a Job" conference in Lake County.

1983   Volga Peace Cruise (Russia).

1984   San Francisco Women's Peace Office receives letter from the Union of Vietnamese Women requesting information about US women who had been active in the anti-war movement. WILPF members among those arrested at Livermore Labs spend two weeks in Santa Rita Detention Center.

1985   Alice takes oral history course at Vista College; interviews Pat Cody, co-founder of Cody's Books, among others; WILPF 70th anniversary.

1986   Alice's book on Pat Cody published; The Western Jewish History Center of the Judah L. Magnes Museum in Berkeley requests Sam's papers; Bay Area WILPF archives sent to Swarthmore, repository of the Jane Addams Collection;

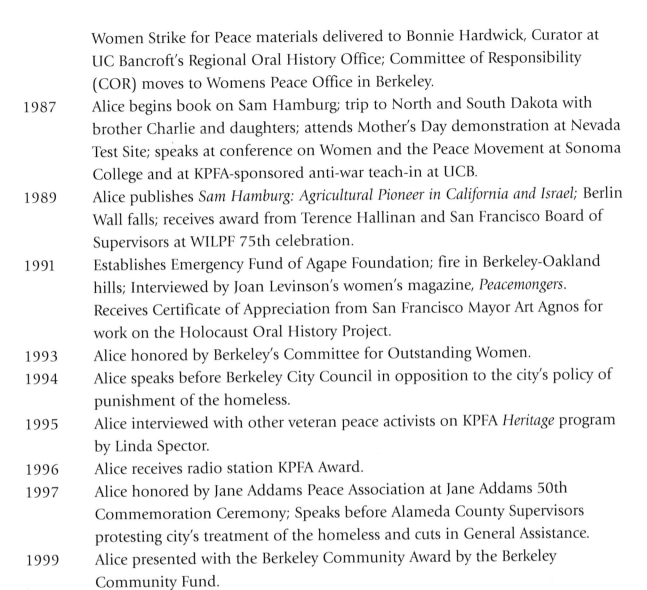

Women Strike for Peace materials delivered to Bonnie Hardwick, Curator at UC Bancroft's Regional Oral History Office; Committee of Responsibility (COR) moves to Womens Peace Office in Berkeley.

1987　Alice begins book on Sam Hamburg; trip to North and South Dakota with brother Charlie and daughters; attends Mother's Day demonstration at Nevada Test Site; speaks at conference on Women and the Peace Movement at Sonoma College and at KPFA-sponsored anti-war teach-in at UCB.

1989　Alice publishes *Sam Hamburg: Agricultural Pioneer in California and Israel*; Berlin Wall falls; receives award from Terence Hallinan and San Francisco Board of Supervisors at WILPF 75th celebration.

1991　Establishes Emergency Fund of Agape Foundation; fire in Berkeley-Oakland hills; Interviewed by Joan Levinson's women's magazine, *Peacemongers*. Receives Certificate of Appreciation from San Francisco Mayor Art Agnos for work on the Holocaust Oral History Project.

1993　Alice honored by Berkeley's Committee for Outstanding Women.

1994　Alice speaks before Berkeley City Council in opposition to the city's policy of punishment of the homeless.

1995　Alice interviewed with other veteran peace activists on KPFA *Heritage* program by Linda Spector.

1996　Alice receives radio station KPFA Award.

1997　Alice honored by Jane Addams Peace Association at Jane Addams 50th Commemoration Ceremony; Speaks before Alameda County Supervisors protesting city's treatment of the homeless and cuts in General Assistance.

1999　Alice presented with the Berkeley Community Award by the Berkeley Community Fund.

2000　The American Friends Service Committee honors Alice and fellow WILPF'er Madeline Duckles at "Two Lifetimes of Peacework" part of "Fallout: Complicated Lies, Simple Acts of Heroism", a series of programs on anti-nuclear activites and art.

Alice completes her autobiography, *Grass Roots, From Praire to Politics*, with the invaluable help of her grandchildren, assistants and colleagues in the ongoing struggle for a better world.

My Progeny

Children

SONYA Hamburg, b. 1935 (married to Ernest Ruehl, d. 1997)

> Their children
> Ernest Junior, b. 1963 (Married to Jennifer Lowery)

> > Their children
> > Henry, b. 1997
> > Elizabeth, b. 2000

> Theodore "Ted," b. 1966 (married to Claudia Svoboda)

> > Their children
> > Nicholas, b. 1995
> > Isabel, b. 1998

> Paul, b. 1969

TANYA Hamburg, b. 1935 (married to Ernest–referred to as "Ernie"–Goldsmith

> Their children
> David, b. 1964
> Julie, b. 1966 (married to Jose Lopez)

> > Their child
> > Samuel, b. 2000

ARON Hamburg, b. 1939, d. 1975

Organizations That Can Make a Difference

"Peace is not only the absence of war, but the conditions under which everyone has an opportunity for a decent job at wages which cover basic needs for food, shelter, clothing, vocational training, health and child care, and for an education to prepare for today's fast-changing world."

> —Alice Hamburg's statement before the Alameda County
> Board of Supervisors, on behalf of the East Bay Women
> Strike for Peace in opposition to cutting General Assistance,
> 1995

The following is a partial list of Bay Area, state, national, and international groups I recommend to readers. Although not all are peace organizations, I believe that each helps to bring about conditions necessary for a peaceful world.

Abolition 2000 Global Network to Eliminate Nuclear Weapons
(see Western States Legal Foundation)

Agape Foundation
1095 Market St. Ste. 304, San Francisco, CA 94103   415-701-8707
Begun in 1969 by Bay Area pacifists, including Joan Baez and Roy Kepler
Raises funds, distributes grants and loans, provides fiscal sponsorship and technical assistance to grassroots peace, justice, social change and environmental projects with focus on nonviolent social change.

American Civil Liberties Union (ACLU)
1663 Mission, #460, San Francisco, CA 94103   415-621-2493
Dorothy Ehrlich, Exec. Dir.
Guardian of the First Amendment, separation of church and state, racial justice, equal opportunity.

265

American Friends Service Committee (AFSC)
65 Ninth Street, San Francisco, CA 94103-1401   415-565-0201
Founded by the Quakers, also known as the "Friends"
Sandra Schwartz, Director,
Publishes Street Spirit, *newspaper by and for the homeless.*
International service organization devoted to peaceful resolution of world problems. Works for welfare of youth and homeless. Early recipient of Nobel Peace Prize.

American Jewish Congress
703 Market Street, Ste. 258, Northern Pacific Region, San Francisco, CA 94103 415-974-1287
A liberal voice in the Jewish community involved in protecting religious liberties.

American Red Cross
85 Second Street 7th Floor, San Francisco, CA 94105   415- 427-8000
Worldwide disaster relief.

Amnesty International
500 Sansome, San Francisco, CA 94111   415-291-9233
Works for prevention of torture and release of prisoners of conscience .

Association of World Citizens
55 New Montgomery Street, Suite 224, San Francisco, CA 94105   415-541-9610
Douglas Mattern, Pres.
Promotes internationalism, works for a more representative UN.

Berkeley Community Fund
2320 Shattuck, Berkeley, CA 94704   510-843-5202
Narsai David, Pres., Bd. of Directors
Grants awards to community activists and organizations.

Berkeley Emergency Food & Housing Project
2140 Dwight Way, Berkeley, CA 94704   510-649-4965
Jenny Abramson
The Multi-Purpose Center feeds hundreds of homeless daily and houses 100 women and children. Runs Transitional House for mentally disabled.

Berkeley Free Clinic
2339 Durant Avenue, Berkeley, CA 94704   510-548-2570
Provides free healthcare and education to those in need.

Berkeley Gray Panthers
1403 Addison Street, Berkeley, CA 94702   510-548-9696
Lillian Rabinowitz and Suse Moyal, co-founders
Works for universal health care, subsidized housing and electoral reform. Their slogan: "Age and Youth in Action."

Berkeley Historical Society
PO Box 1190, Berkeley, CA 94704   510-848-0181
Repository of local history.

Berkeley/Richmond Jewish Community Center
1414 Walnut Street, Berkeley, CA 94709   510-848-0237
Center for culture and welfare, with programs for seniors and youth. Features music and art.

Building Opportunities for Self Sufficiency (BOSS)
2065 Kittredge Street, Ste E, Berkeley, CA 94704   510-649-1931
boona cheema, Director
Provides emergency, transitional and long-term services to the homeless and mentally disabled, including housing, job training, and leadership development.

California Association for Older Americans
Shirley Bierly
325 Clementina St., San Francisco, CA 94103-4104   415-541-9629
Publishes issues concerning senior citizens.

California Council of Churches
2700 L Street, Sacramento, CA 95816-5614   916-442-5447
Ecumenical coalition. Publishes California Church Impact. *Furnishes alerts and guidance on national and state legislative issues and ballot measures*

California Peace Action
2800 Adeline St., Berkeley, CA 94703 3127   510-849-2272
Successor to SANE/Freeze; nation's largest organization for peace, justice, and non-intervention.

Catholic Charities of the East Bay
433 Jefferson Street, Oakland, CA 94607   510-834-5656
Serves poor and homeless.

Center for Constitutional Rights
666 Broadway, New York, NY 10012   212-614-6464
"Defends the weak, powerless and unpopular."

Center for Defense Information (CDI)
1779 Massachusetts Avenue NW, Washington, DC 20036   202-332-0600
Ret. Admiral Gene LaRocque, President
Retired military officers working to reduce military budget and eliminate nuclear weapons.

Center for Economic Conversion
222 View Street, Mt.View, CA 94041-1344   650-968-8798
Dedicated to building a sustainable peace-oriented economy through converting military facilities to civilian use.

Chaplaincy for the Homeless, Ecumenical
2345 Channing, Rm. 207 Congregational Church, Berkeley, CA 94704   510-548-0551
Frances Townes, founder
An interfaith group (over 30 congregations) working to empower poor and homeless and reach runaway youth.

CHRICA
347 Dolores Street #210, San Francisco, CA 94110   415-431-7760
Committee for Health Rights in Central America.

Circle of Concern
Berkeley, CA
Margaret Olney, Founder
Biweekly silent vigil at UCB's West Gate, opposing UC's involvement in nuclear weapons production.

CISPES NW Region/SF
3181 Mission, Box 20, 3382 - 26th Street, San Francisco, CA 94110 415-648-6520
The Committee in Solidarity with the People of El Salvador.

Coalition on Homelessness, San Francisco
433 Turk Street, San Francisco, CA 94102   415-346-3740
Paul Boden, Exec. Dir.

Common Cause
926 J Street, Suite 910, Sacramento, CA 95814
Monitors government policy and works for reforms in campaign financing.

Council for a Livable World
110 Maryland Avenue NE, Ste. 201, Washington, DC 20002   202-546-0795
John Isaacs, President
Works to reduce world nuclear arsenals through research and grassroots activity.

Cuban American Alliance - Jewish Solidarity
3161 Bridle Drive, Hayward, CA 94541
Delvis Levy, Editor
Delivers food and medical supplies to Cuba.

Data Center
1904 Franklin Street, Ste. 900, Oakland, CA 94612-9725   510-835-4692
Fred Goff, Director
Gathers and provides background information to candidates, scholars, and community activists.

Earth Island Institute
300 Broadway, Ste. 28, San Francisco, CA 94133-3312   415-788-3666
David Brower, Founder
Dedicated to preserving the environment.

Ecology Center
2530 San Pablo Avenue, Berkeley, CA 94702   510-548-2220
Responsible for Berkeley's Farmers' Markets and recycling.

Elders Network
1860 Alcatraz Avenue, Berkeley, CA 94703   510-597-8010 x.401
Mobilizes support for frail elders enabling them to remain in their own homes. Affiliated with the Over-60 Health Center.

Emma Goldman Papers
2372 Ellsworth Street University of California, Berkeley, CA 94720 510-642-0658
Candace Falk, Director
Researches and publishes Emma Goldman's papers.

50 Years Is Enough Campaign: US Network for Global Economic Justice
1247 E Street SE Suite 201, Washington DC 20003   202-463-2265
Opposed debt policy of the IMF.

Friends Committee on Legislation (FCL)
926 J Street #707, Sacramento, CA 95814   916-443-3734
Scott Anderson, Exec. Director
The legislative action arm of AFSC. Lobbies for peace and justice issues. Analyzes ballot measures .

Global Exchange
2017 Mission Rm. 202, San Francisco, CA 94110-1285   415-255-7296
Medea Benjamin & Kevin Danaher, Co-Founders
Publicizes labor conditions in Third World and US sweatshops. Conducts visits to trouble spots.

Green Party, Berkeley
2022 Blake Street, Berkeley, CA   510-644-2293
For single payer health care, runs political candidates.

Greenpeace - International
Aggressively promotes environmental causes.   800-326-0959

Holocaust Center of Northern California
639 - 14th Avenue, San Francisco, CA 94118   415-751-6040
Develops education programs and materials for SF's multicultural community.

Institute for Food & Development Policy (Food First)
398 - 60th Street, Oakland, CA 94618   510-654-4400
Peter Rosset, Dir.
Seeks to eliminate poverty in the US, calls for redistribution of land through agrarian reform.

Institute for Policy Studies
733 15th St. NW #1020, Washington, DC 20005-2112   202-234-9382
John Cavanagh, Chair   Fax 202-387-7915
Works with grassroots groups and Congressional Progressive Caucus on labor, environmental and foreign policy issues.

Intertribal Friendship House
523 International Blvd., Oakland, CA   510-452-1235
Cultural center

Jane Addams Peace Association (JAPA)
777 UN Plaza, New York, NY 10017   212-682-8830
WILPF's educational arm. Sponsors Jane Addams Children's Book Award.

Jewish Family & Children's Services East Bay
2484 Shattuck Avenue Suite 210, Berkeley, CA 94704   510-704-7475
Ted Feldman, Director
Offers youth programs and community outreach.

Jewish Federation of the Greater East Bay
401 Grand Avenue, 5th Flr., Oakland, CA 94610   510-839-2900
Umbrella organization soliciting funding for numerous agencies serving the greater Bay Area Jewish communities.

Jewish Peace Lobby
8401 Colesville Road Suite 317, Silver Spring, MD 20910
Jerome Siegel, Director
Represents liberal Jewish thinking.

Judah L. Magnes Museum, Western Jewish History Center
2911 Russell, Berkeley, CA 94705   510-849-2710
Center for Jewish history and research;.

Kehilla Community Synagogue
941 The Alameda, Berkeley, CA 94707   510-527-5452
A progressive Jewish congregation.

KPFA "Free Speech" Radio
1929 Martin Luther King, Jr. Way, Berkeley, CA 94704   510-848-6767
Berkeley FM radio station founded in 1949, originated listener-supported radio and call-in programs.

La Peña Cultural Center
3105 Shattuck Avenue, Berkeley, CA 94705   510-849-2568
Brings artists and communities together to celebrate diversity and link art with social justice.

League of Women Voters (LWV)
1414 University Avenue, Ste. D, Berkeley, CA 94702   510-843-8824
Produces studies on politics, culture, and education.

Livermore Conversion Project
PO. Box 31835, Oakland, CA 94604   510-832-4347
Coalition, seeks to end nuclear weapons work at Livermore Laboratories.

Meiklejohn Civil Liberties Institute
PO Box 673, Berkeley, CA 94701   510-848-0599
Ann Fagan Ginger, Founder/Director
Center for human rights and peace law. Advocates for World Court, maintains resource library.

Middle East Children's Alliance (MECA)
905 Parker Street, Berkeley, CA 94710   510-548-0542
Barbara Lubin, Founder/Director
Raises funds for Palestinian and Iraqi relief; leads travel groups and reports on Middle East conditions.

Mt. Diablo Peace Center
55 Eckley Lane, Walnut Creek, CA 94596   925-933-7850
Darien de Lu, Director
Publishes monthly newsletter.

National Committee Against Repressive Legislation (NCARL)
1313 West 8th St. Suite 313, Los Angeles, CA 90017
Civil liberties watchdog.

National Organization for Women (NOW)
3543 18th Street, San Francisco, CA   415-861-8880
Promotes women's rights, currently involved in struggle to maintain right of choice.

Neighbor to Neighbor
6151 West Century Boulevard, Suite 1024
Los Angeles, CA 90045   310-337-7739
Conducts voter registration; concerned with universal health care.

Neve Shalom/Wahat al-Salam, American Friends of
121 6th Avenue, Ste. 502, New York, NY 10013   212-226-9246
A community of Jews and Palestinians. Maintains a School for Peace and a Center for Conflict Resolution.

New Israel Fund
693 Sutter Street, Suite 500 D, San Francisco, CA 94102   415- 928-1114
Norman S. Rosenberg, Exec. Dir.
US organization works to promote civil liberties and religious pluralism in Israel.

Nicaragua Center for Community Action (NICCA)
2140 Shattuck Avenue, Box 2063, Berkeley, CA 94704   510-704-5242
Works for reconstruction and debt cancellation.

Niebyl-Proctor Library for Social Research
6501 Telegraph Avenue, Oakland, CA 94609   510-595-7417
Jane Hodes-Cohen, Founder
Study center and repository for Marxist literature.

Omega Boys Club
San Francisco, CA   415-826-8664
Promotes welfare and education of urban youth endangered by drugs, gangs, and violence.

Oral History Association
2000 Center Street, Suite 303, Berkeley CA 94704-1223   510 -643-7154
Promotes the recording and publication of individual life stories.

Over 60 Health Center, Lifelong Medical Care
1860 Alcatraz Avenue, Berkeley, CA 94702   510-601-6060
Marty Lynch, Director
Comprehensive health care for low income elderly, also furnishes housing.

Oxfam America
26 West Street, Boston, MA 02111   617-482-1211
John C. Hammock, Director
Works to alleviate global hunger and poverty.

Pastors for Peace
402 W. 145th Street, New York, NY 10031   212-926-5757
Rev. Lucius Walker, Jr., Exec. Director
Provides medical and food supplies to Cuba and Chiapas, Mexico.

People for the American Way
2000 M Street NW, Ste. 400, Washington, DC 20036   800-326-7329
Devoted to defeating intolerance, particularly from the religious right.

Physicians for Social Responsibility (PSR)
2288 Fulton Street Rm. 307, Berkeley, CA 94704   510-845-8395
Lends medical as well as social credibility to the anti-nuclear struggle.

Planned Parenthood
482 MacArthur, Oakland, CA   510-601-4700
Opposes anti-choice extremists; health care clinic offers educational programs.

Ploughshares Fund
Fort Mason Center, San Francisco, CA 94123   415-775-2244
Sally Lilienthal, Founder
Grantmaker dedicated to stopping weapons of war.

Potrero Hill Neighborhood Center
953 de Haro, San Francisco, CA 94107   415-826-8080
Enola Maxwell, Exec. Director
*Community center for drug rehabilitation, political organizing, youth programs,
women's empowerment, and cultural events.*

Regional Oral History Office (ROHO)
Bancroft Library, UC Berkeley, CA 94720   510-642-7395
Willa Baum, Director
Compiles and collects oral histories.

Rosenberg Children's Fund
1145 Main St., Ste 408, Springfield, MA 01103
Robbie Meeropol, Director & Co-founder
Supports children of jailed activists.

Sacred Run
PO Box 315, Newport, KY 41071
Promotes Native American consciousness.

St. Joseph the Worker Church
Father Bill O'Donnell
1640 Addison St., Berkeley, CA 94703   510 843-2244
In the forefront of social change.

Salvation Army
810 Clay Street, Oakland, CA   510-451-5547
Collects clothing and funds for homeless and low income people, provides food and shelter.

San Carlos Foundation
1065 Creston Road, Berkeley, CA 94708   510-525-3787
Davida Coady, MD, Director
Provides medical aid for Central America.

SHANTI Project
1546 Market, San Francisco 94103   415-864-2273
Raises funds and organizes volunteer assistance for HIV-AIDS patients.

Share Foundation
995 Market St. #1400, San Francisco 94103   415 882 1530
Building a new El Salvador Today.

Sierra Club, SF Bay Chapter
85 2nd St., San Francisco, CA, 94103   415-977-5500
Publishes information about and lobbies on environmental issues.

Southern California Library for Social Studies
6120 South Vermont Avenue, Los Angeles, CA 90044
Repository for early California history with emphasis on radical labor, especially ILWU.

Tri-Valley CAREs
2582 Old First Street, Livermore, CA 94550   925-443-7148
Marylia Kelley, Founder/Director
(CAREs—Communities Against a Radioactive Environment). Works closely with Livermore Conversion Project.

Union of Concerned Scientists (UCS)
Two Brattle Square, Cambridge, MA 02238-9105   617-547-5552
Educates about environmental hazards of nuclear development and fossil fuels.

United Farm Workers (UFW)
PO Box 62, Keene, CA 93531   805-822-5571
Cesar Chavez, Founder, Arturo S. Rodriguez, President
Organizes agricultural workers.

United Nations Assoc.-East Bay (UNA)
1403 Addison St. Berkeley, CA 94702   510-849-1752
Mary & Bill Trampleasure, Co-founders
Supports United Nations working to end war and establish universal social justice.

United Nations Children's Fund (UNICEF)
333 E. 38th Street, New York, NY 10016
Dedicated to saving children's lives, worldwide. Disseminates basic medical information and inoculates poor children.

US/Vietnam Friendship Association
P.O. Box 460073, San Francisco, CA 94146
Solicits funds for humanitarian projects and publishes news from Vietnam. Beatrice Eisman, editor.

The Utility Reform Network (TURN)
711 Van Ness Avenue Suite 350, San Francisco, CA 94102   415-929-8876
Nettie Hogue, Exec. Director.
California consumer watchdog organization.

Vanguard Public Foundation
383 Rhode Island Street, Ste. 301, San Francisco, CA 94103   415-487-2111
Funds humanitarian and social action organizations.

Video Project
200 Estates Drive, Ben Lomond, CA 95005   408-336-0160
Ian & Terry Thiermann
Maintains an anti-nuclear and environmental video collection available to schools.

Vietnam Help
Box 2882, Castro Valley, CA 94546   510-426-7094
Anh Tran
Raises funds for victims of the Vietnam War.

Vote Health
PO Box 32185, Oakland, CA 94604-9627   510 835-5803
Works for universal (single payer) health coverage.

War Resisters League West (WRL)
942 Market, San Francisco, CA 94102
Sponsors a YouthPeace project calling for an end to militarization of youth. Publishes annual, "Where Your Income Tax Money Really Goes."

Western States Legal Foundation (WSLF)
1504 Franklin #202, Oakland, CA 94612   510-839-5877
Jackie Cabasso, Exec. Director
Leading opponent of nuclear development, targeting the Livermore Weapons Lab. Local contact for Abolition 2000.

Women in Black
Supports Palestinian rights by protesting in the US and in Israel .   415-434-1304

Women's Daytime Drop-In Center (WDDC)
2218 Acton Street, Berkeley, CA 94702   510-548-6933
Linda Lazzareschi, Director
Daytime refuge center for women and children; offers counseling, telephone , transportation assistance, and mailing address.

Women's Energy Matters
PO Box 12487, Berkeley, CA 94712
Barbara George
Dedicated to solving local energy issues and transitioning to sustainable sources.

Working Assets
101 Market Street, San Francisco, CA 94105   415-788-0777
Long distance telephone company that shares profits with progressive organizations.

World Wall for Peace
1427 Milvia, Berkeley 94709
Carolyna Marks, Founder.
Hand-painted tile walls built throughout the world bearing hopeful messages of peace, nonviolence, and understanding.

My Peace Organizations

Women's International League for Peace & Freedom - International (WILPF)
1 Rue de Varembe 1211, Geneva 20, Switzerland
41-22-733-6175

Women's International League for Peace & Freedom - National (WILPF)
Mary Day Kent, Exec. Director.
1213 Race Street, Philadelphia, PA 19107   215-563-7110
Chapters in thirty-nine countries and 100 plus US branches, all working for total and complete disarmament.
Shares legislative office space in Washington, DC, with Women Strike for Peace.

Women's International League for Peace & Freedom - SF (WILPF)
PO Box 591390, San Francisco, CA 94159-1390

Women's International League for Peace & Freedom (WILPF) - East Bay
2302 Ellsworth, Berkeley, CA 94704   510-849-3020
Locally, Women Strike for Peace and WILPF share an office.
Each organization carries out special programs,
many are jointly conducted.

Women (Strike) for Peace (WSP)
2302 Ellsworth, Berkeley, CA 94704   510-849-3020
Peace education programs in school, sponsors film series; circulates books, videos and other educational materials.

Both WILPF and WSP work for a peaceful and just world, the end of the nuclear threat,
and protection of the environment.

Index